"An eloquent and surprisingly moving tribute not only to libraries, private and public, but to our enduring need for them and for the order they try so hard to impose on a chaotic world. . . . Manguel does all facets of his subject proud in *The Library at Night,* celebrating a treasure we so often take for granted. With this wise and tender book, he also creates a treasure of his own."

—*The Gazette* (Montreal)

"Fluid, rich and consistent."　　　—*Edmonton Journal*

"Anecdotal, often impassioned, filled with fascinating, out-of-the-way information, this paean to books and to the libraries that house them beckons beguilingly to all bibliophiles."　　　—*The Hamilton Spectator*

"The atmosphere in *The Library at Night* is cultivated, but never stodgy. It's the ideal companion volume to his international bestseller *A History of Reading.* . . . Manguel turns the library, both public and private, into a theatre rich in symbolism and associations."　　　—*CBC Arts Online*

"Who better than Alberto Manguel, that globetrotting, multilingual citizen of the world . . . to pay homage to the library as the centre of civilization? . . . *The Library at Night* is filled with odd combinations, unexpected transitions and wandering scraps of esoterica with aphorisms appearing as signposts along the way. . . . This book is utterly sensitive to the experience of reading. . . . Manguel, in this and his other books, comes off as quite the raconteur."　　　—*Toronto Star*

ALBERTO
MANGUEL

THE LIBRARY
AT NIGHT

PAGES II/III: *Aby Warburg's Library, Hamburg, Germany*

VINTAGE CANADA EDITION, 2007

Published in Canada by Vintage Canada, a division of Random House of Canada Limited, Toronto, in 2007. Originally published in hardcover in Canada by Alfred A. Knopf Canada, a division of Random House of Canada Limited, Toronto, in 2006. Distributed by Random House of Canada Limited, Toronto.

Vintage Canada and colophon are registered trademarks of Random House of Canada Limited.

www.randomhouse.ca

Permission to reprint "The Mayan Books" by A.D. Hope from *The Collected Poems 1930–1970*, Angus & Robertson, 1972, granted by arrangement with the Licensor, c/o Curtis Brown (Aust.) Pty. Ltd.

Pages 357–360 constitute a continuation of the copyright page.

Library and Archives Canada Cataloguing in Publication

Manguel, Alberto, 1948–
        The library at night / Alberto Manguel.

Includes bibliographical references and index.

ISBN 978-0-676-97589-5

1. Libraries. 2. Libraries—History. 3. Books and reading.
I. Title.

Z665.M35 2007   027   C2007-903237-0

Printed and bound in the United States of America

10 9 8 7 6 5 4 3 2 1

In the sixteenth century, the Ottoman poet Adbüllatif Çelebi,
better known as Latifi, called each of the books in his library
"a true and loving friend who drives away all cares."

This book is for Craig.

Contents

All that remains of an Athenian library: an inscription stating that opening times are "from the first to the sixth hour" and that "it is forbidden to take works out of the library."

FOREWORD

This roving humor (though not with like success) I have ever had, & like a ranging spaniel, that barks at every bird it sees, leaving his game, I have followed all, saving that which I should, and may justly complain, and truly (for who is everywhere is nowhere) . . . , that I have read many books, but to little purpose, for want of good method; I have confusedly tumbled over divers authors in our Libraries, with small profit, for want of art, order, memory, judgement.

Robert Burton, *The Anatomy of Melancholy*

The starting point is a question.

Outside theology and fantastic literature, few can doubt that the main features of our universe are its dearth of meaning and lack of discernible purpose. And yet, with bewildering optimism, we continue to assemble whatever scraps of information we can gather in scrolls and books and computer chips, on shelf after library shelf, whether material, virtual or otherwise, pathetically intent on lending the world a semblance of sense and order, while knowing perfectly well that, however much we'd like to believe the contrary, our pursuits are sadly doomed to failure.

Why then do we do it? Though I knew from the start that the question would most likely remain unanswered, the quest seemed worthwhile for its own sake. This book is the story of that quest.

Less keen on the tidy succession of dates and names than on our endless collecting efforts, I set off several years ago, not to compile another history of libraries nor to add another tome to the alarmingly extensive collection of bibliotechnology, but merely to give an account of my astonishment. "Surely we should find it both touching and inspiriting," wrote Robert Louis Stevenson over a century ago, "that in a field from which success is banished, our race should not cease to labour."[1]

Libraries, whether my own or shared with a greater reading public, have always seemed to me pleasantly mad places, and for as long as I can remember I've been seduced by their labyrinthine logic, which suggests that reason (if not art) rules over a cacophonous arrangement of books. I feel an adventurous pleasure in losing myself among the crowded stacks, superstitiously confident that any established hierarchy of letters or numbers will lead me one day to a promised destination. Books have long been instruments of the divinatory arts. "A big library," mused Northrop Frye in one of his many notebooks, "really has the gift of tongues & vast potencies of telepathic communication."[2]

Under such agreeable delusions, I've spent half a century collecting books. Immensely generous, my books make no demands on me but offer all kinds of illuminations. "My library," wrote Petrarch to a friend, "is not an unlearned collection, even if it belongs to someone unlearned."[3] Like Petrarch's, my books know infinitely more than I do, and I'm grateful that they even tolerate my presence. At times I feel that I abuse this privilege.

The love of libraries, like most loves, must be learned. No one stepping for the first time into a room made of books can know instinctively how to behave, what is expected, what is promised, what is allowed. One may be overcome by horror—at the clutter or the vastness, the stillness, the mocking reminder of everything one doesn't know, the surveillance—and some of that overwhelming feeling may cling on, even after the rituals and conventions are learned, the geography mapped, the natives found friendly.

In my foolhardy youth, when my friends were dreaming of heroic deeds in the realms of engineering and law, finance and national politics, I dreamt of becoming a librarian. Sloth and an ill-restrained fondness for travel decided otherwise. Now, however, having reached the age of fifty-six (which, according to Dostoyevsky in *The Idiot*, is "the age at which *real* life can be rightly said to begin"), I've returned to that early ideal and, though I cannot properly call myself a librarian, I live among ever-increasing bookshelves whose limits begin to blur or coincide with the house itself. The title of this book should have been *Voyage around My Room*. Regrettably, over two centuries ago, the notorious Xavier de Maistre got there first.

ALBERTO MANGUEL, 30 January 2005

THE LIBRARY

AS MYTH

The library in which I have at long last collected my books began life as a barn sometime in the fifteenth century, perched on a small hill south of the Loire. Here, in the last years before the Christian era, the Romans erected a temple to Dionysus to honour the god of this wine-producing area; twelve centuries later, a Christian church replaced the god of drunken ecstasy with the god who turned his blood into wine. (I have a picture of a stained-glass window showing a Dionysian grapevine growing out of the wound in Christ's right side.) Still later, the villagers attached to the church a house to lodge their priest, and eventually added to this presbytery a couple of pigeon towers, a small orchard and a barn. In the fall of 2000, when I first saw these buildings which are now my home, all that was left of the barn was a single stone wall that separated my property from a chicken run and the neighbour's field. According to village legend, before belonging to the barn, the wall was

part of one of the two castles that Tristan L'Hermite, minister of Louis XI of France and notorious for his cruelty, built for his sons around 1433. The first of these castles still stands, much altered during the eighteenth century. The second burnt down three or four centuries ago, and the only wall left standing, with a pigeon tower attached to its far end, became the property of the church, bordering one side of the presbytery garden. In 1693, after a new cemetery was opened to house the increasing number of dead, the inhabitants of the village ("gathered outside the church doors," says the deed) granted the incumbent priest permission to incorporate the old cemetery and to plant fruit trees over the emptied tombs. At the same time, the castle wall was used to enclose a new barn. After the French Revolution, war, storms and neglect caused the barn to crumble, and even after services resumed in the church in 1837 and a new priest came to live in the presbytery, the barn was not

ABOVE: *The stained-glass window in Chinon depicting Christ as the life-giving vine.*

OPPOSITE: *The Long Hall library at Sissinghurst.*

rebuilt. The ancient wall continued to serve as a property divider, looking onto a farmer's field on one side and shading the presbytery's magnolia tree and bushes of hydrangea on the other.[4]

As soon as I saw the wall and the scattered stones around it, I knew that here was where I would build the room to house my books. I had in mind a distinct picture of a library, something of a cross between the long hall at Sissinghurst (Vita Sackville-West's house in Kent, which I had recently visited) and the library of my old high school, the Colegio Nacional de Buenos Aires. I wanted a room panelled in dark wood, with soft pools of light and comfortable chairs, and an adjacent, smaller space in which I'd set up my writing desk and reference books. I imagined shelves that began at my waist and went up only as high as the fingertips of my stretched-out arm, since, in my experience, the books condemned to heights that require ladders, or to depths that force the reader to crawl on his stomach on the floor, receive far less attention than their middle-ground fellows, no matter their subject or merit. But these ideal arrangements would have required a library three or four times the size of the vanished barn and, as Stevenson so mournfully put it, "that is the bitterness of art: you see a good effect,

and some nonsense about sense continually intervenes."[5] Out of necessity, my library has shelves that begin just above the baseboards and end an octavo away from the beams of the watershed ceiling.

While the library was being built, the masons discovered two windows in the old wall that had been bricked up long ago. One is a slim embrasure from which archers perhaps defended Tristan l'Hermite's son when his angry peasants revolted; the other is a low square window protected by medieval iron bars cut roughly into stems with drooping leaves. From these windows, during the day, I can see my neighbour's chickens hurry from one corner of the compound to another, pecking at this spot and at that, driven frantic by too many offerings, like demented scholars in a library; from the windows on the new wall opposite, I look out onto the presbytery itself and the two ancient sophora trees in my garden. But at night, when the library lamps are lit, the outside world disappears and nothing but this space of books remains in existence. To someone standing outside, in the garden, the library at night appears like a vast vessel of some sort, like that strange Chinese villa that, in 1888, the capricious Empress Cixi caused to be built in the shape of a ship marooned in the garden lake of her Summer Palace. In the dark, with the windows lit and the rows of books glittering, the library is a closed space, a universe of self-serving rules that pretend to replace or translate those of the shapeless universe beyond.

During the day, the library is a realm of order. Down and across the lettered passages I move with visible purpose, in search of a name or a voice, summoning books to my attention according to their allotted rank and file.

The marble boat palace of Empress Cixi.

The structure of the place is visible: a maze of straight lines, not to become lost in but for finding; a divided room that follows an apparently logical sequence of classification; a geography obedient to a predetermined table of contents and a memorable hierarchy of alphabets and numbers.

But at night the atmosphere changes. Sounds become muffled, thoughts grow louder. "Only when it is dark does the owl of Minerva take flight," noted Walter Benjamin, quoting Hegel.[6] Time seems closer to that moment halfway between wakefulness and sleep in which the world can be comfortably reimagined. My movements feel unwittingly furtive, my activity secret. I turn into something of a ghost. The books are now the real presence and it is I, their reader, who, through cabbalistic rituals of half-glimpsed letters, am summoned up and lured to a certain volume and a certain page. The order decreed by library catalogues is, at night, merely conventional; it holds no prestige in the shadows. Though my own library has no authoritarian catalogue, even such milder orders as alphabetical arrangement by author or division into sections by language find their power diminished. Free from quotidian constraints, unobserved in the late hours, my eyes and hands roam recklessly across the tidy rows, restoring chaos. One book calls to another unexpectedly, creating alliances across different cultures and centuries. A half-remembered line is echoed by another for reasons which, in the light of day, remain unclear. If the library in the morning suggests an echo of the severe and reasonably wishful order of the world, the library at night seems to rejoice in the world's essential, joyful muddle.

In the first century A.D., in his book on the Roman civil war that had taken place a hundred years earlier, Lucan described Julius Caesar wandering through the ruins of Troy and remarked how every cave and every barren wood reminded his hero of the ancient Homeric stories. "A legend clings to every stone,"[7] Lucan explained, describing both Caesar's narrative-filled journey and, far in the future, the library in which I am now sitting. My books hold between their covers every story I've ever known and still remember, or have now forgotten, or may one day read; they fill the space around me with ancient and new voices. No doubt these stories exist on the page equally during the day but, perhaps because of nighttime's acquaintance with phantom appearances and telltale dreams, they become more vividly present after the sun has set. I walk down the aisles glimpsing the works of Voltaire and hear in the dark the oriental fable of Zadig; somewhere in the distance William Beckford's *Vathek* picks up the thread of the story and hands it over to Salman Rushdie's clowns behind the blue covers of *The Satanic Verses;* another Orient is echoed in the magical twelfth-century village of Zahiri of Samarkand, which in turn relinquishes the telling to Naguib Mahfouz's sorrowful survivors in present-day Egypt. Lucan's Caesar is told to walk carefully in the Trojan landscape lest he tread on ghosts. At night, here in the library, the ghosts have voices.

And yet, the library at night is not for every reader. Michel de Montaigne, for instance, disagreed with my gloomy preference. His library (he spoke of *librairie*, not *bibliothèque*, since the use of these words was just beginning to change in the vertiginous sixteenth century) was housed on the third floor of his tower, in an ancient storage space. "I spend there most of the days of my life and most of the hours of the day; I am never there at night,"[8] he confessed. At night Montaigne slept, since he believed that the body suffered enough during the day for the sake of the reading mind. "Books have many pleasant qualities for those who know how to choose them, but there is no good without effort; it is not a plain and pure pleasure, not more so than others; it has its discomforts, and they are onerous; the soul disports itself, but the body, whose care I have not forgotten, remains inactive, and grows weary and sad."[9]

Not mine. The various qualities of my readings seem to permeate my every muscle, so that, when I finally decide

Montaigne's Tower.

to turn off the library light, I carry into my sleep the voices and the movements of the book I've just closed. I've learned from long experience that if I want to write on a certain subject in the morning, my reading on that subject at night will feed my dreams not only with the arguments but with the actual events of the story. Reading about Mrs. Ramsay's *boeuf en daube* makes me hungry, Petrarch's ascension of Mount Ventoux leaves me breathless, Keats's account of his swimming invigorates me, the last pages of *Kim* fill me with loving friendship, the first description of the Baskervilles' hound makes me look uneasily over my shoulder. For Coleridge, such recollections elicit in a reader the loftiest of all possible sensations, the sense of the sublime, which, he says, "arises, not from the sight of an outward object, but from the beholder's reflection upon it; not from the sensuous impression, but from the imaginative reflex."[10] Coleridge dismisses the "sensuous impression" too readily; in order for these nightly imaginations to flourish, I must allow my other senses to awaken—to see and touch the pages, to hear the crinkle and the rustle of the paper and the fearful crack of the spine, to smell the wood of the shelves, the musky perfume of the leather bindings, the acrid scent of my yellowing pocket books. Then I can sleep.

During the day, I write, browse, rearrange books, put away my new acquisitions, reshuffle sections for the sake of space. Newcomers are made welcome after a period of inspection. If the book is second-hand, I leave all its markings intact, the spoor of previous readers, fellow-travellers who have recorded their passage by means of scribbled comments, a name on the fly-leaf, a bus ticket to mark a certain page. Old or new, the only sign I always try to rid my books of (usually with little success) is the price-sticker that malignant booksellers attach to the backs. These evil white scabs rip off with difficulty, leaving leprous wounds and traces of slime to which adhere the dust and fluff of ages, making me wish for a special gummy hell to which the inventor of these stickers would be condemned.

During the night, I sit and read, and watch the rows of books tempting me again to establish connections between neighbours, to invent common histories for them, to associate one recalled snippet with another. Virginia Woolf once tried to distinguish between the man who loves learning and the man who loves reading and concluded that "there is no connection whatever between the two." "A learned man," she wrote,

> is a sedentary, concentrated solitary enthusiast, who searches through books to discover some particular grain of truth upon which he has set his heart. If the passion for reading conquers him, his gains dwindle and vanish between his fingers. A reader, on the other hand, must check the desire for learning at the outset; if knowledge sticks to him well and good, but to go in pursuit of it, to read on a system, to become a specialist or an authority, is very apt to kill what it suits us to consider the more humane passion for pure and disinterested reading.[11]

During the day, the concentration and system tempt me; at night I can read with a lightheartedness verging on insouciance.

Day or night, however, my library is a private realm, very unlike public libraries large and small, and also unlike the phantom electronic library of whose universality I remain a moderate sceptic. The geography and customs of the three are different in different ways, even though all have in common the explicit will to lend concord to our knowledge and imagination, to group and to parcel information, to assemble in one place our vicarious experience of the world, and to exclude many other readers' experiences through parsimony, ignorance, incapability or fear.

So constant and far-reaching are these seemingly contradictory attempts at inclusion and exclusion that (at least in the West) they have their distinct literary emblems, two monuments that, it could be said, stand for everything we are. The first, erected to reach the unreachable heavens, rose from our desire to conquer space, a desire punished by the plurality of tongues that even today lays daily obstacles against our attempts at making ourselves known to one another. The second, built to assemble, from all over the world, what those tongues had tried to record, sprang from our hope to vanquish time, and ended in a legendary fire that consumed even the present. The Tower of Babel in space and the Library of Alexandria in time are the twin symbols of these ambitions. In their shadow, my small library is a reminder of both impossible yearnings—the desire to contain all the tongues of Babel and the longing to possess all the volumes of Alexandria.

The story of Babel is told in the eleventh chapter of Genesis. After the Flood, the people of the earth journeyed east to the land of Shi'nar, and there decided to build a city and a tower that would reach into the heavens. "And the Lord came down to see the city and the tower, which the children of men builded. And the Lord said, Behold, the people is one, and they have all one language; and this they begin to do: and now nothing will be restrained from them, which they have imagined to do. Go to, let us go down, and there confound their language, that they may not understand one another's speech."[12] God, the legend tells us, invented the multiplicity of languages in order to prevent us from working together, so we would not overreach our powers. According to the Sanhedrin (a council of Jewish elders set up in Jerusalem in the first century), the place where the tower once rose never lost its peculiar quality and, even today, whoever passes it forgets all he knows.[13]

Years ago, I was shown a small hill of rubble outside the walls of Babylon and told that this was all that remained of what had once been Babel.

The Library of Alexandria was a learning centre set up by the Ptolemaic kings at the end of the third century B.C. better to follow the teachings of Aristotle. According to the Greek geographer Strabo,[14] writing in the first century B.C., the library may have contained the philosopher's own books, left to one of his disciples, Theophrastus, who in turn bequeathed them to another, Neleus of Scepsis, who eventually became involved in the establishment of the library. Up until the founding of the Library of Alexandria, the libraries of the ancient world were either private collections of one man's readings, or government storehouses where legal and literary documents were kept for official reference. The impulse for setting up these earlier libraries was one less of curiosity than of safekeeping, and stemmed from the

La tour de babiloi

Nembrot

need for specific consultation rather than from the desire to be all-embracing. The Library of Alexandria revealed a new imagination that outdid all existing libraries in ambition and scope. The Attalid kings of Pergamum, in northwestern Asia Minor, attempted to compete with Alexandria and built a library of their own, but it never achieved the grandeur of that of Alexandria. To prevent their rivals from creating manuscripts for their library, the Ptolemies banned the exportation of papyrus, to which the Pergamum librarians responded by inventing a new writing material which was given the city's name: *pergamenon,* or parchment.[15]

A curious document from the second century B.C., the perhaps apocryphal *Letter of Aristeas,* records a story about the origins of the Library of Alexandria that is emblematic of its colossal dream. In order to assemble a universal library (says the letter), King Ptolemy I wrote "to all the sovereigns and governors on earth" begging them to send to him every kind of book by every kind of author, "poets and prose-writers, rhetoricians and sophists, doctors and soothsayers, historians, and all others too." The king's scholars had calculated that five hundred thousand scrolls would be required if they were to collect in Alexandria "all the books of all the peoples of the world."[16] (Time magnifies our ambitions; in 1988, the Library of Congress in Washington alone was receiving that number of items a year, from which it sparingly kept about four hundred thousand.)[17] Today, the Library of Alexandria has been rebuilt by the Egyptian government following a design competition won by the Norwegian architectural studio Snøhetta. Costing US$220 million, rising thirty-two metres high

The new Library of Alexandria, whose first stone was laid in 1988.

and encompassing a circumference of 160 metres, with enough shelf space to hold over eight million volumes, the new Library of Alexandria will also house audio-visual material and virtual collections in its capacious rooms.[18]

The Tower of Babel stood (while it stood) as proof of our belief in the unity of the universe. According to the story, in the growing shadow of Babel humankind inhabited a world with no linguistic borders, believing heaven to be as much within its rights as solid earth. The Library of Alexandria (on ground firmer perhaps than that of Babel) rose to prove the contrary, that the universe was of a bewildering variety and that this variety possessed a secret order. The first reflected our intuition of a single, continuous, monolingual divinity whose words were spoken by all from earth to heaven; the second, the belief that each of the books made up of these words was its own complex cosmos, each presuming in its singularity to address the whole of creation. The Tower of Babel collapsed in the prehistory of storytelling; the Library of Alexandria rose when stories took on the shape of books, and strove to find a syntax that would lend each word, each tablet, each scroll its illuminating and necessary place. Indistinct, majestic, everpresent, the tacit architecture of that infinite Library continues to haunt our dreams of universal order. Nothing like it has ever again been achieved, though other libraries (the Web included) have tried to copy its astonishing ambition. It stands unique in the history of the world as the only place which, having set itself up to record everything, past and future, might also have foreseen and stored the chronicle of its own destruction and resurrection.

Divided into thematic areas by categories devised by its librarians, the Library of Alexandria became a multitude of libraries, each insistent on one aspect of the world's variety. Here (the Alexandrians boasted) was a place where memory was kept alive, where every written thought had its niche, where each reader could find his own itinerary traced line after line in books perhaps yet unopened, where the universe itself found its worded reflection. As a further measure to accomplish his ambition, King Ptolemy decreed that any book arriving in the port of Alexandria was to be seized and copied, with the solemn promise that the original would be returned (like so many solemn kingly promises, this one was not always kept, and often it was the copy that was handed back). Because of this despotic measure, the books assembled in the Library became known as "the ships' collection."[19]

The first reference to the Library is by Herodas, a poet from Cos or Miletus who lived in the second half of the third century B.C., in a text that mentions a building known as the Museion, or House of the Muses, that almost certainly lodged the famous Library. Curiously, in a dizzying game of Chinese boxes, Herodas lends the kingdom of Egypt an all-englobing universal-library nature, so that Egypt includes the Museum, which in turn includes the Library, which in turn includes everything:

And [Egypt] resembles the house of Aphrodite:
Everything that exists and everything that is possible
Is found in Egypt: money, games, power, the blue sky above,
Fame, spectacles, philosophers, gold, young men and maidens,
The temple of the sibling gods, the benevolent king,
The Museum, wine and whatever else one might imagine.[20]

Unfortunately, in spite of passing references like this one, the truth is that we don't know what the Library of Alexandria looked like. We have an image of the Tower of Babel, probably inspired by the ninth-century spiral minaret of the Abu Dulaf mosque in Samarra and rendered in dozens of paintings, mainly by sixteenth-century Dutch artists such as Breughel: a snail-like, unfinished building crawling with industrious workers. We have no familiar image, however fantastical, of the Library of Alexandria.

The Italian scholar Luciano Canfora, after surveying all the sources available to us, concludes that the Library itself must have consisted of a very long, high hall or passageway in the Museion. Along its walls were endless *bibliothekai,* a term which originally designated not the room but the shelves or niches for the scrolls. Above the shelves there was an inscription: "The place of the cure of the soul." On the other side of the *bibliothekai* walls were a number of rooms, used perhaps by the scholars as residences or meeting places. There was also a room for communal meals.

The Museion stood in the royal neighbourhood, by the seafront, and provided bed and board to scholars invited to the Ptolemaic court. According to the Sicilian historian Diodorus Siculus, writing in the first century B.C., Alexandria boasted a second library, the so-called daughter library, intended for the use of scholars not affiliated with the Museion. It was situated in the southwestern neighbourhood of Alexandria, close to the temple of Serapis, and was stocked with duplicate copies of the Museion library's holdings.

It is infuriating not to be able to tell what the Library of Alexandria looked like. With understandable hubris, every one of its chroniclers (all those whose testimony has reached us) seems to have thought its description superfluous. The Greek geographer Strabo, a contemporary of Diodorus, described the city of Alexandria in detail but, mysteriously, failed to mention the Library. "The Museion too forms part of the royal buildings and comprises a *peripatos* [deambulatory], an exedra with seats, and a large building housing the common room where scholars who are members of the Museion take their meals,"[21] is all he tells us. "Why need I even speak of it, since it is imperishably held in the memory of all men?" wrote Athenaeus of Naucratis, barely a century and a half after its destruction. The Library that wanted to be the storehouse for the memory of the world was not able to secure for us the memory of itself. All we know of it, all that remains of its vastness, its marbles and its scrolls, are its various raisons d'être.

One forceful reason was the Egyptian pursuit of immortality. If an image of the cosmos can be assembled and preserved under a single roof (as King Ptolemy must have thought), then every detail of that image—a grain of sand, a drop of water, the king himself—will have a place there, recorded in words by a poet, a storyteller, a historian, forever, or at least as long as there are readers who may one day open the appointed page. There is a line of poetry, a sentence in a fable, a word in an essay, by which my existence is justified; find that line, and immortality is assured. The heroes of Virgil, of Herman Melville, of Joseph Conrad, of most epic literature, embrace this Alexandrian belief. For them, the world (like the Library) is made up of myriad stories that, through tangled mazes, lead to a revelatory moment set up for them alone—even if in that last moment the revelation itself is denied, as Kafka's pilgrim realizes, standing outside the Gates of Law (so oddly reminiscent of library gates) and finding in the instant of dying that "they are to be closed forever, because they were meant for you alone."[22] Readers, like epic heroes, are not guaranteed an epiphany.

In our time, bereft of epic dreams—which we've replaced with dreams of pillage—the illusion of immortality is created by technology. The Web, and its promise of a voice and a site for all, is our equivalent of the *mare incognitum,* the unknown sea that lured ancient travellers with the temptation of discovery. Immaterial as water, too vast for any mortal apprehension, the Web's outstanding qualities allow us to confuse the ungraspable with the eternal. Like the sea, the Web is volatile: 70 percent of its communications last less than four months. Its virtue (its virtuality) entails a constant present—which for medieval scholars was one of the definitions of hell.[23] Alexandria and its scholars, by contrast, never mistook the true nature of the past; they knew it to be the source of an ever-shifting present in which new readers engaged with old books which became new in the reading process. Every reader exists to ensure for a certain book a modest immortality. Reading is, in this sense, a ritual of rebirth.

But the Library of Alexandria was set up to do more than merely immortalize. It was to record everything that had been and could be recorded, and these records were to be digested into further records, an endless trail of readings and glosses that would engender in turn new glosses and new readings. It was to be a readers' workshop, not just a place where books were endlessly preserved. To ensure its use, the Ptolemies invited the most celebrated scholars from many countries—such as Euclid and Archimedes—to take up residence in Alexandria, paying them a handsome retainer and not demanding anything in exchange except that they make use of the Library's treasures.[24] In this way, these specialized readers could each become acquainted with a large number of texts, reading and summing up what they had read, producing critical digests for future generations who would then reduce these readings to further digests. A satire from the third century B.C. by Timon of Phlius describes these scholars as *charakitai,* "scribblers," and says that "in the populous land of Egypt, many well-fed *charakitai* scribble on papyrus while squabbling incessantly in the Muses' cage."[25]

In the second century, and as a result of the Alexandrian summaries and collations, an epistemological rule for reading was firmly established, decreeing that "the most recent text replaces all previous ones, since it is supposed to contain them."[26] Following this exegesis and closer to our time, Stéphane Mallarmé suggested that "the world was made to conclude in a handsome book,"[27] that is to say, in a single book, any book, a distillation or summing-up of the world that must encompass all other books. This method proceeds by foreshadowing certain books, as the *Odyssey* foresees the adventures of Holden Caulfield, and the story of Dido foretells that of Madame Bovary, or by echoing them, as the sagas of Faulkner hold the destinies of the House of Atreus, and the peregrinations of Jan Morris pay homage to the voyages of Ibn Khaldun.

This intuition of associative readings allowed the librarians of Alexandria to establish complex literary genealogies, and later readers to recognize, in the most trivial accounts of a hero's life (*Tristram Shandy* or *The Confessions of Zeno*) or in the most fantastical nightmares (of Sadegh Hedayat or Julio Cortázar), a description of the universe at large, and of their own triumphs and tribulations. In any of the pages of any of my books may lie a perfect account of my secret experience of the world. As the librarians of Alexandria perhaps discovered, any single literary moment necessarily implies all others.

But more than anything else, the Library of Alexandria was a place of memory, of necessarily imperfect memory. "What memory has in common with art," wrote Joseph Brodsky in 1985,

> is the knack for selection, the taste for detail. Complimentary though this observation may seem to art (that of prose in particular), to memory it should appear insulting. The insult, however, is well deserved. Memory contains precisely details, not the whole picture; highlights, if you will, not the entire show. The conviction that we are somehow remembering the whole thing in a blanket fashion, the very conviction that allows the species to go on with its life, is groundless. More than anything, memory resembles a library in alphabetical disorder, and with no collected works by anyone.[28]

Honouring Alexandria's remote purpose, all subsequent libraries, however ambitious, have acknowledged this piecemeal mnemonic function. The existence of any library, even mine, allows readers a sense of what their craft is truly about, a craft that struggles against the stringencies of time by bringing fragments of the past into their present. It grants them a glimpse, however secret or distant, into the minds of other human beings, and allows them a certain knowledge of their own condition through the stories stored here for their perusal. Above all, it tells readers that their craft consists of the power to remember, actively, through the prompt of the page, selected moments of the human experience. This was the great practice established by the Library of Alexandria. Accordingly, centuries later, when a monument was suggested to honour the victims of the Holocaust in Germany, the most intelligent proposal (unfortunately not chosen) was to build a library.[29]

And yet, as a public space the Library of Alexandria was a paradox, a building set aside for an essentially private craft (reading) which now was to take place communally. Under the Library's roof, scholars shared an illusion of freedom, convinced that the entire reading realm was theirs for the asking. In fact, their choice was censored in a number of ways: by the stack (open or closed) on which the book sat, by the section of the library in which it had been catalogued, by privileged notions of reserved rooms or special collections, by generations of librarians whose ethics and tastes had shaped the collection, by official guidelines based on what Ptolemaic society considered "proper" or "valuable," by bureaucratic rulings whose reasons were lost in the dungeons of time, by considerations of budget and size and availability.

The Ptolemies and their librarians were certainly aware that memory was power. Hecateus of Abdera, in his semi-fictional book of travels, the *Egyptiaca,* had claimed that Greek culture owed its existence to Egypt, whose culture was more ancient and morally far superior.[30] Mere assertion was not enough, and the librarians of Alexandria dutifully set up a vast collection of Greek works to confirm the debt of these to Egyptian authority. Not just Greek; through the collection of books of various pasts, the librarians hoped to grant their readers knowledge of the interwoven roots and branches of human culture, which (as Simone Weil was much later to declare) can be defined as "the formation of attention."[31] For this purpose, they trained themselves to become attentive to the world beyond their borders, gathering and interpreting information, ordering and cataloguing all manner of books, seeking to associate different texts and to transform thought by association.

By housing as many books as possible under one single roof, the librarians of Alexandria also tried to protect them from the risk of destruction that might result if left in what were deemed to be less caring hands (an argument adopted by many Western museums and libraries today). Therefore, as well as being an emblem of man's power to act through thought, the Library became a monument intended to defeat death, which, as poets tell us, puts an end to memory.

And yet, in spite of all the concern of its rulers and librarians, the Library of Alexandria vanished. Just as we know almost nothing of the shape it had when it was erected, we know nothing certain about its disappearance, sudden or gradual. According to Plutarch, during Julius Caesar's stay in Alexandria in 47 B.C. a fire spread from the Arsenal and "put an end to the great Library," but his account is faulty. Other historians (Dio Cassius and Orosius, drawing their information from Livy and from Caesar's own *De bello alexandrino*) suggested that Caesar's fire destroyed not the Library itself but some forty thousand volumes stored near the Arsenal, where they were possibly awaiting shipment to Rome. Almost seven centuries later, another possible ending was offered. A Christian chronicle, drawn from the *Ta'rikh al-Hukuma* or *Chronicle of Wise Men* by Ibn al-Kifti and now discredited, blamed the destruction on the Muslim general Amr ibn al-As, who, upon entering Alexandria in A.D. 642, was supposed to have ordered Caliph Omar I to set fire to the contents of the Library. The books, always according to the Christian narrator, were used to feed the stoves of the public baths; only the works of Aristotle were spared.[32]

Historically, in the light of day, the end of the Library remains as nebulous as its true aspect; historically, the Tower, if it ever existed, was nothing but an unsuccessful if ambitious real estate enterprise. As myths, however, in the imagination at night, the solidity of both buildings is unimpeachable. We can admire the mythical Tower rising visibly to prove that the impossible is worth attempting, no matter how devastating the result; we can see it working its way upwards, the fruit of a unanimous, all-invading, antlike society; we can witness its end in the dispersion of its individuals, each in the isolation of his own linguistic circle. We can roam the bloated stacks of the Library of Alexandria, where all imagination and knowledge are assembled; we can recognize in its destruction the warning that all we gather will be lost, but also that much of it can be collected again; we can learn from its splendid ambition that what was one man's experience can become, through the alchemy of words, the experience of all, and how that experience, distilled once again into words, can serve each singular reader for some secret, singular purpose.

The Library of Alexandria, implicit in travellers' memoirs and historians' chronicles, re-invented in works of fiction and of fable, has come to stand for the riddle of human identity, posing shelf after shelf the question "Who am I?" In Elias Canetti's 1935 novel *Die Blendung*

(*Auto da Fé*), Peter Kien, the scholar who in the last pages sets fire to himself and to his books when he feels that the outside world has become too unbearably intrusive, incarnates every inheritor of the Library, as a reader whose very self is enmeshed in the books he possesses and who, like one of the ancient Alexandrian scholars, must himself become dust in the night when the library is no more. Dust indeed, the poet Francisco de Quevedo noted, early in the seventeenth century. And then added, with the same faith in the survival of the spirit that the Library of Alexandria embodied, "Dust it shall be, but dust in love."[33]

THE LIBRARY

AS ORDER

Sitting in my library at night, I watch in the pools of light the implacable plankton of dust shed by both the pages and my skin, hourly casting off layer after dead layer in a feeble attempt at persistence. I like to imagine that, on the day after my last, my library and I will crumble together, so that even when I am no more I'll still be with my books.

The truth is, I can't remember a time when I did not live surrounded by my library. By the age of seven or eight, I had assembled in my room a minuscule Alexandria, about one hundred volumes of different formats on all sorts of subjects. For the sake of variety, I kept changing their groupings. I would decide, for instance, to place them by size so that each shelf contained only volumes of the same height. I discovered much later that I had an illustrious predecessor, Samuel Pepys, who in the seventeenth century built little high heels for his smaller volumes, so that the tops all

followed a neat horizontal line.[34] I began by placing on my lowest shelf the large volumes of picture-books: a German edition of *Die Welt, in der wir leben,* with detailed illustrations of the world under the sea and life in an autumn undergrowth (even today I can perfectly recall the iridescent fish and the monstrous insects), a collection of stories about cats (from which I still remember the line "Cats' names and cats' faces/ Are often seen in public places"), the several titles of Constancio C. Vigil (an Argentine children's writer who was also a secret collector of pornographic literature), a book of tales and poems by Margaret Wise Brown (it included a terrifying story about a boy who is successively abandoned by the animal, vegetable and mineral kingdoms) and a treasured old edition of Heinrich Hoffmann's *Struwwelpeter* in which I carefully avoided the picture of a tailor cutting off a boy's thumbs with a huge pair of scissors. Next came my books with odd shapes: single volumes of folk tales, a few pop-up books on animals, a tattered atlas which I studied carefully, trying to discover microscopic people in the tiny cities that dotted its continents. On a separate shelf I grouped what I called my "normal-size" books: May Lamberton Becker's Rainbow Classics, Emilio Salgari's pirate adventures, a two-volume *Childhood of Famous Painters*, Roy Rockwood's Bomba saga, the complete fairy tales of Grimm and Andersen, the children's novels of the great Brazilian author Monteiro Lobato, Edmundo de Amicis's infamously sentimental *Cuore*, full of heroic and long-suffering infants. A whole shelf was given over to the many embossed red-and-blue volumes of a Spanish-language encyclopedia, *El Tesoro de la juventud*. My Golden Books series, slightly smaller, went on a lower shelf. Beatrix Potter and a German collection of tales from the *Arabian Nights* formed the last, miniature section.

But sometimes this order would not satisfy me and I'd reorganize my books by subject: fairy tales on one shelf, adventure stories on another, scientific and travel volumes on a third, poetry on a fourth, biographies on a fifth. And sometimes, just for the sake of change, I would group my books by language, or by colour, or according to my degree of fondness for them. In the first century A.D., Pliny the Younger described the joys of his place in the country, and among these a sunny room where "one wall is fitted with shelves like a library to hold the books I read and reread."[35] At times, I've thought of having a library that consisted of nothing but my most thumbed volumes.

Then there would be groupings within groupings. As I learned then, but was not able to articulate until much later, order begets order. Once a category is established, it suggests or imposes others, so that no cataloguing method, whether on shelf or on paper, is ever closed unto itself. If I decide on a number of subjects, each of these subjects will require a classification within its classification. At a certain point in the ordering, out of fatigue, boredom or frustration, I'll stop this geometrical progression. But the possibility of continuing it is always there. There are no final categories in a library.

A private library, unlike a public one, presents the advantage of allowing a whimsical and highly personal classification. The invalid writer Valéry Larbaud would have his books bound in different colours according to the language in which they were written, English novels in blue, Spanish in red, etc. "His sickroom was a rainbow," said one of his admirers, "that allowed his eye and his memory surprises and expected pleasures."[36] The novelist Georges Perec once listed a dozen ways in which to classify one's library, "none satisfactory in itself."[37] He halfheartedly suggested the following orders:

~ alphabetically
~ by continent or country
~ by colour
~ by date of purchase
~ by date of publication
~ by format
~ by genre
~ by literary period
~ by language
~ according to our reading priorities
~ according to their binding
~ by series

Such classifications may serve a singular, private purpose. A public library, on the other hand, must follow an order whose code can be understood by every user and which is decided upon before the collection is set up on the shelves. Such a code is more easily applied to an electronic library, since its cataloguing system can, while serving all readers, also allow a superimposed program to classify (and therefore locate) titles entered in no predetermined order, without having to be constantly rearranged and updated.

Sometimes the classification precedes the material ordering. In my library in the reconstructed barn, long before my books were put away in obedient rows, they clustered in my mind around specific subject-headings that probably made sense to me alone. It seemed therefore an easy task, when in the summer of 2003 I started to arrange my library, to file into specific spaces the volumes already consigned to a clear set of categories. I soon discovered that I had been overly confident.

For several weeks I unpacked the hundreds of boxes that had, until then, taken up the whole of the dining-room, carried them into the empty library and then stood bewildered among teetering columns of books that seemed to combine the vertical ambition of Babel with the horizontal greed of Alexandria. For almost three months I sifted through these piles, attempting to create some kind of order, working from early in the morning to very late at night. The thick walls kept the room cool and peaceful, and the rediscovery of old and forgotten friends made me oblivious of the time. Suddenly I would look up and find that it was dark outside, and that I had spent the entire day filling only a few expectant shelves.

Sometimes I worked throughout the night, and then I would imagine all kinds of fantastical arrangements for my books that later, in the light of day, I dismissed as sadly impractical.

Unpacking books is a revelatory activity. Writing in 1931, during one of his many moves, Walter Benjamin described the experience of standing among his books "not yet touched by the mild boredom of order,"[38] haunted by visions of the times and places he had collected them, of the circumstantial evidence that rendered each volume truly his. I too, during those summer months, was overwhelmed by these visions: a ticket fluttering away from an opened book reminded me of a tram ride in Buenos Aires (trams stopped running in the late sixties) when I first read Julian Green's *Moira;* a name and phone number inscribed on a fly-leaf brought back the face of a friend long lost who gave me a copy of the *Cantos* of Ezra Pound; a paper napkin with the logo of the Café de Flore, folded inside Hermann Hesse's *Siddhartha,* attested to my first trip to Paris in 1966; a letter from a teacher inside a collection of Spanish poetry made me think of distant classes where I first heard of Góngora and Vicente Gaos. *"Habent sua fata libelli,"* says Benjamin, quoting the forgotten medieval essayist Maurus. "Books have their own fates." Some of mine have waited half a century to reach this tiny place in western France, for which they were seemingly destined.

I had, as I have said, previously conceived of organizing my library into several sections. Principal among these were the languages in which the books were written. I had formed vast mental communities of those works written in English or Spanish, German or French, whether poetry or prose. From these linguistic pools I would exclude certain titles that belonged to subjects of interest to me, such as Greek Mythology, Monotheistic Religions, Legends of the Middle Ages, Cultures of the Renaissance, First and Second World Wars, History of the Book. . . . My choice of what to lodge under these categories might seem whimsical to many readers. Why stash the works of Saint Augustine in the Christianity section rather than under Literature in Latin or Early Medieval Civilizations? Why place Carlyle's *French Revolution* in Literature in English rather than in European History, and not Simon Schama's *Citizens?* Why keep Louis Ginzberg's seven volumes of *Legends of the Jews* under Judaism but Joseph Gaer's study on the Wandering Jew under Myths? Why place Anne Carson's translations of Sappho under Carson but Arthur Golding's *Metamorphoses* under Ovid? Why keep my two pocket volumes of Chapman's Homer under Keats?

Ultimately, every organization is arbitrary. In libraries of friends around the world, I have found many odd classifications: Rimbaud's *Le Bateau ivre* under Sailing, Defoe's *Robinson Crusoe* under Travel, Mary McCarthy's *Birds of America* under Ornithology, Claude Lévi-Strauss's *The Raw and the Cooked* under Cuisine. But public libraries have their own odd approaches. One reader was upset because, in the London Library, Stendhal was listed under "B" for his real name, Beyle, and Gérard de Nerval under "G." Another complained that, in the same library, Women were classed "under the Miscellaneous end of Science," after Witchcraft and before Wool and Wrestling.[39] In the Library of Congress's catalogues, the subject-headings include such curious categories as:

~ banana research
~ bat binding
~ boots and shoes in art
~ chickens in religion and folklore
~ sewage: collected works

It is as if the contents of the books matter less to these organizers than the uniqueness of the subject under which they are catalogued, so that a library becomes a collection of thematic anthologies. Certainly, the subjects or categories into which a library is divided not only change the nature of the books it contains (read or unread) but also, in turn, are changed by them. To place Robert Musil's novels in a section on Austrian Literature circumscribes his work by nationalistic definitions of novel-writing; at the same time, it illuminates neighbouring sociological and historical works on the Austro-Hungarian Empire by expanding their restrictive scholarly views on the subject. Inclusion of Anton Chekhov's *Strange Confession* in the section of Detective Novels forces the reader to follow the story with the requisite attention to murder, clues and red herrings; it also opens the notion of the crime genre to authors such as Chekhov, not usually associated with the likes of Raymond Chandler and Agatha Christie. If I place Tomás Eloy Martínez's *Santa Evita* in my section on Argentinian History do I diminish the book's literary value? If I place it under Fiction in Spanish am I dismissing its historical accuracy?

Sir Robert Cotton, an eccentric seventeenth-century English bibliophile, ranged his books (which included many rare manuscripts, such as the only known manuscript of *Beowulf,* and the Lindisfarne Gospels, from about A.D. 698) in twelve bookcases, each adorned with the bust of one of the first twelve Caesars. When the British Library acquired some of his collection, it kept Cotton's strange cataloguing system, so that the Lindisfarne Gospels can today be requested as "Cotton MS. Nero D. IV" because it was once the fourth book on the fourth shelf down in the bookcase topped by the bust of Nero.[40]

And yet order of almost any kind has the merit of containing the uncontainable. "There is probably many an old collector," G.K. Chesterton observed, "whose friends and relations say that he is mad on Elzevirs, when as a matter of fact it is the Elzevirs that keep him sane. Without them he would drift into soul-destroying idleness and hypochondria; but the drowsy regularity of his notes and calculations teaches something of the same lesson as the swing of the smith's hammer or the plodding of the ploughman's horses, the lesson of the ancient commonsense of things."[41] The ordering of a collection of thrillers, or of books printed by Elzevir, grants the manic behaviour of the collector a certain degree of sanity. At times I feel as if the exquisite pocket-sized leather-bound Nelsons, the flimsy Brazilian booklets known as *literatura de cordel* (because they were sold by hawkers who strung their wares on thin cords), the early editions of the Séptimo Círculo detective series edited by Borges and Bioy Casares, the small square volumes of the New Temple Shakespeare published by Dent and illustrated with wood engravings by Eric Gill—all these books that I sporadically collect—have kept me sane.

~~~

Several examples of literatura de cordel.

The broader the category, the less circumscribed the book. In China, at the beginning of the third century, the books in the Imperial Library were kept under four modest and comprehensive headings agreed upon by eminent court scholars—canonical or classical texts, works of history, philosophical works, and miscellaneous literary works—each bound in a specific and symbolic colour, respectively green, red, blue and grey (a chromatic division curiously akin to that of the early Penguins or the Spanish Colección Austral). Within these groupings, the titles were shelved following graphic or phonetic orderings. In the first case, many thousands of characters were broken into a few basic elements—the ideogram for earth or water, for instance—and then placed in a conventional order that followed the hierarchies of Chinese cosmology. In the second, the order was based on the rhyme of the last syllable of the last word in a title. Equivalent to the Roman alphabetical system, which fluctuates between 26 (English) and 28 (Spanish) letters, the number of possible rhymes in Chinese varied between 76 and 206. The largest manuscript encyclopedia in the world, the *Yongle Dadian*, or *Monumental Compendium from the Era of Eternal Happiness*, commissioned in the fifteenth century by the Emperor Chengzu with the purpose of recording in one single publication all existing Chinese literature, used the rhyming method to order its thousands of entries. Over two thousand scholars worked on the ambitious enterprise. Only a small portion of that monstrous catalogue survives today.[42]

Entering a library, I am always struck by the way in which a certain vision of the world is imposed upon the reader through its categories and its order. Some categories, of course, are more evident than others, and Chinese libraries in particular have a long history of classification that reflects, in its variety, the changing ways in which China has conceived the universe. The earliest catalogues follow the hierarchy imposed by a belief in the supreme rule of the gods, beneath whose primordial, all-encompassing vault—the realm of the heavenly bodies—stands the subservient earth. Then, in decreasing order of importance, come human beings, animals, plants and, lastly, minerals. These six categories govern the divisions under which the works of 596 authors, preserved in 13,269 scrolls, are classified in the first-century bibliographic study known as the *Hanshu Yiwenzhi*, or *Dynastic History of the Han*, an annotated catalogue

One of the volumes of the monumental Yongle Dadian encyclopedia.

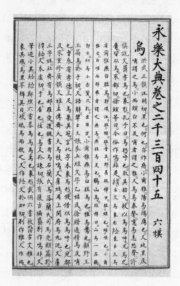

One of the volumes of the monumental Yongle Dadian encyclopedia.

based on the research of two imperial librarians, Liu Xiang and his son Liu Xin,[43] who, alone, dedicated their lives to recording what others had written. Other Chinese catalogues stem from different hierarchies. The *Cefu Yuangui,* or *Archives of the Divinatory Tortoise,* compiled by imperial command between 1005 and 1013, follows not a cosmic order but rather a bureaucratic one, beginning with the emperor and descending through the various state officials and institutions down to lowly citizens.[44] (In Western terms, we could conceive of a library of English literature that began, for instance, with the *Prayers and Poems* of Elizabeth I and ended with the complete works of Charles Bukowski.) This bureaucratic or sociological order was employed to assemble one of the first Chinese encyclopedias to call itself exhaustive: the *Taiping Yulan,* or *Imperial Readings from the Era of the Great Peace*. Finished in 982, it explored all fields of knowledge; its sequel, *Vast Compendium from the Era of the Great Peace*, covered under fifty-five subject-headings more than five thousand biographical entries, and listed over two thousand titles. Song Taizong, the emperor who commanded its writing, is said to have read three chapters a day for one whole year. A more complex ordering system appears in what is known as the largest encyclopedia ever printed: the *Qinding Gujin Tushu Jicheng*, or *Great Illustrated Imperial Encyclopedia of Past and Present Times*, of 1726, a gigantic biographical library divided into more than ten thousand sections. The work was attributed to Jiang Tingxi, a court proofreader who used wooden blocks with cut-out pictures and movable characters specially designed for the enterprise. Each section of the encyclopedia covers one specific realm of human concern, such as Science or Travel, and is divided into subsections containing biographical entries. The section on Human Relations, for instance, lists the biographies of thousands of men and women according to their occupation or position in society, among them sages, slaves, playboys, tyrants, doctors, calligraphers, supernatural beings, great drinkers, notable archers and widows who did not marry again.[45]

Five centuries earlier, in Iraq, the renowned judge Ahmad ibn Muhammad ibn Khalikan had compiled a similar "mirror of the world." His *Obituaries of Celebrities and Reports of the Sons of Their Time* encompassed 826 biographies of poets, rulers, generals, philologists, historians, prose writers, traditionalists, preachers, ascetics, viziers, Koranic expositors, philosophers, physicians, theologians, musicians and judges—providing, among other features, the subject's sexual preferences, professional merits and social standing. Because Khalikan's "biographical library" was meant to "entertain as well as edify," he omitted from his great work entries on the Prophet and his companions.[46] Unlike the Chinese encyclopedias, Khalikan's opus was arranged in alphabetical order.

The alphabetical classification of books was first used over twenty-two centuries ago, by Callimachus, one of the most notable librarians of Alexandria, a poet admired by Propertius and Ovid, and the author of over eight hundred books, including a 120-volume catalogue of the most important Greek authors in the Library.[47] Ironically, given that he so laboriously strove to preserve the works of the past for future readers, all that remains of Callimachus's own work today is six hymns, sixty-four epigrams, a fragment of a little epic and, most important, the method he used to catalogue his voluminous readings. Callimachus had devised a system for his critical inventory of Greek literature that divided the material into tables or *pinakes*, one for each genre: epic, lyric, tragedy, comedy, philosophy, medicine, rhetoric, law and, finally, a grab-bag of miscellany.[48] Callimachus's main contribution to the art of keeping books, inspired perhaps by methods employed in the vanished Mesopotamian libraries, was to list the chosen authors alphabetically, with biographical notes and a bibliography (also alphabetically ordered) appended to each consecrated name. I find it moving to think that, were Callimachus to wander into my library, he would be able to find the two volumes of what remains of his own works, in the Loeb series, by following the method he himself conceived to shelve the works of others.

The alphabetical system entered the libraries of Islam

by way of Callimachus's catalogues. The first such work composed in the Arab world, in imitation of the *pinakes*, was the *Book of Authors*, by the Baghdad bookseller Abu Tahir Tayfur, who died in A.D. 893. Though only the title has come down to us, we know that the writers selected by Tayfur were each given a short biography and a catalogue of important works listed in alphabetical order.[49] About the same time, Arab scholars in various learning centres, concerned with lending order to Plato's dialogues so as to facilitate translation and commentaries, discovered that Callimachus's alphabetic method, which enabled readers to find a certain author in his allotted shelf, did not lend the same rigour to the placement of the texts themselves. Consulting the various bibliographies of Plato's work compiled by the long-gone librarians of Alexandria, they discovered to their astonishment that these ancient sages, in spite of following Callimachus's system, had rarely been in agreement as to what went where. All had agreed that Plato's works, for example, were to be classified under "P," but in what order or within which subgroupings? The scholarly Aristophanes of Byzantium, for instance, had gathered Plato's work in triads (excluding several dialogues for no clear reason), while the learned Thrasylus had divided what he assumed to be "the genuine dialogues" into sets of four, saying that Plato himself had always "published his dialogues in tetralogies."[50] Other librarians had listed the collected works in one single grouping but in different sequences, some beginning with the *Apology*, others with the *Republic*, others still with *Phaedrus* or *Timaeus*. My library suffers from the same confusion. Since my authors are listed in alphabetical order, all of Margaret Atwood's books are to be found under the letter "A," on the third shelf down of the English language section, but I don't pay much attention to whether *Life before Man* precedes *Cat's Eye* (for the sake of respecting the chronology), or *Morning in the Burned House* follows *Oryx and Crake* (separating her poetry from her fiction).

In spite of such minor frailties, the Arab libraries that flourished in the late Middle Ages were catalogued using alphabetical order. It would otherwise have been impossible to consult a repertoire of books as lengthy as that of the Nizamiyya College in Damascus, where, we are told, a Christian scholar was able to peruse, in 1267, the fifty-sixth volume of a catalogue that listed nothing but works on several subjects "written during the Islamic period up to the reign of Caliph Mustansir in 1241."[51]

If a library is a mirror of the universe, then a catalogue is a mirror of that mirror. While in China the notion of listing all a library's books between the covers of a single book was imagined almost from the start, in the Arab world it did not become common until the fifteenth century, when catalogues and encyclopedias frequently bore the name "Library." The greatest of these annotated catalogues, however, was compiled at a much earlier date. In 987, Ibn al-Nadim (of whom we know little, except that he was probably a booksellerin the service of the Abbasid rulers of Baghdad) set out to assemble

> the catalogue of all the books of all peoples, Arab and foreigners, existing in the Arab tongue, as well as their writings on the various sciences, together with an account of the life of those who composed them and the social standing of these authors with their genealogies, the date of their birth, the length of their life, the time

of their death, and their cities of origin, their virtues and their faults, from the beginning of the invention of each science up to our own age, the year 377 of the Hegira.

Al-Nadim did not work only from previous bibliographies; his intention, he tells us in his preface, is to "see for himself" the works in question. For this purpose he visited as many libraries as he had knowledge of, "opening volume after volume and reading through scroll after scroll." This all-encompassing work, known as the *Fihrist,* is in fact the best compendium we have of medieval Arab knowledge; it combines in one volume "memory and inventory" and is "a library in its own right."[52]

The *Fihrist* is a unique literary creation. It does not follow Callimachus's alphabetical order, nor is it divided according to the location of the volumes it lists. Meticulously chaotic and delightfully arbitrary, it is the bibliographical record of a boundless library dispersed throughout the world and visible only in the shape al-Nadim chose to give it. In its pages, religious texts sit side by side with profane ones, scientific works grounded in arguments of authority are listed together with writings belonging to what al-Nadim called the rational sciences, while Islamic studies are paired with studies of the beliefs of foreign nations.[53] Both the unity and the variety of the *Fihrist* lie in the eye and mind of its omnivorous author.

But a reader's ambition knows no bounds. A century later, the vizier Abul-Qasim al-Maghribi, dissatisfied with what he deemed to be an incomplete work, composed a *Complement to the Catalogue of al-Nadim* that extended the already inconceivable repertory to an even more astonishing length. The volumes listed in this exaggerated catalogue were likewise, of course, never collected in one place.

Looking for more practical ways to find their path through a maze of books, Arab librarians often allowed themes and disciplines to override the strictures of the alphabetical system and to impose subject divisions on the physical space itself. Such was the library visited towards 980 by a contemporary of al-Nadim, the distinguished doctor Abou Ali El-Hossein Ibn Sina, known in the West as Avicenna. Paying a visit to his patient the Sultan of Bukhara, in what is today Uzbekistan, Avicenna discovered a library conveniently divided into scholarly subjects of all sorts. "I entered a building of many rooms," he tells us.

In each room there were chests full of books, piled one on top of the other. In one room were poetry books in Arabic, in another books of law, and so forth; each room was given over to books of one specific science. I consulted the catalogue of Ancient Works [i.e., Greek] and asked the librarian, keeper of the live memory of the books, for what I wanted. I saw books whose very titles are for the most part unknown, books I had never seen before and which I have never seen since. I read these books and I profited from them, and I was able to recognize each one's position inside its proper scientific category.[54]

These thematic divisions were commonly used together with the alphabetical system in the Islamic Middle Ages. The subjects themselves varied, as did the place in which the books were kept, whether open shelves, closed cupboards or (as in the case of the Bukhara Library) wooden chests. Only the category of sacred books—the Koran, in a variety of copies—was always kept separate, since the word of God is not to be mixed with the word of men.

The cataloguing methods of the Library of Alexandria, with its space organized according to the letters of the alphabet and its books subjected to hierarchies imposed by the selected bibliographies, reached far beyond the borders of Egypt. Even the rulers of Rome created libraries in Alexandria's image. Julius Caesar, who had lived in Alexandria and had certainly frequented the Library, sought to establish in Rome "the finest possible public library," and charged Marcus Terence Varro (who had written an unreliable handbook of library science, quoted approvingly by Pliny) "to collect and classify all manner of Greek and Latin books."[55] The task was not carried out until after Caesar's death; in the first years of the reign of Augustus, Rome's first public library was opened by Asinius Pollio, a friend of Catullus, Horace and Virgil. It was housed in the so-called Atrium of Freedom (its exact location has not yet been established) and decorated with portraits of famous writers.

Roman libraries like that of Asinius Pollio, specially designed to suit the learned reader in spite of names such as "Atrium of Freedom," must have felt powerfully like a place of containment and order. The earliest remains we have of such a library were unearthed on the Palatine Hill in Rome. Because Roman book collections such as Pollio's were bilingual, architects had to design in duplicate the buildings housing them. The Palatine ruins, for instance, reveal one chamber for Greek works and one for works in Latin, each with openings for statues and deep niches for wooden bookcases (*armaria*), while the walls appear to have been lined with shelves and protected by doors. The *armaria* were labelled and their codes inscribed in the catalogues next to the titles of the books they contained. Flights of stairs allowed readers to reach the different thematic areas and, since some of the shelves were higher than arm's length, portable steps were available for those who required them. A reader would have picked up the desired scroll, aided perhaps by the cataloguing librarian, and unfurled it on one of the tables in the middle of the room, to examine it in the midst of a communal mumbling, in the days before silent reading became common, or carried it out and read it under the colonnade, as was customary in the libraries of Greece.[56]

But this is only guesswork. The single depiction we have of a Roman library derives from a line drawing, made in the nineteenth century, of a relief from the Augustan period found in Neumagen, Germany, and now lost.[57] It shows the scrolls lying in tiers of three on deep shelves, probably in alphabetical order within their subject section, their triangular identifying tags clearly visible to the reader, who is stretching his right arm towards them. Unfortunately, the titles on the tags cannot be read. As in any library I visit, I am curious to know what the books are, and even here, faced with the image of an image of a long-vanished collection, my eyes peer into the drawing, trying to make out the names of those ancient scrolls.

A library is an ever-growing entity; it multiplies seemingly unaided, it reproduces itself by purchase, theft, borrowings, gifts, by suggesting gaps through association, by demanding completion of sorts. Whether in

Engraving copied from a no longer extant Roman bas-relief, depicting the method for storing scrolls.

Alexandria, Baghdad or Rome, this expanding mass of words eventually requires systems of classification that allow it space to grow, movable fences that save it from being restricted by the limits of the alphabet or rendered useless by the sheer quantity of items it might hold under a categorical label.

Numbers seem perhaps better suited than letters or subject-headings to maintain order in this unstoppable growth. Even in the seventeenth century, Samuel Pepys realized that, to allow for this surfeit, the infinite universe of numbers was more efficient than the alphabet, and he enumerated his volumes for his "easy finding them to read."[58] The numerical classification I remember from my visits to the school library (and the one most widely used throughout the world) is Dewey's, which lends the spines

Portrait of Melvil Dewey.

of books the aspect of licence plates on rows of parked cars.

Melvil Dewey's story is a curious combination of a generous vision and narrow views. In 1873, while still a student at Amherst College, Massachusetts (where he soon after became acting librarian), the twenty-two-year-old Dewey realized the need for a system of classification that would combine both common sense and practicality. He disliked arbitrary methods, such as that of the New York State Library he had frequented, by which books were arranged alphabetically but "paying no attention to subjects," and so he set himself the task of conceiving a better system. "For months I dreamed night and day that there must be somewhere a satisfactory solution," he wrote fifty years later. "One Sunday during a long sermon . . . the solution flasht over me so that I jumpt in my seat and came very near shouting 'Eureka!' Use *decimals* to number a classification of all human knowledge in print."[59]

Following the subject divisions of earlier scholars, Dewey ambitiously divided the vast field of "all human knowledge in print" into ten thematic groups, and then assigned to each group one hundred numbers which in turn were broken down into a further ten, allowing for a progression *ad infinitum*. Religion, for instance, received the number 200; the Christian Church, the number 260; the Christian God, the number 264.[60] The advantage of what became known as the Dewey Decimal Classification System is that, in principle, each division can be subjected to countless further divisions. God himself can suffer being broken down into his attributes or his avatars, and each attribute and each avatar can undergo yet another fragmentation. That Sunday in church, young Dewey discovered a method of great simplicity and effectiveness that allowed for the huge measure of its task. "My heart is open to anything that's either decimal or about libraries," he once confessed.[61]

Though Dewey's method could be applied to any grouping of books, his vision of the world, reflected in his thematic divisions, was surprisingly restricted. According to one of his biographers, Dewey "espoused 'Anglo-Saxonism,' an American doctrine that touted the unique virtues, mission and destiny of the Anglo-Saxon 'race. . . .' So convinced was he of the rightness of 'Anglo-Saxonism' that he based his definition of 'objectivity' on it."[62] It never seems to have occurred to him that to conceive a universal system that limited the universe to what appeared important to the inhabitants of a small northern island and their descendants was at best insufficient, and at worst defeated its own all-embracing purpose. Mr. Podsnap, in *Our Mutual Friend*, constructs his sense of identity by dismissing everything he doesn't understand or care for as "not English!," believing that what he puts behind him, he instantly puts out of existence, with "a peculiar flourish of his right arm."[63] Dewey understood that he could not do this in a library, especially a limitless library, but he decided instead that everything "not Anglo-Saxon" could somehow be forced to fit into categories of Anglo-Saxon devising.

For practical reasons, however, Dewey's system, a reflection of his time and place, became hugely popular, mainly because it was easily memorized since its pattern was repeated in every subject. The system has been variously revised, simplified and adapted, but essentially Dewey's basic premise remains unchanged: everything conceivable can be attributed a number, so that the infinity of the universe can be contained within the infinite combination of ten digits.

Dewey continued working on his system throughout his life. He believed in adult education for those not fully schooled, in the moral superiority of the Anglo-Saxon race, in simplified spelling that would not force students to memorize the irregularities of the English language (he dropped the "le" at the end of "Melville" shortly after graduating) and would "speed the assimilation of non-English-speaking immigrants into the dominant American culture." He also believed in the importance of public libraries. Libraries, he thought, had to be instruments of easy use "for every soul." He argued that the cornerstone of education was not just the ability to read but the knowledge of how "to get the meaning from the printed page."[64] It was in order to facilitate access to that page that he dreamt up the system for which he is remembered.

Ordered by subject, by importance, ordered according to whether the book was penned by God or by one of God's creatures, ordered alphabetically or by numbers or by the language in which the text is written, every library translates the chaos of discovery and creation into a structured system of hierarchies or a rampage of free associations. Such eclectic classifications rule my own library. Ordered alphabetically, for instance, it incongruously marries humorous Bulgakov to severe Bunin (in my Russian Literature section), and makes formal Boileau follow informal Beauchemin (in Writing in French), properly allots Borges a place next to his friend Bioy Casares (in Writing in Spanish) but opens an ocean of letters between Goethe and his inseparable friend Schiller (in German Literature).

Not only are such methods arbitrary, they are also confusing. Why do I place García Márquez under "G" and García Lorca under "L"?[65] Should the pseudonymous Jane Somers be grouped with her alter ego, Doris Lessing? In the case of books written by two or more writers, should the hierarchy of ABC dictate the book's position, or (as with Nordhoff and Hall) should the fact that the authors are always mentioned in a certain order override the system? Should a Japanese author be listed according to Western or Eastern nomenclature, Kenzaburo Oe under "O" or Oe Kenzaburo under "K"? Should the once-popular historian Hendrik van Loon go under "V" or "L"? Where should I keep the delightful Logan Pearsall Smith, author of my much-loved *All Trivia?* Alphabetical order sparks peculiar questions for which I can offer no sensible answer. Why are there more writers whose names (in English, for instance) begin with "G" than "N" or "H"? Why are there more Gibsons than Nichols and more Grants than Hoggs? Why more Whites than Blacks, more Wrights than Wongs, more Scotts than Frenches?

The novelist Henry Green, attempting to explain his difficulty in putting names to faces in his fiction, had this to say:

Names distract, nicknames are too easy and if leaving both out as it often does makes a book look blind then that to my mind is no disadvantage. Prose is not to be read aloud but to oneself alone at night, and it is not quick as poetry but rather a gathering web of insinuations which go further than names however shared can ever go. Prose should be a long intimacy between strangers with no direct appeal to what both may have known. It should slowly appeal to feelings unexpressed, it should in the end draw tears out of the stone, and feelings are not bounded by the associations common to place names or to persons with whom the reader is unexpectedly familiar.[66]

My thematic and alphabetic library allows me that long intimacy *in spite* of names and *in spite* of appealing to what I have known, awakening feelings for which I have no words except those on the page, and experience of which I have no memory except that of the printed story. To know whether a certain book exists in my library, I have to either rely on my memory (did I once buy that book? did I lend it? was it returned?) or on a cataloguing system like Dewey's (which I am reluctant to undertake). The former forces me to exercise a daily relationship with my books, many unopened for long periods, unread but not forgotten, by going repeatedly through the shelves to see what is there and what is not. The latter lends certain books, which I have acquired from other libraries, mysterious notations on their spines that identify them as having belonged to a nameless phantom reader from the past, cabbalistic concatenations of letters and numbers that once gave them a place and a category, far away and long ago.

Some nights I dream of an entirely anonymous library in which books have no title and boast no author, forming a continuous narrative stream in which all genres, all styles, all stories converge, and all protagonists and all locations are unidentified, a stream into which I can dip at any point of its course. In such a library, the hero of *The Castle* would embark on the *Pequod* in search of the Holy Grail, land on a deserted island to rebuild society from fragments shored against his ruins, speak of his first centenary encounter with ice and recall, in excruciating detail, his early going to bed. In such a library there would be one single book divided into a few thousand volumes and, *pace* Callimachus and Dewey, no catalogue.

THE LIBRARY

AS SPACE

"No room! No room!" they cried out when they saw Alice coming. "There's *plenty* of room!" said Alice indignantly, and she sat down in a large arm-chair at one end of the table.

Lewis Carroll, *Alice's Adventures in Wonderland*

The very fact of knowing that the books in a library are set up according to a rule, whichever that may be, grants them preconceived identities, even before we open their first pages. Before my *Wuthering Heights* unfolds its misty story, it already proclaims itself a work of Literature in English (the section in which I've placed it), a creation of the letter B, a member of some now forgotten community of books (I bought this copy second-hand in Vancouver, where it was allotted the mysterious number 790042B inscribed in pencil on the fly-leaf, corresponding to a classification with which I'm not familiar). It also boasts a place in the aristocracy of chosen books which I take down by design and not by chance (since it sits on the highest shelf, unreachable except with a ladder). Though books are chaotic creations whose most secret meaning lies always just beyond the reader's grasp, the order in which I keep them lends them a certain definition (however trivial) and a certain sense (however arbitrary)—a humble cause for optimism.

Yet one fearful characteristic of the physical world tempers any optimism that a reader may feel in any ordered library: the constraints of space. It has always been my experience that, whatever groupings I choose for my books, the space in which I plan to lodge them necessarily reshapes my choice and, more important, in no time proves too small for them and forces me to change my arrangement. In a library, no empty shelf remains empty for long. Like Nature, libraries abhor a vacuum, and the problem of space is inherent in the very nature of any collection of books. This is the paradox presented by every general library: that if, to a lesser or greater extent, it intends to accumulate and preserve as comprehensive as possible a record of the world, then ultimately its task must be redundant, since it can only be satisfied when the library's borders coincide with those of the world itself.

In my adolescence, I remember watching with a kind of fascinated horror, how night after night the shelves on the wall of my room would fill up, apparently on their own, until no promissory nooks were left. New books, lying flat as in the earliest codex libraries, would begin to pile up one on top of the other. Old books, occupying their measured place during the day, would double and quadruple in volume and keep any newcomers at bay. All around me—on the floor, in the corners, under the bed, on my desk—columns of books would slowly rise and transform the space into a saprophyte forest, its sprouting trunks threatening to crowd me out.

Later, in my home in Toronto, I put up bookshelves

just about everywhere—in bedrooms and kitchen, corridors and bathroom. Even the covered porch had its
shelves, so that my children complained that they felt
they required a library card to enter their own home. But
my books, in spite of any pride of place granted to them,
were never satisfied. Detective Writing, housed in the
basement bedroom, would suddenly outgrow the space
allotted to it and would have to be moved upstairs to one
of the corridor walls, displacing French Literature.
French Literature would now have to be reluctantly
divided into Literature of Quebec, Literature of France
and Literature of Other Francophone Countries. I found
it highly irritating to have Aimé Césaire, for instance,
separated from his friends Eluard and Breton, and to be
forced to exile Louis Hémon's *Maria Chapdelaine*
(Quebec's national romantic epic) into the company of
books by Huysmans and Hugo, just because Hémon happened to have been born in Brittany and I had no room
left in the Québécois section.

Old books that we have known but not possessed
cross our path and invite themselves over. New books
try to seduce us daily with tempting titles and tantalizing
covers. Families beg to be united: volume XVIII of the
Complete Works of Lope de Vega is announced in a catalogue, calling to the other seventeen that sit, barely
leafed through, on my shelf. How fortunate for Captain
Nemo to be able to say, during his twenty-thousand-
league journey under the sea, that "the world ended for
me the day when my Nautilus sank underwater for the
first time. On that day I bought my last volumes, my last
pamphlets, my last periodicals, and since then, it is for
me as if humanity no longer thought nor wrote a single

word."[67] But for readers like myself, there are no "last" purchases this side of the grave.

The English poet Lionel Johnson was so pressed for room that he devised shelves suspended from the ceiling, like chandeliers.[68] A friend of mine in Buenos Aires constructed columns of four-sided shelves that spun on a central axis, quadrupling the space for his books; he called the shelves his dervish-cases. In the library of Althorp, the Northampton estate of Earl Spencer (which before its sale in 1892 comprised forty thousand volumes, including fifty-eight titles by the first English printer, William Caxton), the bookshelves rose to such dizzying heights that in order to consult the top rows a gigantic ladder was required, consisting of "a sturdy pair of steps on wheels, surmounted by a crow's nest containing a seat and small lectern, the general effect resembling a medieval siege-machine."[69] Unfortunately, the inventors of these enthusiastic pieces of furniture, like mad geographers intent on

extending geography to fit ever-expanding maps, are always defeated. Ultimately, the number of books always exceeds the space they are granted.

In the second chapter of *Sylvie and Bruno*, Lewis Carroll dreamt up the following solution: "If we could only *apply* that Rule to books! You know, in finding the Least Common Multiple, we strike out a quantity wherever it occurs, except in the term where it is raised to its highest power. So we should have to erase every recorded thought, except in the sentence where it is expressed with the greatest intensity." His companion objects: "*Some* books would be reduced to blank paper, I'm afraid!" "They would," the narrator admits. "Most libraries would be terribly diminished in *bulk*. But just think what they would gain in *quality!*"[70] In a similar spirit, in Lyons, at the end of the first century, a strict law demanded that, after every literary competition, the losers be forced to erase their poetic efforts with their tongues, so that no second-rate literature would survive.[71]

In a manuscript kept in the Vatican Library (and as yet unpublished), the Milanese humanist Angelo Decembrio describes a drastic culling system by which the young fifteenth-century prince Leonello d'Este furnished his library in Ferrara under the supervision of his teacher, Guarino da Verona.[72] Leonello's system was one of exclusion, rejecting everything except the most precious examples of the literary world. Banished from the princely shelves were monastic encyclopedic works ("oceans of story, as they are called, huge burdens for donkeys,")[73] French and Italian translations of classic texts (but not the originals), and even Dante's *Commedia*, "which may be read on winter nights, by the fire, with the wife and the children, but which does not merit being placed in a scholarly library."[74] Only four classical authors were admitted: Livy, Virgil, Sallust and Cicero. All others were considered minor authors whose work could be bought from any street vendor and lent to friends without fear of losing anything of great worth.

In order to find ways to cope with volume growth (though not always concerned with gaining quality), readers have resorted to all manner of painful devices: pruning their treasures, double-shelving, divesting themselves of certain subjects, giving away their paperbacks, even moving out and leaving the house to their books. Sometimes none of these options seems endurable. Shortly after Christmas 2003, a forty-three-year-old New York man, Patrice Moore, had to be rescued by firefighters from his apartment after spending two days trapped under an avalanche of journals, magazines and books that he had stubbornly accumulated for over a decade. Neighbours heard him moaning and mumbling through the door, which had been blocked by all the paper. Not until the lock was broken with a crowbar and rescuers began digging into the entombing piles of publications was Moore found, in a tiny corner of his apartment, literally buried in books. It took over an hour to extricate him; fifty bags of printed material had to be hauled out before this constant reader could be reached.[75]

In the 1990s, conscious that their old, stately buildings were no longer able to contain the flood of printed matter, the directors of several major libraries decided to erect new premises to lodge their vast collections.

In Paris and London, Buenos Aires and San Francisco (among others), plans were laid out and construction began. Unfortunately, in several cases the design of the new libraries proved ill suited to house books. To compensate for the deficient planning of the new main San Francisco Public Library, in which the architect had not allowed for a sufficiently large amount of shelving space, the administrators pulled hundreds of thousands of books from the library's hold and sent them to a landfill. Since books were selected for destruction on the basis of the length of time they had sat unrequested, in order to save as many books as possible, heroic librarians crept into the stacks at night and stamped the threatened volumes with false withdrawal dates.[76]

To sacrifice the contents in order to spare the container—not only the San Francisco Public Library suffered from such an inane action. Even the Library of Congress in Washington, "the purported library of last resort," became the victim of equally irresponsible behaviour. In 1814, during negotiations by the American Congress to purchase the private library of former American president Thomas Jefferson—to replace the books British troops had burned earlier that year after occupying the Capitol Building in Washington—Cyril

King, the Federalist Party lawmaker, objected, "The Bill would put $23,900 into Mr Jefferson's pocket for about 6,000 books—good, bad and indifferent; old, new and worthless, in languages which many cannot read, and most ought not to." Jefferson answered, "I do not know that my library contains any branch of science which Congress would wish to exclude from their collection: there is, in fact, no subject to which a Member of Congress may not have occasion to refer."[77]

Over a century and a half later, Jefferson's observation has been all but forgotten. In 1996, the *New Yorker* reporter (and best-selling novelist) Nicholson Baker heard that the Library of Congress was replacing most of its enormous collection of late-nineteenth-century and early-twentieth-century newspapers with microfilms and then destroying the originals. The justification for this official act of vandalism was based on "fraudulent" scientific studies on the acidity and embrittlement of paper, something like defending a murder by calling it a case of assisted suicide. Several years of research later, Baker reached the conclusion that the situation was even worse than he had at first feared. Nearly all major university libraries in the United States, as well as most large public libraries, had followed the Library of Congress's example, and some of the rarest periodicals no longer existed except in microfilmed versions.[78] And these versions are faulty, in many ways. Microfilms suffer from smudges, stains and scratches; they cut off text at the margins, and often skip entire sections.

The microfilming culprits were not all American. In 1996 the British Library, whose collection of newspapers had, to a large degree, escaped the bombings of the

Second World War, got rid of more than sixty thousand volumes of collected newsprint, mainly non-Commonwealth journals printed after 1850. A year later, it chose to discard seventy-five runs of Western European publications; shortly afterwards, it gave away its collections of periodicals from Eastern Europe, South America and the United States. In each case, the papers had been microfilmed; in each case, the reason given for the removal of the originals was space. But as Baker argues, microfilms are difficult to read and their reproduction qualities are poor. Even the newer electronic technologies cannot approach the experience of handling an original publication. As any reader knows, a printed page creates its own reading space, its own physical landscape in which the texture of the paper, the colour of the

The Library of Congress, Washington, D.C.

ink, the view of the whole ensemble acquire in the reader's hands specific meanings that lend tone and context to the words. (Columbia University's librarian Patricia Battin, a fierce advocate for the microfilming of books, disagreed with this notion. "The value," she wrote, "in intellectual terms, of the proximity of the book to the user has never been satisfactorily established."[79] There speaks a dolt, someone utterly insensitive, in intellectual or any other terms, to the experience of reading.)

But above all, the argument that calls for electronic reproduction on account of the endangered life of paper is a false one. Anybody who has used a computer knows how easy it is to lose a text on the screen, to come upon a faulty disk or CD, to have the hard drive crash beyond all appeal. The tools of the electronic media are not immortal. The life of a disk is about seven years; a CD-ROM lasts about ten. In 1986, the BBC spent two and a half million pounds creating a computer-based, multimedia version of the Domesday Book, the eleventh-century census of England compiled by Norman monks. More ambitious than its predecessor, the electronic Domesday Book contained 250,000 place names, 25,000 maps, 50,000 pictures, 3,000 data sets and 60 minutes of moving pictures, plus scores of accounts that recorded "life in Britain" during that year. Over a million people contributed to the project, which was stored on twelve-inch laser disks that could only be deciphered by a special BBC microcomputer. Sixteen years later, in March 2002, an attempt was made to read the information on one of the few such computers still in existence. The attempt failed. Further solutions were sought to retrieve the data,

The Domesday Book in sections, in its present state.

but none was entirely successful. "There is currently no demonstrably viable technical solution to this problem," said Jeff Rothenberg of the Rand Corporation, one of the world experts on data preservation, called in to assist. "Yet, if it is not solved, our increasingly digital heritage is in grave risk of being lost."[80] By contrast, the original Domesday Book, almost a thousand years old, written in ink on paper and kept at the Public Record Office in Kew, is in fine condition and still perfectly readable.

The director for the electronic records archive program at the National Archives and Records Administration of the United States confessed in November 2004 that the preservation of electronic material, even for the next decade, let alone for eternity, "is a global problem for the biggest governments and the biggest corporations all the way down to individuals."[81] Since no clear solution is available, electronic experts recommend that users copy their materials onto CDs, but even these are of short duration. The lifespan of data recorded on a CD with a CD burner could be as little as five years. In fact, we don't know for how long it will be possible to read a text inscribed on a 2004 CD. And while it is true that acidity and brittleness, fire and the legendary bookworms threaten ancient codexes and scrolls, not everything written or printed on parchment or paper is condemned to an early grave. A few years ago, in the Archeological Museum of Naples, I saw, held between two plates of glass, the ashes of a papyrus rescued from the ruins of Pompeii. It was two thousand years old; it had been burnt by the fires of Vesuvius, it had been buried under a flow of lava—and I could still read the letters written on it, with astonishing clarity.

And yet, both libraries—the one of paper and the electronic one—can and should coexist. Unfortunately, one is too often favoured to the detriment of the other. The new Library of Alexandria, inaugurated in October 2003, proposed, as one of its major projects, a parallel virtual library—the Alexandria Library Scholars Collective. This electronic library was set up by the American artist Rhonda Roland Shearer, and requires an annual operating budget of half a million American dollars, a sum likely to increase considerably in the future. These two institutions, both attempts to reincarnate the ancient library of Callimachus's time, present a paradox. While the shelves of the new stone and glass library stand almost empty for lack of financial resources, displaying a meagre collection of paperbacks and castoffs plus donations from international publishers, the virtual library is being filled with books from all over the world, scanned for the most part by a team of technicians at Carnegie-Mellon University and using software called CyberBook Plus, developed by Shearer herself and designed to allow for different formats and languages "with heavy emphasis on visual rather than posted texts."[82]

The Alexandria Library Scholars Collective is not unique in its ambition to compete with paper libraries. In 2004 the most popular of all Internet search services, Google, announced that it had concluded agreements with several of the world's leading research libraries— Harvard, the Bodleian, Stanford, the New York Public Library—to scan part of their holdings and make the books available on-line to researchers, who would no longer have to travel to the libraries themselves or dust their way through endless stacks of paper and ink.[83] Though, for financial and administrative reasons, Google cancelled its project in July 2005, it will doubtless be resurrected in the future, since it is so obviously suited to the capabilities of the Web. In the next few years, in all probability, millions of pages will be waiting for their on-line readers. As in the cautionary tale of Babel, "nothing will be restrained from them, which they have imagined to do,"[84] and we shall soon be able to summon up the whole of the ghostly stock of all manner of Alexandrias past or future, with the mere tap of a finger.

The practical arguments for such a step are irrefutable. Quantity, speed, precision, on-demand availability are obviously important to the researching scholar. And the birth of a new technology need not mean the death of an earlier one: the invention of photography did not eliminate painting, it renewed it, and the screen and the codex can feed off each other and coexist amicably on the same reader's desk. In comparing the virtual library to the traditional one of paper and ink, we need to remember several things: that reading often requires slowness, depth and context; that our electronic technology is still fragile and that, since it keeps changing, it prevents us many times from retrieving what was once stored in now superseded containers; that leafing through a book or roaming through shelves is an intimate part of the craft of reading and cannot be entirely replaced by scrolling down a screen, any more than real travel can be replaced by travelogues and 3-D gadgets.

Perhaps this is the crux. Reading a book is not perfectly equivalent to reading a screen, no matter what the text. Watching a play is not equivalent to seeing a film, seeing a film is not equivalent to viewing a DVD or videotape, gazing upon a painting is not equivalent to examining a photograph. Every technology provides a medium (the dictum was pronounced in 1964 by Marshall McLuhan[85]) that characterizes the work it embodies, and defines its optimum storage and access. Plays can be performed in circular spaces that are ill-suited for the projection of films; a DVD seen in an intimate room has a different quality from the same film seen on a large screen; photos well-reproduced in a book can be fully appreciated by the viewer, while no reproduction allows the full experience of seeing an original painting.

Baker ends his book with four useful recommendations: that libraries be obliged to publish the lists of the publications they intend to discard; that all publications sent to and rejected by the Library of Congress

be indexed and stocked in ancillary buildings provided by the state; that newspapers routinely be bound and saved; that either the program to microfilm or digitize books should be abolished, or it should become obligatory not to destroy the originals after they are electronically processed. Together, electronic storage and the physical preservation of printed matter grant a library the fulfillment of at least one of its ambitions: comprehensiveness.

Or, if nothing else, a certain measure of comprehensiveness. The nineteenth-century American scholar Oliver Wendell Holmes admonished, "Every library should try to be complete on something, if it were only the history of pinheads,"[86] echoing the sentiments of the

French scholar Gabriel Naudé, who in 1627 published a modest *Advice for Setting Up a Library* (revised and expanded several years later) in which he went even further in the reader's demands. "There is nothing," Naudé wrote, "that renders a Library more recommendable, than when every man finds in it that which he is looking for and cannot find anywhere else; therefore the perfect motto is, that there exists no book, however bad or badly reviewed, that may not be sought after in some future time by a certain reader."[87] These remarks demand from us an impossibility, since every library is, by needs, an incomplete creation, a work-in-progress, and every empty shelf announces the books to come.

And yet it is for those empty spaces that we hoard knowledge. In the year 764, after the suppression of the Emi Rebellion, the Japanese Empress Shotoku, believing that the end of the world was near, decided to leave a record of her times for whatever new generations might rise from the ashes. Following her orders, four *dharani-sutra* (essential words of wisdom transcribed into Chinese from the Sanskrit) were printed from woodblocks on strips of paper and inserted into small wooden stupas—representations of the universe that depict the square base of the earth and the ascending circles of the heavens fixed around the staff of the Lord Buddha. These stupas were then distributed among the ten leading Buddhist temples of the empire.[88]

The empress imagined that she could preserve in this way a distillation of the accumulated knowledge up to her time. Ten centuries later, in 1751, her project was unknowingly restated by Denis Diderot, the co-editor (with Jean le Rond d'Alembert) of the greatest publishing project of the French Enlightenment, the *Encyclopédie, ou, Dictionnaire raisonné des sciences, des arts, et des métiers.*

It is odd that the man who would later be accused of being one of the Catholic Church's fiercest enemies (the *Encyclopédie* was placed on the Church's *Index of Forbidden Books* and Diderot was threatened with excommunication) should have begun his scholarly career as a devout Jesuit student. Diderot was born in 1713, seventy-six years before the beginning of the French Revolution. Having attended the Jesuit College at Langres as a child, in his early twenties he became an ardent and pious believer. He refused the comforts of his family home (his father was a wealthy master cutler of international fame), took to wearing a hair shirt and sleeping on straw, and eventually, urged on by his religious instructors, decided to run away and enter holy orders. Alerted to the plan, his father barred the door and demanded to know where his son was going at midnight. "To Paris, to join the Jesuits," said Diderot. "Your wishes will be granted," his father replied, "but it will not be tonight."[89]

Diderot Senior kept his promise only in part. He sent his son to complete his education in Paris, where he attended not the Jesuit Collège Louis-le-Grand but the Collège d'Harcourt, founded by the Jansenists (followers of an austere religious school of thought whose tenets were similar in many ways to those of Calvinism), and later the University of Paris. Diderot's intention to obtain a doctorate in theology was never fulfilled. Instead, he studied mathematics, classical literature and foreign languages without a definite goal in mind, until his father, alarmed at the prospect of having an eternal student on his hands, cut off all financial support and ordered the young man home. Diderot disobeyed, and for the next several years earned his living in Paris as a journalist and a teacher.

Diderot and d'Alembert met when the former had just turned thirty. D'Alembert was four years younger but had already distinguished himself in the field of mathematics. He possessed (according to a contemporary account) a "luminous, profound and solid mind"[90] that much appealed to Diderot. A foundling who had been abandoned as a baby on the steps of a Paris church, d'Alembert was someone with little concern for social prestige; he maintained that the motto of every man of letters should be "Liberty, Truth and Poverty," the latter achieved, in his case, with no great effort.

Some fifteen years before their meeting, in 1728, the Scottish scholar Ephraim Chambers had published a fairly comprehensive *Cyclopedia* (the first in the English language, and no relation to the present-day *Chambers*) that inspired various other such works, among them Dr. Johnson's *Dictionary*. Early in 1745, the Paris bookseller André-François Le Breton, unable to secure the translation of the *Cyclopedia* into French, engaged the services first of d'Alembert and then of Diderot to edit a similar work but on a vaster scale. Arguing that the *Cyclopedia* was, to a large extent, a pilfering of a number of French texts, Diderot suggested that to translate the work back into what was effectively its original tongue would be a senseless exercise; better to collect new material and offer readers a comprehensive and up-to-date panorama of what the arts and sciences had produced in recent times.

In a game of self-reflecting mirrors, Diderot defined his grand twenty-eight-volume publication (seventeen volumes of text and eleven of illustrations) in an article titled "Encyclopédie" in that same *Encyclopédie:* "The goal of the *Encyclopédie*," he wrote, "is to assemble the knowledge scattered over the surface of the globe and to expose its general system to the men who come after us, so that the labours of centuries past do not prove useless to the centuries to come. . . . May the *Encyclopédie* become a sanctuary in which human knowledge is protected from time and from change."[91] The notion of an encyclopedia as a sanctuary is appealing. In 1783, eleven years after the completion of Diderot's monumental project, the writer Guillaume Grivel imagined this sanctuary as the cornerstone of a future society which, like the one imagined by the Japanese empress, must rebuild itself from its ruins. In the first volume of a novel recounting the adventures of a group of new Crusoes shipwrecked on an uncharted island, Grivel describes how the new colonists rescue several volumes of Diderot's *Encyclopédie* from their wreck and, on the basis of its learned articles, attempt to reconstruct the society they have been forced to leave behind.[92]

The *Encyclopédie* was also conceived as an archival and interactive library. In the prospectus that announced the vast project, Diderot declared that it would "serve all the purposes of a library for a professional man on any subject apart from his own." Defending his decision to arrange this comprehensive "library" in alphabetical order, Diderot explained that it would not destroy liaison between subjects nor violate "the tree of knowledge" but, on the contrary, the system would be made visible in "the disposition of the materials within each article and by the exactitude and frequency of cross-references."[93] What he was proposing by these cross-references was to present the diverse articles not as independent texts, each occupying the exclusive field of a given subject, but as a crossweaving of subjects that would in many cases "occupy the same shelf." Thus he imagined his "library" as a room in which different "books" were placed in a single space. A discussion of CALVINISM, which, on its own, would have aroused the censorious eye of the Church, is included in an entry on GENEVA; a critical assessment of the Church's sacraments is implied in a cross-reference such as "ANTHRO-POPHAGY: see EUCHARIST, COMMUNION, ALTAR, etc." Sometimes he quoted a foreign character (a Chinese savant, a Turk) to voice criticism of religious dogma, simultaneously including the description of other cultures or philosophies; sometimes he took a word in its broadest sense, so that, for example, under ADORATION he was able to discuss both the worship of God and that of a beautiful woman, daringly associating one with the other.

The first volume of the *Encyclopédie* sold quickly, in spite of its high price. By the time the second volume appeared, in 1752, the Jesuits were so enraged by what was in their eyes obvious blasphemy that they urged Louis XV to issue a royal ban. Since one of Louis's daughters had fallen deathly ill, his confessor convinced him that "God might save her if the King, as a token of piety, would suppress the *Encyclopédie*."[94] Louis obeyed, but the *Encyclopédie* resumed publication a year later, thanks to the efforts of the Royal Director of

Publications (a sort of minister of Communications), the enlightened Lamoignon de Malesherbes, who had gone as far as suggesting to Diderot that he hide the manuscripts of future volumes in Malesherbes's own house until the conflict blew over.

Though Diderot does not explicitly mention space in his statement of purpose, the notion of knowledge occupying a physical place is implicit in his words. To assemble scattered knowledge is, for Diderot, to ground that knowledge on a page, and the page between the covers of a book, and the book on the shelves of a library. An encyclopedia can be, among many other things, a space-saving device, since a library endlessly divided into books requires an ever-expanding home that can take on nightmare dimensions. Legend has it that Sarah Winchester, widow of the famous gun-maker whose rifle "won the West," was told by a medium that as long as construction on her California house continued, the ghosts of the Indians killed by her husband's rifle would be kept at bay. The house grew and grew, like a thing in a dream, until its hundred and sixty rooms covered six acres of ground; this monster is still visible in the heart of Silicon Valley.[95] Every library suffers from this urge to increase in order to pacify our literary ghosts, "the ancient dead who rise from books to speak to us" (as Seneca described them in the first century A.D.),[96] to branch out and bloat until, on some inconceivable last day, it will include every volume ever written on every subject imaginable.

One warm afternoon in the late nineteenth century, two middle-aged office clerks met on a bench on the

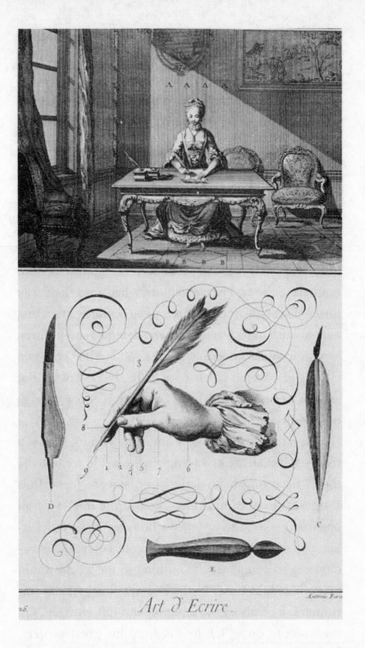

A page from Diderot's Encyclopédie, illustrating the entry on "Writing."

Boulevard Bourdon in Paris and immediately became the best of friends. Bouvard and Pécuchet (the names Gustave Flaubert gave to his two comic heroes) discovered through their friendship a common purpose: the pursuit of universal knowledge. To achieve this ambitious goal, next to which Diderot's achievement appears delightfully modest, they attempted to read everything they could find on every branch of human endeavour, and cull from their readings the most outstanding facts and ideas, an enterprise that was, of course, endless. Appropriately, *Bouvard and Pécuchet* was published unfinished one year after Flaubert's death in 1880, but not before the two brave explorers had read their way through many learned libraries of agriculture, literature, animal husbandry, medicine, archaeology and politics, always with disappointing results. What Flaubert's two clowns discovered is what we have always known but seldom believed: that the accumulation of knowledge isn't knowledge.[97]

Bouvard and Pécuchet's ambition is now almost a reality, when all the knowledge in the world seems to be there, flickering behind the siren screen. Jorge Luis Borges, who once imagined the infinite library of all possible books,[98] also invented a Bouvard-and-Pécuchet-like character who attempts to compile a universal encyclopedia so complete that nothing in the world would be excluded from it.[99] In the end, like his French forerunners, he fails in his attempt, but not entirely. On the evening on which he gives up his great project, he hires a horse and buggy and takes a tour of the city. He sees brick walls, ordinary people, houses, a river, a marketplace, and feels that somehow all these things are his own work. He realizes that his project was not impossible but merely redundant. The world encyclopedia, the universal library, exists, and is the world itself.

THE LIBRARY

AS POWER

The power of readers lies not in their ability to gather
information, in their ordering and cataloguing capabil-
ity, but in their gift to interpret, associate and transform
their reading. For the Talmudic schools, as for those of
Islam, a scholar can turn religious faith into an active
power through the craft of reading, since the knowledge
acquired through books is a gift from God. According to
an early *hadith*, or Islamic tradition, "one scholar is more
powerful against the Devil than a thousand worship-
pers."[100] For these cultures of the Book, knowledge lies
not in the accumulation of texts or information, nor in
the object of the book itself, but in the experience rescued from the page and transformed again into experience, in the words reflected both in the outside world and
in the reader's own being.

In the seventeenth century, Gottfried Wilhelm Leibnitz,
the celebrated German mathematician, philosopher and

jurist, declared that a library's value was determined only by its contents and the use readers made of that contents, not by the number of its volumes or the rarity of its treasures. He compared the institution of a library to a church or a school, a place of instruction and learning, and campaigned in favour of collecting, above all, scientific titles, while doing away with books that he considered merely decorative or entertaining, and therefore useless. "A treatise of architecture or a collection of periodicals," he wrote, "is worth a hundred volumes of literary classics,"[101] and he preferred small books to the larger folios because they saved space and avoided, he thought, superfluous embellishments. He argued that the mission of libraries was to help communication between scholars, and he conceived the idea of a national bibliographical organization that would assist scientists in learning of the discoveries made by their contemporaries. In 1690 he was appointed librarian to the ducal library of Brunswick-Lüneberg in Hanover, and later he became librarian at the important Herzog August Bibliothek at Wolfenbüttel, a post he retained until his death in 1716. Leibnitz was responsible for transferring the Wolfenbüttel collection from its original site to a building he judged better suited to the housing of books, with a glass roof that let in natural light, and several storeys of shelving space. The wooden structure of the building, however, did not allow for heating, and those readers who bravely sought out the books' wise words during the winter months did so with trembling hands and chattering teeth.[102]

Despite Leibnitz's contention that a library should be valued strictly for its contents, books as objects have often been granted spurious authority, and the edifice

The Herzog August Wolfenbüttel Library.

of a library has superstitiously been seen as that authority's symbolic monument. When, in Emile Zola's *L'Assommoir,* an enthusiast of the Emperor Napoleon III is shown a book that portrays the monarch as a lecherous seducer, the poor man is incapable of finding words to defend his king because "it was all in a book; he could not deny it!"[103] Even today, when little or no importance is accorded to the intellectual act, books, read or unread, whatever their allotted use or value, are often lent such awe-inspiring prestige. Fat volumes of memoirs are still authored by those who wish to be seen as powerful, and libraries are still founded by (and named after) politicians who, like the ancient kings of Mesopotamia, wish to be remembered as purveyors of that power. In the United States, a string of presidential libraries testifies to this desire for intellectual immortality (as well as tax relief). In France, every year offers a crop of confessional writings, candid recollections and even fiction by leading politicians; in 1994 ex-president Valéry Giscard d'Estaing went as far as demanding membership in the exclusive Académie Française, reserved for the elite of French intellectuals, on the strength of a slim romantic novel, *Le Passage.*[104] He succeeded. In Argentina, both Evita and Juan Perón prided themselves on their auto-biographies—cum—political testaments, which everyone knew had been ghost-written. Wishing to dispel the image of an illiterate ruler, early on in his career Perón had himself invited by the Argentinian Academy of Letters to pronounce a speech on the four hundredth anniversary of the birth of Cervantes—an author whose work, he laughingly confessed later in life, he hadn't ever bothered to read,[105] but whose large leather-bound,

The last great king of Assyria, Ashurbanipal.

gold-lettered tomes could be seen behind him in several official photographs.

King Ashurbanipal, Assyria's last important monarch, who ruled from 668 to 633 B.C., was fully aware of the association between rulers and the written word. He boasted that he himself was a scribe, though "among the kings, my forerunners, none had learned such an art." His collection of tablets assembled in his palace in Nineveh, while meant for private use, nevertheless stated in the colophon of tablet after tablet, for all to read, that the power granted by the art of letters had been bestowed into his hands:

> Palace of Ashurbanipal, King of the World, King of Assyria, who trusts in Ashur and Ninlil, whom Nabu and Tashmetu gave wide-open ears and who was given profound insight. . . . The wisdom of Nabu, the signs of writing, as many as have been devised, I wrote on tablets, I arranged the tablets in series, I collated [them], and for my royal contemplation and recital I placed them in my palace.[106]

Though Ashurbanipal, like hosts of rulers after him, claimed to be proud of his talents as a scribe and reader, what clearly mattered most to him was not the transformation of experience into learning but the emblematic representation of the powerful qualities associated with books. Under such rulers, libraries become not "temples of learning" (as the commonplace has it) but temples to a benefactor, founder or provider.

Centuries after Ashurbanipal, the symbolic value of funding a library has not much changed. Even during the Renaissance, when libraries in Europe became officially public (beginning with the Ambrosiana in Milan, in 1609), the prestige of funding, endowing or building such an institution remained the privilege of a benefactor, not a community. The notorious millionaires who, in the nineteenth and twentieth centuries, made their fortunes in the factories, mills and banks of the United States assiduously used their money to establish schools, museums and, above all, libraries which, beyond their importance as cultural centres, became monuments to their founders.

"What is the best gift which can be given to a community?" asked the most famous of these benefactors, Andrew Carnegie, in 1890. "A free library occupies the first place," he declared in answer to his own question.[107] Not everyone was of his opinion. In Britain, for instance, the truism that "a public library is essential for the welfare of a community" was not officially proclaimed until 1850, when the MP for Dumfries, William Ewart, forced a bill through Parliament establishing the right of every town to have a free public library.[108] As late as 1832, Thomas Carlyle was angrily asking, "Why is there not a Majesty's library in every county town? There is a Majesty's jail and gallows in every one!"[109]

Andrew Carnegie's story does not allow for simple conclusions. His relationship to wealth and the culture of books was complex and contradictory. Implacable in his pursuit of financial gain, he donated almost 90 percent of his enormous fortune to fund all manner of public institutions, including over 2,500 libraries in a dozen English-speaking countries, from his native Scotland to Fiji and the Seychelles. He worshipped but did not love intellectual pursuits. "The public library was his temple," wrote one of his biographers, "and the 'Letters to the Editor' column his confessional."[110] Brutal in the treatment of his workers, he established a private pension list to assist financially over four hundred artists, scientists and poets, among them Walt Whitman, who described his benefactor as a source "of kindest good will." Though he believed in the sanctity of capitalism (what he called "the Gospel of Wealth"), he insisted that "a working man is a more useful citizen and ought to be more respected than an idle prince."[111]

Carnegie's beginnings, as he himself was quick to remind his listeners, were desperately poor. Two men exerted the greatest influence over his childhood in Scotland. One was his father, an able weaver of damask cloth, whose skills were soon made redundant by the new manufacturing technology of the Industrial Revolution. Will Carnegie was by all accounts a man of spirit who, in spite of being forced to work ten to twelve hours a day, found time to create with his fellow-weavers a small communal library in Dunfermline, a courageous act that must have strongly impressed his young son. The other was Carnegie's uncle Thomas Morrison, a land-reform evangelist who preached non-violent opposition to the abusive industrialists and the end of what he saw as the enduring feudal system in Scotland. "Our rule," he taught, "is *Each shall possess; all shall enjoy;* Our principle, *universal and equal right;* and our 'law of the land' shall be *Every man a lord; every woman a lady;* and *every child an heir.*"[112] During one of the riots against the large linen manufacturers who were threatening, once again, to cut the wages of the weavers, Uncle Thomas was arrested. Though he was never formally charged, the incident marked the young Carnegie powerfully, though not enough to colour his business ethics. Years later, he displayed in his study the framed handbill with the charges, calling it his "title to nobility." From such experiences, he said, he developed "into a violent young Republican whose motto was 'death to privilege.'"[113] And yet, when Carnegie ruled over his own factories and mills in Pittsburgh, his employees were forced to work seven days a week, were denied all holidays except Christmas and the Fourth of July, were paid miserly wages and were forced to live in insalubrious housing estates where the sewers ran alongside the water pipes. One-fifth of Carnegie's men died due to accidents.[114]

In 1848, when Carnegie was barely thirteen, his parents became destitute. To escape famine, the family emigrated to the United States and, after a difficult crossing, settled in Pittsburgh, where they discovered that the situation of the weavers was scarcely better than back home. At length the young Carnegie found work, first at the Atlantic and Ohio Telegraph Company and later with the Pennsylvania Railroad. In the railroad offices, work ended early in the evening, leaving the boy time "for self-improvement."

In downtown Pittsburgh, Carnegie discovered a free public library founded by a certain Colonel Anderson "for apprentices for whom school was not an option." "Colonel Anderson opened to me the intellectual wealth of the world," he recalled in 1887. "I became fond of reading. I reveled week after week in the books. My toil was light, for I got up at six o'clock in the morning, contented to work until six in the evening if there was then a book for me to read."[115]

But in 1853 Anderson's library changed locale and the new administration decided to charge all customers, except "true apprentices" (that is to say, those bound to an employer), a fee of two dollars. The sixteen-year-old Carnegie, an apprentice not officially "bound," felt that the measure was unjust and, after uselessly arguing with the librarian, wrote an open letter to the editor of the *Pittsburgh Dispatch*. It appeared on 13 May 1853.

Mr Editor:

Believing that you take a deep interest in whatever tends to elevate, instruct and improve the youth of this country, I am induced to call your attention to the following. You will remember that some time ago Mr. Anderson (a gentleman of this city) bequested a large sum of money to establish and support a Library for working boys and apprentices residing here. It has been in successful operation for over a year, scattering precious seeds among us, and although fallen [sic] "by the wayside and in stony places," not a few have found good ground. Every working boy has been freely admitted only requiring his parents or guardian to become surety. But its means of doing good have recently been greatly circumscribed by new directors who refuse to allow any boy who *is not learning a trade* and *bound* for a stated time to become a member. I rather think that the new directors have misunderstood the generous donor's *intentions*. It can hardly be thought that he meant to exclude boys employed in stores merely because they are not bound.

A Working Boy though not bound.[116]

After a brisk exchange of letters, the harried librarian was forced to call a meeting of trustees, in which the question was settled in the boy's favour. For Carnegie, it was a question of what he himself considered "fair usage." As he was later repeatedly to prove, any argument of justice, any question of rights, any effort of self-improvement only carried weight if it ultimately succeeded in procuring Carnegie himself greater savings or greater power. "Money no object compared to power," he said to one of his business partners some twenty-five years later.[117]

The United States of the late nineteenth century provided Carnegie with an ideal setting for his convictions. Called upon on one occasion to exalt the merits of American institutions in comparison to those of his native Scotland, he described his adopted country as "the perfect place to pursue one's business." In the United States, he argued, "the mind is freed from superstitious reverence to old customs, unawed by gorgeous and unmeaning show and form." As his biographer Peter Krass points out, in Carnegie's description of the American utopia "there was no mention of the cotton and iron riots in which the police forces were routed, no word of slavery, Indian relocation, or women's suffrage in discussing equality of voice.

Carnegie presenting his trust as "a Trustworthy Beast" to Uncle Sam,
a cartoon from Harper's Weekly.

[Carnegie] had a selective memory; he preferred to
ignore America's underside, as he would when making
his millions in steel while his exploited workers died by
the dozens."[118]

Carnegie believed that a man must be ruthless if he
was to become wealthy, but he also believed that such
wealth should be employed in "illuminating the spirit" of
the community he exploited. To his detractors, the
libraries he funded were merely stepping-stones to personal glorification. He very rarely gave money for books,
only for the building in which they were to be lodged,

and even then he stipulated that the town provide the site and the cash to maintain the library. He insisted that his libraries run as efficiently as his mills, and that no extravagance be indulged in. Nor did he give to state libraries or subscription libraries, because these institutions had access to alternative funding. "He has bought fame and paid cash for it," Mark Twain once quipped.[119]

Many criticized the Carnegie libraries as anti-democratic, judging them "centres for exerting social control on the working-classes," "forcing upon the readers capitalistic ideas and values in an attempt to control their thoughts and actions."[120] Whatever the case, these libraries served a purpose well beyond Carnegie's self-aggrandizement. When the architect who designed Carnegie's first library asked for the millionaire's coat of arms to be carved over the entrance, Carnegie, who had no such distinction, suggested instead an allegorical rising sun surrounded by the words "Let There Be Light."[121] For decades the Carnegie libraries remained a paradox: a monument to their founder, and a fruitful cultural instrument that helped awaken thousands of intellectual lives.

Dozens of writers have acknowledged their debt to the Carnegie libraries. John Updike, describing his own experiences as a teenager at the Carnegie Library of Reading, Pennsylvania, spoke of his gratitude "for the freedom given me in those formative years when we, generally speaking, become lifelong readers or not." He concluded, "A kind of heaven opened up for me there."[122] Eudora Welty traced back to the Carnegie Library of Jackson, Mississippi, the beginnings of her literary life. As Carnegie had stipulated, his donation was conditional

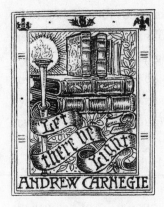

on the community's undertaking to guarantee the upkeep and smooth administration of the library; in Jackson, in 1918, the librarian in charge of these tasks was a certain Mrs. Calloway. Mrs. Calloway, Welty recalled, "ran the Library absolutely by herself, from the desk where she sat with her back to the books and facing the stairs, her dragon eye on the front door, where who knew what kind of person might come in from the public? SILENCE in big black letters was on signs tacked up everywhere." Mrs. Calloway made her own rules about books. "You could not take back a book to the Library on the same day you'd taken it out; it made no difference to her that you'd read every word in it and needed another to start. You could take out two books at a time and two books only; this applied as long as you were a child and also for the rest of your life." But such arbitrary rules made no difference to Welty's reading passion; what counted was that someone (she did not then know who this distant benefactor was) had set up a treasure trove for her personally (she believed), through which her "devouring wish to read" was instantly granted.[123]

The sarcastic critic H.L. Mencken objected. "Go to the nearest Carnegie Library," he instructed, "and examine its catalog of books. The chances are five to one that you will find the place full of literary bilge and as bare of good books as a Boston bookshop."[124] But for most writers, even if the stock of books is not formidable, to be able to enter a place where books are seemingly numberless and available for the asking is a joy in itself. "I knew this was bliss," Welty wrote late in life, "knew it at the time. Taste isn't nearly so important; it comes in its own time. I wanted to read *immediately*. The only fear was that of books coming to an end."

Carnegie himself may have believed that the buildings he paid for would serve as proof of "my efforts to make the earth a little better than I found it."[125] Whatever his desire may have been, for hundreds of thousands of readers the Carnegie libraries became not the proof of any selfless or egotistical concern, or of a millionaire's magnanimity, but the necessary intellectual stronghold at the heart of any literate society, a place where all citizens, provided they can read, are granted the basic right to make themselves "powerful against the Devil."

THE LIBRARY

AS SHADOW

But that's the price we have to pay for stability. You've got to choose between happiness and what people used to call high art. We've sacrificed the high art.

Aldous Huxley, *Brave New World*

We dream of a library of literature created by everyone and belonging to no one, a library that is immortal and will mysteriously lend order to the universe, and yet we know that every orderly choice, every catalogued realm of the imagination, sets up a tyrannical hierarchy of exclusion. Every library is exclusionary, since its selection, however vast, leaves outside its walls endless shelves of writing that, for reasons of taste, knowledge, space and time, have not been included. Every library conjures up its own dark ghost; every ordering sets up, in its wake, a shadow library of absences. Of Aeschylus's 90 plays only 7 have reached us; of the 80-odd dramas of Euripides, only 18 (if we include the *Rhesus,* of doubtful authenticity); of the 120 plays of Sophocles, a mere 7.

If every library is in some sense a reflection of its readers, it is also an image of that which we are not, and cannot be. Even within the strictest circumscriptions, any choice of books will be greater than its label, and

A book-burning in Warsaw, Indiana.

an inquiring reader will find danger (salutary or reprehensible) in the safest, most invigilated places. Our mistake, perhaps, has been to look upon a library as an all-encompassing but neutral space. "The keepers," wrote the American poet Archibald MacLeish during his posting as librarian of Congress, "whether they wish so or not, cannot be neutral."[126] Every library both embraces and rejects. Every library is by definition the result of choice, and necessarily limited in its scope. And every choice excludes another, the choice not made. The act of reading parallels endlessly the act of censorship.

This implicit censorship starts with the earliest Mesopotamian libraries we know of, from the beginning of the third millennium B.C.[127] Unlike official archives, set up to preserve the daily transactions and ephemeral dealings of a particular group, these libraries collected works of a more general nature, such as the so-called royal inscriptions (commemorative tablets of stone or metal that retold important political events, akin to the broadsheets of seventeenth-century Europe or today's current events best-sellers). In all probability these libraries were privately owned—personal spaces set up by lovers of the written word, who would often instruct the scribes to copy the owner's name on the tablets as a mark of possession. Even libraries attached to a temple usually carried the name of a high priest or some other important personage responsible for the collection. So as to preserve the order established by a particular shelving or cataloguing method, certain library books carried a warning colophon intended to dissuade anyone wishing to tamper with the assigned category. A dictionary from the seventh century B.C. carries this prayer: "May Ishtar bless the reader who will not alter this tablet nor place it elsewhere in the library, and may She denounce in anger he who dares withdraw it from this building."[128] I have placed this warning on the wall of my own library to ward off borrowers in the night.

Most of the owners of these collections were of royal blood, and they kept their libraries stocked through the agency of buyers and looters. King Ashurbanipal, in order to supplement his already considerable library, was known to dispatch representatives throughout his vast kingdom to search for whatever volumes might be missing. He had no guiding principle defined by categories (later imposed on the collection); his was a haphazard hoarding of anything at hand.[129] We have a letter in which Ashurbanipal, after listing the books he is seeking, insists that the task should be carried out without delay. "Find them and dispatch them to me. Nothing should detain them. And in the future, if you discover other tablets not herewith mentioned, inspect them and, if you consider them of interest for the library, collect them and send them on to me."[130] A similar all-inclusive impulse governed the composition of other Mesopotamian lists and catalogues. Commenting on the celebrated Code of Hammurabi, that compendium of laws from the eighteenth century B.C., the historian Jean Bottéro stressed the fact that it included in its enumerations "not only the common and commonly observable reality, but also the exceptional, the aberrant: in the end, everything *possible*."[131]

Though a library such as that of Ashurbanipal was the visible expression of earthly power, no single person, however royal, could hope to read through it all. To read every book and to digest all the information, the king recruited other eyes and other hands to scan the tablets and summarize their findings, so that in reading these digests he might be able to boast that he was familiar with the library's entire contents. Scholars extracted the meat from the texts and then, "like pelicans," regurgitated it for the benefit of others.

Four centuries after Ashurbanipal, in the first half of the second century B.C., a couple of the principal librarians of Alexandria, Aristophanes of Byzantium and his disciple

A contemporary cartoon depicting a book-burning in Nazi Germany.

Aristarchus of Samothrace, decided to assist their readers in a similar fashion. Not only did they select and gloss all manner of important works, but they also set out to compile a catalogue of authors who, in their opinion, surpassed all others in literary excellence.[132] The qualifications of the two scholars were impeccable. Aristophanes had edited the works of Homer and Hesiod,[133] and to his edition of the latter he had added brief critical notes in which he listed other writers who had dealt with the same material; these notes, known as *hypotheseis*, were essentially annotated bibliographies that allowed readers a quick and exact overview of a certain subject. Aristarchus had also edited the works of Homer, with a rigour that was legendary, so that any exacting critic who followed him became known as an *aristarchus*. These lists of "best authors" (lists which, almost two thousand years later, the scholar David Ruhnken would call "canons"[134]) were copied out well into the Middle Ages and the Renaissance, and granted the included authors literary immortality, since their works were sought after and assiduously studied. On the other hand, authors not present in these lists were considered unworthy of attention and were allowed to fade into ashes and oblivion. This lengthy, never-compiled catalogue of neglected authors haunts us by its absence.

The weight of absence is as much a feature of any library as the constriction of order or space. In the library of my Colegio Nacional de Buenos Aires, we felt it behind the imposing wooden doors, in the welcoming gloom, and under the green-shaded lamps that reminded me vaguely of the lamps in sleeping-car compartments. Up the marble staircase, down the tiled floor, between the grey columns, the library seemed a parallel universe, both fearful and comforting, in which my own story had other adventures and other endings. Above all, absence (of the books deemed improper, dangerous, provocative) gaped in the dark holes that pierced the countless shelves of books towering up to the ceiling.

And yet, many seemingly innocent titles deceived the librarian's censorious eye. I remember, in the silence

MAY ISHTAR BLESS
THE READER WHO
WILL NOT ALTER THIS
TABLET NOR PLACE IT
ELSEWHERE IN THE
LIBRARY, AND MAY
SHE DENOUNCE IN
ANGER HE WHO DARES
WITHDRAW IT FROM
THIS BUILDING.

Warning sign in the library at Le Presbytère.

broken by whispered snatches of conversation, the pages at which certain books would spontaneously fall open: Lorca's *Romancero gitano* at "The Unfaithful Bride," *La Celestina* at the brothel scene, Cortázar's *Los Premios* at the chapter in which a young boy is seduced by a wicked sailor. How these forbidden texts had found their way into our scrupulous library we never knew, and we wondered how long it would be before the librarian discovered that, under his very nose, generation after generation of corruptible students filled the absence on the shelves by selectively reading these scandalous books.

It may be, as Primo Levi suggests in his memoirs, that the unspoken purpose of librarians is to make sure that only those truly wishing access to books be allowed into the sanctum. For Levi, the library of Turin's Chemical Institute in the 1930s was

at that time, like Mecca, impenetrable to infidels and even hard to penetrate for such faithful as I. One had to think that the administration followed the wise principle according to which it is good to discourage the arts and sciences: only someone impelled by absolute necessity, or by an overwhelming passion, would willingly subject himself to the trials of abnegation that were demanded of him in order to consult the volumes. The library's schedule was brief and irrational, the lighting dim, the file cards in disorder; in the winter, no heat; no chairs but uncomfortable and noisy metal stools; and finally, the librarian was an incompetent, insolent boor of exceeding ugliness, stationed at the threshold to terrify with his appearance and his howl those aspiring to enter.[135]

Like Levi's unwelcoming library, and like the far less forbidding one of my school, every library, including those under strictest surveillance, contains secretly rebellious texts that escape the librarian's eye. As a prisoner in a Russian camp near the polar circle doing what he called "my own time in the North,"[136] Joseph Brodsky read W.H. Auden's poems, and they strengthened his resolve to defy his jailers and survive for the sake of a glimpsed-at freedom. Haroldo Conti, tortured in the cells of the Argentinian military of the 1970s, found solace in the novels of Dickens, which his jailer had allowed him to keep.[137] For the writer Varlam Chalamov, sent by Stalin to work in the gold mines of Kolyma because of his "counter-revolutionary activities," the prison library was itself a gold mine that "for incomprehensible reasons, had escaped the innumerable inspections and 'purges' systematically inflicted upon all of Russia's libraries." On its miserable shelves Chalamov found unexpected treasures such as Bulgakov's writings and the poems of Mayakovski. "It was," he said, "as if the authorities had wished to offer the prisoners a consolation for the long road ahead, for the Calvary awaiting them. As if they thought: 'Why censor the reading of those condemned?'"[138]

Sometimes, those who take upon themselves the task of guarding the entrance to the library's stacks find danger where others see none. During the hunt for "subversive elements" under the military regimes in Argentina, Uruguay and Chile in the 1970s, anyone in possession of a "suspicious" book could be arrested and detained without charge. "Suspicious" were the poems of Neruda and Nâzim Hikmet (they were communists), the novels of Tolstoy and Dostoevsky (they were Russian) and any book with a dangerous word in its title, such as Stendhal's *The Red and the Black* or the sixteenth-century Japanese classic *Comrade Loves of the Samurai*. In fear of sudden police raids, many people burnt their libraries by lighting bonfires in their toilets, and plumbers became suddenly perplexed by an epidemic of broken toilet bowls (the heat of burning paper causes the porcelain to crack). "He has children who saw him burn his books" is how the novelist Germán García defines the generation that was killed, tortured or forced into exile.[139]

Those in power can ban books for peculiar motives. General Pinochet famously excluded *Don Quixote* from the libraries of Chile because he read in that novel an argument for civil disobedience, and the Japanese minister of Culture, several years ago, objected to *Pinocchio* because it showed unflattering pictures of handicapped people in the figures of the cat who pretends to be blind and the fox who pretends to be lame. In March 2003 Cardinal Joseph Ratzinger (who was to become Pope Benedict XVI) argued that the Harry Potter books "deeply distort Christianity in the soul, before it can grow properly."[140] Other idiosyncratic reasons have been given for banning all manner of books, from *The Wizard of Oz* (a hotbed of pagan beliefs) to *The Catcher in the Rye* (a dangerous adolescent role model). In the words of William Blake,

Both read the Bible day and night,

But thou read'st black where I read white.[141]

As I've said, any library, by its very existence, conjures up its forbidden or forgotten double: an invisible but formidable library of the books that, for conventional reasons of quality, subject matter or even volume, have been deemed unfit for survival under this specific roof.

At the end of the sixteenth century, the stern Jesuit Jacob Gretser published a defence of censorship under the explicit title *Of the Laws and Customs Concerning the Banning, Expurgation and Destruction of Heretical and Noxious Books*. Gretser's erudition led him to be appointed advisor to the Catholic Church when the *Index of Forbidden Books* was being compiled in Madrid in 1612; he employed that same erudition to support the argument (evident to many) that censorship of books is common to all peoples in all times. Gretser's infamous genealogy begins with the pagans who burned Cicero's treatise *On the Nature of the Gods* (for being too inclined to monotheism, according to an old, unproven story), and leads up to the book-burnings of the followers of Luther and Calvin.[142] Had Gretser been able to look into the future, he could have added to his list the "degenerate" books condemned to the pyre by the Nazis, the works of the "bourgeois" writers proscribed by Stalin, the publications of the "Communist scribblers" exiled by Senator McCarthy, the books destroyed by the Taliban, by Fidel Castro, by the government of North Korea, by the officials of Canada Customs. Gretser's book is in fact the unacknowledged history of those colossal libraries that whisper from the gaps on the bookshelves.[143]

Earlier, I mentioned the legend that accused Amr ibn al-As of ordering Caliph Omar I to set fire to the books in Alexandria. Omar's apocryphal response deserves to be quoted here because it echoes the curious logic of every book-burner then and now. He is said to have acquiesced by saying, "If the contents of these books agree with the Holy Book, then they are redundant. If they disagree, then they are undesirable. In either case, they should be consigned to the flames."[144] Omar was addressing—somewhat stridently, it is true—the essential fluidity of literature. Because of it, no library is what it is set up to be, and a library's fate is often decided not by those who created it for its merits but by those who wish to destroy it for its supposed faults.

This is true of the native literature of the Americas, of which hardly anything has reached us. In Mexico and

Central America, particularly, the great libraries and archives of the pre-Columbian peoples were systematically destroyed by the Europeans, both to deprive them of an identity and to convert them to the religion of Christ. The Australian poet A.D. Hope tells the story of how the Spanish conquistadores set fire to the books of the Maya:

Diego de Landa, archbishop of Yucatán
—The curse of God upon his pious soul—
Placed all their Devil's picture books under ban
And, piling them in one sin-heap, burned the whole;

But he took the trouble to keep the calendar
By which the Devil had taught them to count time.
The impious creatures tallied back as far
As ninety million years before Eve's crime.

That was enough: they burned the Mayan books,
Saved souls and kept their own in proper trim.
Diego de Landa in heaven always looks
Towards God: God never looks at him.[145]

Diego de Landa's contemporary Friar Juan de Zumárraga, "a name that should be as immortal as that of Omar," says William Prescott in his classic *Conquest of Mexico*,[146] did likewise with the books of the Aztecs. Zumárraga was born in Durango, Spain, in 1468 and studied in the Franciscan monastery of Aránzazu, in the Basque Country. Appointed to the Most Holy Office of the Inquisition, he received his first inquisitorial commission from the Emperor Charles v "to hunt the witches of Biscay" in northern Spain. Zumárraga proved himself so

A nineteenth-century engraving based on a sixteenth-century portrait of Archbishop Juan de Zumárraga.

successful that shortly afterwards he was posted to the Viceroyalty of Mexico as bishop-elect. In 1547, Pope Paul II crowned him first archbishop of Mexico.

Zumárraga spent seven years as head of the Mexican Inquisition, from 1536 to 1543, during which time he wrote a catechism for native neophytes and a brief manual of Christian doctrine for use in the missions, supervised the translation of the Bible into a number of native languages and founded the Colegio de Santa Cruz in Tlaltelolco, where the sons of the native nobility were taught Latin, philosophy, rhetoric and logic so that they could become "good Christians." Zumárraga's name, however, is mainly associated with two events that profoundly affected the history of Mexico: he was responsible for creating the first printing press in the New World, and for destroying most of the vast literature of the Aztec Empire.

Zumárraga had long been convinced of the need to print locally the books required for the conversion of the natives, since he felt that it was difficult to control, across the ocean, the accuracy of translations into native languages, and the contents of doctrinal books for a native audience. In 1533, on a return voyage to Spain, he visited several printers in Seville in order to find one willing to assist him in establishing a printing press in Mexico. He found his partner in the person of Jacobo Cromberger, a converted Jew with long experience in the making of books, who was willing to invest in the overseas enterprise "a press, ink, type and paper, as well as other implements of the trade, the whole estimated at 100,000 *maravedis*,"[147] and to send as his representative one of his assistants, an Italian known as Juan Pablos or Giovanni Paoli.

The ways of censors are mysterious. Zumárraga's obligation as Inquisitor was to seek out and punish all those perceived to be enemies of the Catholic Church—idolaters, adulterers, blasphemers, witches, Lutherans, Moors and Jews—and he did so with extraordinary ferocity. Converted Jews had, since the days of Columbus, been denied permission to establish themselves in the colonies. But since the financial capital required to set up business in the New World was often in the hands of Jewish and Moorish converts, illegal immigration became common in the early years of the sixteenth century, and by 1536 there was a sizable Jewish community in Mexico. The first Mexican ordinance against heretics and Jews dates from 1523, decreeing that those who denounced a converted Jew who practised his religion secretly would benefit from a third of the Jew's confiscated property (the other two-thirds going to the royal treasurer and to the judge). Accordingly, accusations flourished, and Zumárraga in particular persecuted the Jews with relentless determination, often condemning them to be burnt at the stake on the flimsiest of evidence.[148] It is therefore puzzling to learn that Zumárraga chose the services of a converted Jew to establish his Mexican press. Though he must have been aware of his partner's bloodline, Zumárraga left no comment on his choice, and we can wonder, at a distance of almost five centuries, how the Inquisitor justified his relationship with the "impure" Cromberger.

Nor do we know whether Zumárraga understood the paradox of on the one hand creating books, and on the other hand destroying them. Shortly after his appointment as head of the Inquisition, he sent troops to the farthest corners of the colony to ferret out anyone suspected of possessing Aztec religious objects or illuminated books. Through bribes and torture he discovered the location of important collections of art and entire native libraries the Aztec notables had hidden away, "especially from Tezcuco," Prescott writes, "the most cultivated capital in Anahuac, and the great depository of the national archives." Finally, after an astonishing number of paintings and books had been collected by his emissaries, Zumárraga had them piled in a tall heap in the marketplace of Tlaltelolco, and burnt. The fire, witnesses say, lasted several days and nights.

Thanks to the efforts of other, more enlightened Spaniards (of Friar Bernardino de Sahagún, for example, who preserved and translated a number of Aztec texts), we have an approximate idea of what was lost: a complex vision of the universe, with its theology, its songs, its stories, its historical chronicles, its works of philosophy and divination, its scientific treatises and astronomical charts.[149] Among the treasures that miraculously survived, in 1924 scholars discovered, in the so-called Secret Archives of the Vatican, fourteen of the thirty chapters of the *Book of Dialogues*, the last major work in Nahuatl (one of the many languages spoken in the Aztec Empire), written in the mid-sixteenth century. In this book, a group of native priests and scholars defend the Aztec view of the world against Catholic dogma, in a dramatic series of dialogues reminiscent of those of Plato. Works like the *Book of Dialogues* (and there were no doubt many) would have helped Europeans understand the people they were encountering, and allowed for an exchange of wisdom and experience.

Even from a political and religious point of view, the destruction of an opposing culture is always an act of stupidity, since it denies the possibility of allegiance, conversion or assimilation. The Spanish Dominican Diego Durán, writing shortly before his death in 1588, argued that in order to attempt to convert the natives of the New World it was necessary to know their customs and religion, and he blamed those who, like Diego de Landa and Zumárraga, burnt the ancient books:

> Those who with fervent zeal (though with little prudence) in the beginning burned and destroyed all the ancient Indian pictographic documents were mistaken. They left us without a light to guide us— to the point that the Indians worship idols in our presence, and we understand nothing of what goes on in their dances, in their market-places, in their bathhouses, in the songs they chant (when they lament their ancient gods and lords), in their repasts and banquets; these things mean nothing to us.[150]

Few of those in power paid attention to Durán's warnings. The destruction of the books of pre-Columbian America exemplify the fear that those in power have of the subversive capabilities of the written word. Sometimes they believe that even committing books to the flames is not enough. Libraries, in their very being, not only assert but also question the authority of power. As repositories of history or sources for the future, as guides or manuals for difficult times, as symbols of authority past or present, the books in a library stand for more than their collective contents, and have, since the beginning of writing, been considered a threat. It hardly matters why a library is destroyed: every banning, curtailment, shredding, plunder or loot gives rise (at least as a ghostly presence) to a louder, clearer, more durable library of the banned, looted, plundered, shredded or curtailed. Those books may no longer be available for consultation, they may exist only in the vague memory of a reader or in the vaguer-still memory of tradition and legend, but they have acquired a kind of immortality. "We scorn," wrote Tacitus in the first century, "the blindness of those who believe that with an arrogant act even the memory of posterity can be extinguished.

In fact, the sentence increases the prestige of the noble spirits they wish to silence, and foreign potentates, or those others who have used similar violence, have obtained nothing other than shame for themselves and lasting fame for their enemies."[151]

The libraries that have vanished or have never been allowed to exist greatly surpass in number those we can visit, and form the links of a circular chain that accuses and condemns us all. Three and a half centuries after Omar's riposte, the notorious Abi-Amir al-Mansur, Moorish regent of Córdoba, condemned to the flames a rare collection of scientific and philosophical works collected in the Andalusian libraries by his predecessors. As if answering across the ages Omar's pitiless judgment, the historian Sa'id the Spaniard was moved to observe, "These sciences were despised by the old and criticized by the mighty, and those who studied them were accused of heresy and heterodoxy. Thereafter, those who had the knowledge held their tongue, went into hiding and kept secret what they knew for a more enlightened age."[152] We are still waiting. Five centuries later, in 1526, Ottoman soldiers led by Sultan Suleiman II rode into Buda and set fire to the Great Corvina Library, founded by King Matthias Corvinus in 1471 and said to have been one of the jewels of the Hungarian crown, in an attempt to annihilate the culture of the people they had conquered.[153] A further three centuries after that destruction, in 1806, Suleiman's descendants emulated them by burning the extraordinary Fatimid Library in Cairo, containing over a hundred thousand precious volumes.[154]

~~~

In our time, a government's methods of censorship are less drastic but still effective. In March 1996 the French minister of Culture, Philippe Douste-Blazy, objecting to the cultural policies of the Mayor of Orange, a member of Jean-Marie Le Pen's far-right-wing party, ordered the inspection of the municipal library of that city. The report, published three months later, concluded that the Orange librarians were under orders from the mayor to withdraw certain books and magazines from the library shelves: any publications of which Le Pen's followers might disapprove, any books by authors critical of the party, and certain foreign literature (North African folk tales, for example) that was considered not part of true French cultural heritage.[155]

Readers, censors know, are defined by the books they read. In the aftermath of 11 September 2001, the Congress of the United States passed a law, Section 215 of the U.S.A. Patriot Act, allowing federal agents to obtain records of books borrowed at any public library or bought at any private bookstore. "Unlike traditional search warrants, this new power does not require officers to have evidence of any crime, nor provide evidence to a court that their target is suspected of one. Nor are library staff allowed to tell targeted individuals that they are being investigated."[156] Under such requirements, a number of libraries in the United States, kowtowing to the authorities, reconsidered the purchase of various titles.

Sometimes, it is nothing but a random act that determines the fate of a library. In 1702, the scholar Arni Magnusson learned that the impoverished inhabitants of Iceland, starving and naked under Danish rule, had raided the ancient libraries of their country—in which unique copies of the *Eddas* had been kept for over six hundred years—in order to turn the poetic parchment into winter clothes. Alerted to this vandalism, King Frederick IV of Denmark ordered Magnusson to sail to Iceland and rescue the precious manuscripts. It took Magnusson ten years to strip the thieves and reassemble the collection, which, though soiled and tailored, was shipped back to Copenhagen, where it was carefully guarded for another fourteen-odd years—until a fire reduced it to illiterate ashes.[157]

Will libraries always exist under such uncertainties? Perhaps not. Virtual libraries, if they become technologically resilient, can circumvent some of these threats; there would no longer be any justification for culling, since cyberspace is practically infinite, and censorship would no longer affect the majority of readers, since a censor, confined to one administration and one place, cannot prevent a reader from calling up a forbidden text from somewhere faraway, beyond the censor's rule. A caveat, however: the censor can employ the Internet as his own instrument and punish the reader after the act. In 2005 the Internet giant Yahoo! provided information that helped Chinese state security officials convict a journalist, Shi Tao, for supposedly using a New York–based website to obtain and post forbidden texts, for which he was sentenced to ten years' imprisonment.[158]

But in spite of such dangers, examples of the freedom offered by the Web are numerous. In Iran, under the tyranny of the mullahs, students could still read on-line all kinds of forbidden literature; in Cuba, dissidents have Internet access to the published reports of Amnesty

International and other human rights organizations; in Rhodesia, readers can open onscreen the books of banned writers.

And even paper and ink can sometimes survive a death sentence. One of the lost plays of Sophocles is *The Loves of Achilles*, copies of which must have perished one after another, century after century, destroyed in pillaging and fires or excluded from library catalogues because perhaps the librarian deemed the play of little interest or of poor literary quality. A few words were, however, miraculously preserved. "In the Dark Ages, in Macedonia," Tom Stoppard has one of his characters explain in his play *The Invention of Love*, "in the last guttering light from classical antiquity, a man copied out bits from old books for his young son, whose name was Septimius; so we have one sentence from *The Loves of Achilles*. Love, said Sophocles, feels like the ice held in the hand by children."[159] I trust that book-burners' dreams are haunted by such modest proof of the book's survival.

THE LIBRARY

AS SHAPE

The first view I had of what was to be my library was one of rocks and dust covering a rectangular space of approximately six by thirteen metres. The toppled stones lay between the pigeon tower and the furnace room that was to become my study; powdery sand showered the leaves of the creeper every time a bird settled on the dividing wall. The architect who eventually drew the library's plans (fortunately for me) lives in the village. She insisted that traditional methods be used to clean the wall and rebuild the space, and she contracted masons knowledgable in the handling of the local stone, *tuffeau,* which is soft as sandstone and the colour of butter. It was an extraordinary sight to see these men work row by row, placing stone next to stone with the ability of skilled typographers in an old-fashioned printing shop. The image came to mind because in local parlance the large stones are known as upper case (*majuscules*) and the small ones as lower case (*minuscules*), and during the

building of the library it seemed utterly appropriate that these inheritors of the bricklayers of Babel should mix stones and letters in their labours. *"Passe-moi une majuscule!"* they would call to one another, while my books waited silently in their boxes for the day of resurrection.

Books lend a room a particular identity that can, in some cases, usurp that of their owner—a peculiarity well known to oafish personalities who demand to be portrayed against the background of a book-lined wall, in the hope that it will grant them a scholarly lustre. Seneca mocked ostentatious readers who relied on such walls to lend them intellectual prestige; he argued for possessing only a small number of books, not "endless bookshelves for the ignorant to decorate their dining-rooms."[160] In turn, the space in which we keep our books changes our relationship to them. We don't read books in the same way sitting inside a circle or inside a square, in a room

with a low ceiling or in one with high rafters. And the mental atmosphere we create in the act of reading, the imaginary space we construct when we lose ourselves in the pages of a book, is confirmed or refuted by the physical space of the library, and is affected by the distance of the shelves, the crowding or paucity of books, by qualities of scent and touch and by the varying degrees of light and shade. "Every librarian is, up to a certain point, an architect," observed Michel Melot, director of the Centre Pompidou Library in Paris. "He builds up his collection as an ensemble through which the reader must find a path, discover his own self, and live."[161]

The library I had imagined for my books, long before its walls were erected, already reflected the way in which I wished to read. There are readers who enjoy trapping a story within the confines of a tiny enclosure; others for whom a round, vast, public space better allows them to imagine the text stretching out towards far horizons;

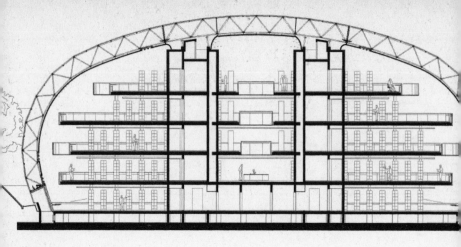

ABOVE: *Design for the library of the brain-shaped Freie Universität in Berlin.*

OPPOSITE BOTTOM: *The book-shaped towers of the Bibliothèque de France, Paris.*

others still who find pleasure in a maze of rooms through which they can wander, chapter after chapter. I had dreamt of a long, low library where there would always be enough darkness around the pools of light on the desk to suggest that it was night outside, a rectangular space in which the walls would mirror one another and in which I could always feel as if the books on either side were almost at arm's length. I read in a haphazard way, allowing books to associate freely, to suggest links by their mere proximity, to call to one another across the room. The shape I chose for my library encourages my reading habits.

The idea of a library set down on paper, still unpeopled by readers and books, as yet devoid of shelves and partitions, is nothing but the frame of a given style of reading, the

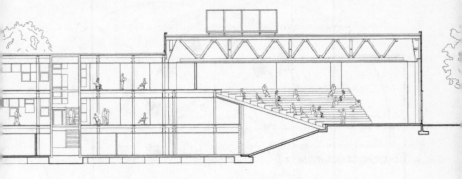

reduction of an as yet shapeless universe to its minimum expression: pure geometrical form. Square spaces contain and dissect; circular spaces proclaim continuity; other shapes evoke other qualities. The Toronto Reference Library is a progression of ascending disks. The library

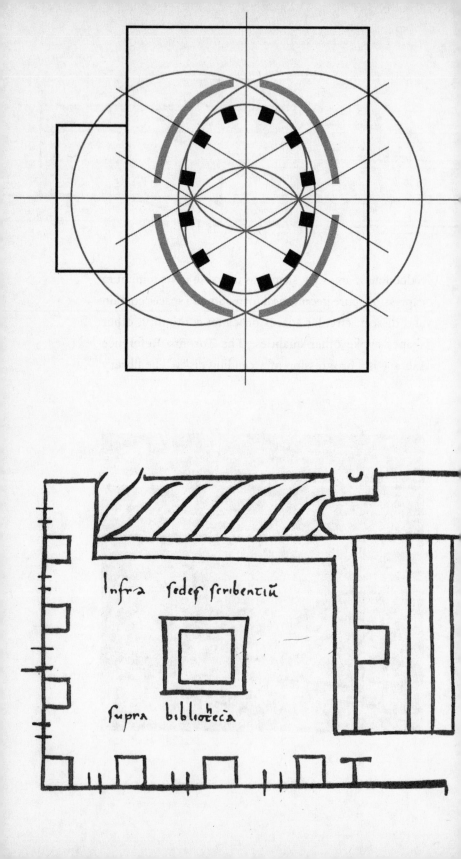

Infra ſedeſ ſcribentiũ

ſupra bibliotheca

of Buckingham House (where King George III kept his books) was octagonal. The first Ambrosiana Library in Milan, lodged in three refurbished houses barely fit for "pigs and cheeky prostitutes,"[162] occupied a narrow rectangle. The library of the Freie Universität in Berlin was designed by Norman Foster to resemble a skull and is now nicknamed The Brain. The Bibliothèque de France, in Paris, has the shape of an inverted table. The Biblioteca de Catalunya, in Barcelona, is a cylinder cut lengthwise in half. The Wolfenbüttel Library in Germany was designed by the architect Hermann Korb in the shape of an oval. The Freiburg University Library, built in 1902, is in the shape of a triangle.

The first plan we have of a medieval library is a square. Drawn in the Monastery of Reichenau for the Abbey of St. Gall in Switzerland, it dates from around 820 and is divided into two storeys. On the ground floor is the scriptorium, two sides of which are occupied by seven small tables set under the same number of windows, with a large desk in the centre of the room. Above is the storage space for books, from which a corridor leads to the great choir where the liturgical volumes are kept.[163] The result (barring the corridor and the choir) is a perfect cube in which the upper section reflects the lower one: the books produced below are stored above, and are in turn used to supply the copyists, in an endless chain of literary reproduction. We do not know whether this plan was ever carried out, but for the anonymous architect the harmonious shape of the square must have seemed the perfect space for the creation, preservation and consultation of books.

A library of straight angles suggests division into parts or subjects, consistent with the medieval notion of a compartmentalized and hierarchical universe; a circular library more generously allows the reader to imagine that every last page is also the first. Ideally, for many readers, a library would be a combination of both, an intersection of circle and rectangle or oval and square, like the ground floor of a basilica. The idea is not a new one.

Towards the end of the seventeenth century, the Royal Library of France had grown from the private collection established by Louis XI in the fifteenth century to a vast assembly of collections, the result of donations, booty and the royal decree of *dépôt légal*, signed in December 1537, requiring that two copies of every book printed in France be deposited at the Château de Blois.[164] By the time of the French Revolution, it was obvious that this rapidly growing national library required a new home, and over the next century a great number of proposals were put forward to solve the problem of lodging the many books. Certain enthusiasts suggested moving the collection to a pre-existing Paris structure, such as the church of La Madeleine (then under construction), the Louvre (Napoleon signed a decree to this effect, which was never executed), the government offices on the Quai d'Orsay, the Marché aux Veaux, where meat was butchered, or even the Hôpital de la Charité, from which the patients would have had to be evacuated. Others imagined erecting new buildings of various styles and sizes, and their proposals, from the most eccentric to the most practical, bear witness to the search for an ideal shape that would allow readers a necessary freedom of movement, and at the same time lend their working space the best influential qualities.

Etienne-Louis Boullée, one of the most imaginative architects of all time, proposed in 1785 a long, high-roofed gallery of gigantic proportions, inspired by the ruins of ancient Greece, in which the rectangle of the gallery would be topped by an arched ceiling, and readers would wander up and down long, terraced mezzanines in search of their volume of choice. The project never went beyond the drafting stage, but little in the design suggested possibilities of privacy and concentration. Boullée's magnificent library had the features of a tunnel, and resembled a passageway more than a stopping place, a building intended less for leisured reading than for rapid consultation.

OVERLEAF: *Boullée's fantastical design for an ideal library.*

Fifty years later, the architect Benjamin Delessert imagined an elliptical library enclosed in a rectangular building, with spokelike shelves radiating from the centre in all directions. The staff would be seated in the middle in order to keep an eye on the readers, but it was objected that "unless the librarian, armed with a telescope and a loudspeaker, could be made to turn on an incessantly gyrating pivot,"[165] security would always be wanting. Furthermore, the reading desks, set in the spaces between the shelves, would feel uncomfortably constrained and give the reader a feeling of entrapment or claustrophobia. In spite of the objections, the idea of a centralized service point surrounded by desks and bookshelves never lost its appeal.

Finally, in 1827, the chance vacating of several buildings on the right bank of the Seine provided planners with a ready-made site. The ancient Hôtel Tubeuf, at the corner of Vivienne and Petits-Champs, was abandoned by the Treasury, and at the same time some adjacent houses and shops were conveniently made available to the city. It took the authorities some thirty more years before the plans for the transformation of the locale were accepted. The architect in charge of the final project was Henri Labrouste, who had made his reputation with the renovation of another important Paris library, the Bibliothèque Saint-Geneviève.[166]

Labrouste was aware that a national library is both a monument and a place of everyday common labours, both the symbol of a country's intellectual wealth and the practical space in which ordinary readers need to pursue their craft comfortably and efficiently. The shape and size had therefore to reflect both immensity and intimacy, majesty and unobtrusive seclusion. Labrouste conceived the main reading room—the library's core— as a circle within a square, or rather as a series of circles looming high above the square of assembled readers— nine round glass domes that allowed sunlight to enter and illuminate the right-angled space below. As in Delessert's project, the librarian surveyed his flock from the middle of the room, from within a banistered booth in which he could turn around as needed. Tall metal columns supported the arches of the domes, giving the interior the look of a winter garden, while five storeys of bookshelves covered the walls on all sides, creating storage for over a million volumes.

Thirty years later, on the other side of the Channel, the new reading room of the British Museum Library in London was being completed according to a similar pattern, except that a single cupola crowned the circular space and the desks radiated from the centre, controlled by the ever-conspicuous librarian. By then, the British Museum (the institution that housed it) had been in existence for over a century and had worked its way through six previous, much-deplored reading rooms. The first had been a narrow, dark room with two small windows which the trustees had ordered, in 1785, to "be appropriated for the reading-room, and that a proper wainscot table, covered with green bays [sic] . . . be prepared for the same with twenty chairs." The sixth, in use from 1838 to 1857, had consisted of two squarish high rooms with over ten thousand reference books and twenty-four tables. Ventilation was inefficient; readers complained that while their feet were cold, their heads were always too hot. Many suffered from what became known as "Museum headache," and from the unpleasant "Museum flea," which one reader said was "larger than any to be found elsewhere except in the receiving rooms of work-houses."[167] The seventh reading room, inaugurated in May 1857, was designed both to avoid these problems and to ensure more space for books. The shape—a circle within a square—had been suggested by Antonio Panizzi, the British Museum Library's most eminent librarian, who once declared that "every shelf and peg and pivot of the new building was thought of and determined in the wakeful hours of the night."[168]

Like Panizzi, Labrouste, a keen bibliophile himself, was convinced of the importance of lending this ample space a human measure, even in the areas behind the reading room. In the stacks, the enormous number of books were not only to be housed; they were to remainaccessible to an ordinary reader. The width of each shelving section

OPPOSITE: *The British Library Reading Room, as depicted in* The Illustrated London News.

BELOW: *The intial sketch of the Reading Room drawn by Panizzi himself and dated "April 18th 1852."*

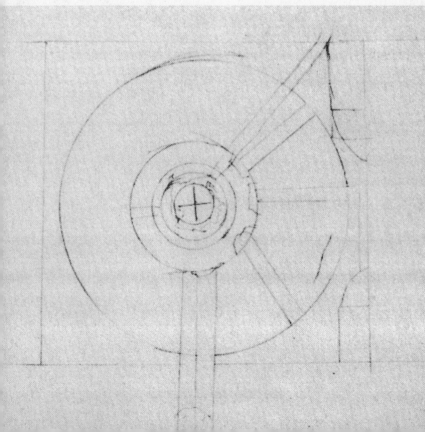

The stalls at the Bibliothèque Nationale required no stepladders: their
dimensions were determined by the breadth and height of a man's body.

was therefore determined by an average person's arms' span (so that readers could pull out books on either side without having to move), and the height by the reach of a hand (so that readers would have access to the highest shelf without requiring steps or a sliding ladder). In spite of the vastness, there was no sense of crowding under the arched glass domes. Though the reading room could accommodate hundreds of readers at one time, each inhabited a private realm, seated at a numbered desk that had been fitted with an inkstand and a penholder, and was kept warm in winter by a combination of metal stoves and hot-water radiators that also served as footrests. Having worked both in the Salle Labrouste and in the British Library reading room, I know the mixed feeling of expansion and containment, grandiosity and seclusion, that the combination of square and circle grants such spaces.

~~~

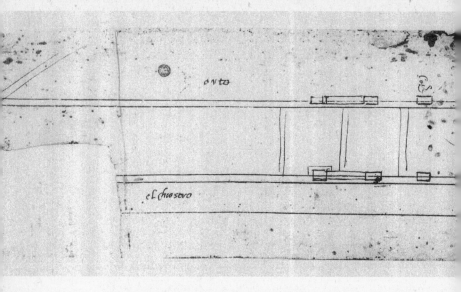

Michelangelo's first sketch for the Laurentian Library.

Other shapes imply other physical qualities. A simple rectangle, for instance, can suggest a different kind of limit and endlessness, continuity and separation, as proven by one of the loveliest libraries ever built, the Laurentian Library in Florence. Miraculously, we have a sketch of its conception: a scrap of paper, slightly larger than a dollar bill, kept in the Buonarroti Archives, one corner torn off where the artist perhaps jotted down a quick message. The sketch shows nothing but a rectangle of double lines interrupted by a few short strokes representing, we are told, intermittent stone buttresses. Drawn by the hand of Michelangelo, it is the earliest draft we possess of what would be his "first and most completely realized building and arguably his most original contribution to Renaissance architecture."[169] Only two words are written on the paper, one above the rectangle, *orto* (garden) and one below, *chiostro* (cloister). Though at the beginning of the project the exact site of the library had not been decided upon, once Michelangelo imagined its future shape he was able to give it a precise location as well—the middle section of the main building of the Monastery of San Lorenzo, somewhere between the garden and the courtyard cloister.

The idea for a grand monastic library in San Lorenzo, to lodge the superb collection amassed by the Medicis, had been put forward by Cardinal Giulio de' Medici as early as 1519, several years before the actual commission, which, for financial reasons, had to wait until 1523 to be made official. That was the year in which the cardinal became Pope Clement VII. In the eyes of Pope Clement, a library was truly a library: not an ostentatious chamber lined with luxurious volumes, but a place to keep books and make use of the written word, an institution whose purpose was to serve the scholarly public, complementing with its treasures the lesser holdings of the university collections.

Clement was the grandson of Lorenzo the Magnificent, who was to lend his name to the great Medici collection. He was the bastard son of Giuliano de' Medici and his mistress Fioretta, but his illegitimacy was ignored by his cousin Pope Leo x, who, dismissing all objections, made him Archbishop of Florence as well as cardinal. Though lacking the political talents of his grandfather, Clement was, like him, a man of letters and a lover of fine art. He doggedly opposed the movements of reform spreading throughout the Catholic

Church, and implemented the measures taken against Luther and the Protestant princes in Germany. He was above all a Medici and a Florentine, strongly set against change, a ruler who sought instead to claim the social and artistic comforts of his position. An ambitious but discriminating patron, he supported writers such as Francesco Guicciardini and Niccolò Machiavelli, and artists such as Benvenuto Cellini, Raphael and Michelangelo.[170]

Clement was a connoisseur, not a mere admirer of the works he commissioned. The correspondence between him and Michelangelo, from the beginning of the building of the library to its completion, bears witness to his detailed preoccupation. For three full years, from 1523 to 1526, Pope Clement in Rome and Michelangelo in Florence exchanged letters three or four times a week. In letter after letter, Clement suggested to Michelangelo—though papal suggestions carried the weight of orders—all manner of arrangements and dispositions: that the Latin texts be separated from the Greek, that rare books be kept in small individual cabinets, that the foundations of the building be reinforced, that the ceiling be vaulted to help prevent fires. With nagging concern, he insisted on knowing everything: how many desks Michelangelo was planning for the reading room, how many books could be kept on each desk, where Michelangelo intended to obtain the walnut for the tables and by what process the wood was to be treated. He offered opinions on everything, from the design of the doors to the importance of the lighting, on where the best travertine could be found to make lime and how many coats of stucco should be applied to the walls. Most of the time, Michelangelo responded readily and diplomatically, sometimes accepting these suggestions and sometimes ignoring them completely.[171]

Conservative in politics, Clement was more open to innovation in matters of design, but he remained a practical man. When Michelangelo explained that he wanted to light the library vestibule through circular skylights, Clement expressed delight at the idea but observed that at least two persons would have to be employed "just to keep the glass clean."[172] However, Michelangelo (whose stubbornness was one of his most notorious traits) did not wait for the pope's agreement on everything, and started raising the walls in December 1525, three months before the final design was approved by His Holiness.

When Michelangelo received the commission for the library in November 1523, he was forty-eight years old. Celebrated throughout Europe, he was in the eyes of patrons and fellow artists a painter, sculptor, architect and poet whose talents were beyond question. In all these areas, he coupled the physical world to the world of thought, so that the laws of one intermingled with the laws of the other. For Michelangelo, the properties of wood and marble were mirrored in the properties of imagination and reason; in his eyes, aesthetics and physics, ethics and mathematics shared the same matter and substance. In an unfinished sonnet composed around the time of his work at San Lorenzo, he wrote:

> Since no piece of wood can preserve
> Its proper moisture out of its proper place,
> It cannot help, touched even slightly by some great heat,

The monumental staircase of the Laurentian Library, designed by Michelangelo.

Being dried up or bursting into flame or burning.

Just like the heart, taken by one who will never return it,

Living in tears and fed by flames—

Now that it's far from its home and proper place,

What blow will not be fatal to it?[173]

Michelangelo's confidence in the ability of material things to reproduce or translate thought and feeling according to objective rules is evident in the Laurentian Library. Three separate building commissions were entrusted to him. The first, the façade of San Lorenzo, was never completed. The second, the Medici Chapel interior, was a project he undertook belatedly, after other artists had worked on it for years, and though he achieved some of his best work here, his contribution remained only partial. However, the third, the library, is entirely Michelangelo's own creation.

Since the library was to be used primarily as a workplace, the interior was given greater aesthetic importance than the exterior. Erected (due to the fear of floods) on the third floor, it consists of an entrance vestibule, a magnificent and startlingly original staircase, and a lofty reading room that seemingly stretches towards a point of perspective on the hidden horizon. The entire space of the library is built out of rectangles: the columned openings on the walls holding the windows, open or blind; the rows of desks on either side of the room; the majestic central aisle; the divided and carved ceiling. It is easy to imagine the effect created by the great illuminated codexes or the smaller octavo volumes open on the inclined desktops, duplicated by equal rectangular shapes on walls, floor and ceiling, so that every element of the architecture and decoration recalls for the reader the intimate relationship between the world and the book, the unlimited physical space which, in the library, is divided into pagelike areas. The central motif of the carved wooden ceiling of the vestibule is, however, not a rectangle, but four interlinked circles representing the Medici diamond ring, a pattern repeated in the yellow and red tiled floor of the library itself, reminding readers of the four related corners of God's universe, reflected in God's word penned by the four Evangelists.

Michelangelo's contemporary Giorgio Vasari speaks of the "licence" that the artist allowed himself when he departed from classical notions of proportion and order, a licence to which, says Vasari, "all artists are under a great and permanent obligation." According to Vasari, nowhere did Michelangelo better demonstrate these new ideas than in the Laurentian Library,

> namely, in the beautiful distribution of the windows, the pattern of the ceiling, and the marvelous entrance of the vestibule. Nor was there ever seen such resolute grace, both in detail and overall effect, as in the consoles, tabernacles, and cornices, nor any stairway more commodious. And in this stairway, he made such strange breaks in the design of the steps, and he departed in so many details and so widely from normal practice, that everyone was astonished.[174]

The stairway that Vasari so admired is indeed a marvel. Michelangelo had conceived it in walnut, not in the grey stone in which it was finally executed by the Florentine sculptor Bartolomeo Ammanati in 1559, twenty-five years after Michelangelo's departure from Florence

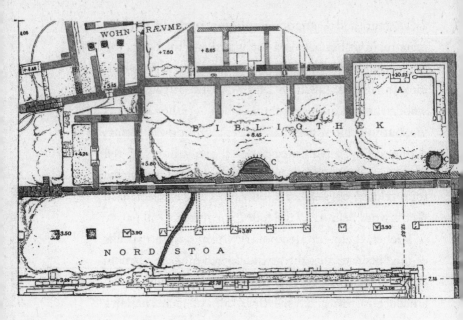

Ground plan of the Pergamon Library.

in 1534. But even in grey stone rather than dark wood, which would have introduced the visitor to the material of the desks and the ceiling of the reading room beyond, the stairway suggests a spatial complexity that seems almost impossible in so restricted a space, a laboriously intricate passage proposing at least three different routes, an obligation of choice entirely appropriate for someone entering the realm of books. The area of the vestibule is small; Michelangelo's design treats it as if it were vast, so that the stairs cascade from between the balustrades outside the door onto three descents with no railings, the middle one made of curving steps each finished with a volute, the side ones rectangular but, as they reach the floor, gently metamorphosing into lozenges. Writing to Vasari from Rome before construction had begun, Michelangelo said that he indeed remembered his original design for the stairway but only "as if in a dream." That is the quality that best defines the finished work.

However, what Vasari saw as startling novelty was rather the perfecting of primitive conceptions of the shape a library should occupy. The examples are many. One of the earliest dates from 2300 B.C. Archaeological digging performed in 1980 at the site of the royal palace of Ebla, in Syria, unearthed a rectangular room containing the remains of a library: more than fifteen thousand clay tablets which had apparently been kept on wooden shelves along the walls; when the shelves burnt after invaders set fire to the palace, the tablets fell in heaps to the floor.[175] The library of Pergamum was discovered to have followed the same pattern twenty-five centuries later. Its ruins show that it consisted of a rectangle formed by a succession of chambers: the first and largest one used for meetings, the following three housing the stacks. Readers consulted the scrolls in the space before the chambers, sheltered by a colonnade. In Rome, in the library of the Forum of Trajan, built in A.D. 112, the design changed somewhat: the rectangular shape was maintained, but the division into small rooms was eliminated.[176] Designing the Laurentian Library, Michelangelo was aware that he was evolving a practical, ancient design familiar to Plato and to Virgil.

Throughout his life, Michelangelo seems to have pursued two conflicting yet complementary ideals of the ancient world. One was the ideal of perfection, the finished quality of Greek art that he and his contemporaries believed gave each of its masterpieces the durable impression of a thing complete unto itself. The other was its fragmentary nature, the result of time and chance that, in the eyes of the Renaissance artists, allowed certain ruins and myriad broken remains to reflect a vanished perfection now implicit in the surviving headless torsos and details of columns[177]—an aesthetic discovery much exploited later by the inventors of the Gothic revival in the eighteenth century. The Laurentian Library displays both qualities.

Among the many discoveries made by the artists of the Renaissance was the "golden section." Though the concept had been known in ancient Greece and had been used in both Greek and Roman architecture, it was not clearly articulated until 1479, when the mathematician Luca Pacioli, in a book illustrated by Leonardo da Vinci and not printed until ten years later, defined it as "a line cut in such a way that the smaller section is to the greater as the greater is to the whole."[178] The pleasing perfection of such a measure cannot be explained mathematically, and therefore held (and still holds today) a magical aesthetic quality, as a physical equilibrium for which there exists no formula. The rectangle of the reading room designed by Michelangelo, whose sides correspond to the ideal proportions dictated by this "golden section," pays homage to the balanced beauty of a Greek temple or a Roman courtyard, and reduces the lovely proportions of our vast universe to a measure pleasing to our human eyes. The stern windows and recurrent volutes, and the complex and dynamic stairway perfectly illustrate the paradoxical nature of a library. The first suggests that it can be an ordered, contained place where our knowledge of the universe can be gracefully stored; the second implies that no order, no method, no elegant design can ever fully hold it.

THE LIBRARY

AS CHANCE

A library is not only a place of both order and chaos; it is also the realm of chance. Books, even after they have been given a shelf and a number, retain a mobility of their own. Left to their own devices, they assemble in unexpected formations; they follow secret rules of similarity, unchronicled genealogies, common interests and themes. Left in unattended corners or on piles by our bedside, in cartons or on shelves, waiting to be sorted and catalogued on some future day many times postponed, the stories held by books cluster around what Henry James called a "general intention" that often escapes readers: "the string the pearls were strung on, the buried treasure, the figure in the carpet."[179]

For Umberto Eco, a library should have a haphazard, flea-market quality. Sunday morning, a *brocante* is set up in one of my neighbouring villages. It has none of the pretensions of the well-established flea markets of Paris, nor the prestige of the antiquarian fairs regularly scheduled throughout France. The *brocante* is a hodgepodge of everything from massive nineteenth-century country furniture to bits of ancient brocade and lace, from chipped pieces of china and crystal to rusty screws and gardening tools, from regrettable oil paintings and anonymous family photos to one-eyed plastic dolls and battered miniature cars. These commercial encampments have the feel of the ancient ruined cities imagined by Stevenson from a child's point of view:

> There I'll come when I'm a man
> With a camel caravan;
> Light a fire in the gloom
> Of some dusty dining-room;
> See the pictures on the walls,
> Heroes, fights, and festivals;
> And in a corner find the toys
> Of the old Egyptian boys.[180]

At the *brocante,* my own interest usually lies in the cratefuls of postcards, prints, calendars and especially books. Sometimes the books are displayed under an obvious banner: history of the region or New Age arcana, animal husbandry or love stories. But most of the time they pile up haphazardly, single volumes of leather-bound eighteenth-century translations of Homer together with shabby wartime Simenons, fine editions of signed novels (I found a 1947 copy of Colette's *Chéri,* mysteriously inscribed "To Gloriane, who attempts to 'repair' women and who miraculously succeeds," in a box of "2 x 8 euros"), together with countless long-forgotten American bestsellers.

~~~

Books come together because of the whims of a collector, the avatars of a community, the passing of war and time, because of neglect, care, the imponderability of survival, the random culling of the rag-and-bone trade, and it may take centuries before their congregation acquires the identifiable shape of a library. Every library, as Dewey discovered, must have an order, and yet not every order is willed or logically structured. There are libraries that owe their creation to affectations of taste, to casual offerings and encounters. In the desert of Adrar, in central Mauritania, the oasis cities of Chinguetti and Ouadane still house dozens of age-old libraries whose very existence is due to the whims of passing caravans laden with spices, pilgrims, salt and books. From the fifteenth to the eighteenth century, these cities were obligatory halting points on the route to Mecca. The books deposited here throughout the years, for reasons of trade or safety—treasures that included works from the celebrated Koranic schools of Granada and Baghdad, Cairo and Meknès, Córdoba and Byzantium—are lodged now in the private homes of several distinguished families. In Chinguetti, for instance—an oasis that boasted twelve mosques and twenty-five thousand inhabitants during its golden age in the eighteenth century—five or six families among the remaining three thousand souls now keep, for the curious reader, over ten thousand volumes of astronomy, sociology, commentaries on the Koran, grammar, medicine and poetry.[181] Many of these were borrowed from travelling scholars and copied by the librarians of these erudite cities; sometimes, reversing the process, students would arrive here and spend

Reading-room in the Habott Library, Mauritania.

months copying out one of the books kept on the library shelves.

A story is told in Ouadane of a beggar who, early in the fifteenth century, appeared at the city gates, famished and dressed in tatters. He was taken into the mosque, fed and clothed, but no one succeeded in making him reveal his name or the city of his birth. All the man seemed to care for was spending long hours among the books of Ouadane, reading in complete silence. Finally, after several months of such mysterious behaviour, the imam lost his patience and said to the beggar, "It is written that he who keeps knowledge to himself shall not be made welcome in the Kingdom of Heaven. Each reader is but one chapter in the life of a book, and unless he passes his knowledge on to others, it is as if he condemned the book to be buried alive. Do you wish such a fate for the books who have served you so well?" Hearing this, the man opened his mouth and gave a lengthy and marvellous commentary on the sacred text he happened to have before him. The imam realized that his visitor was a certain celebrated scholar who, despairing of the deafness of the world, had promised to hold his tongue until he came to a place where learning was truly honoured.[182]

The starting point of a library is sometimes imponderable. In the year A.D. 336, a Buddhist monk whose name has failed to reach us ventured on a pilgrimage along the Great Silk Road, between the Gobi Desert and the wastes of Taklimakan, in that vast area of Central Asia which, two centuries earlier, had been named the land of the Seres by the Greek geographer Pausanias, after the word for silkworm.[183] Here, amid the sand and stones, the monk had a vision of his Lord in a constellation of a thousand points of light (which unbelievers have attempted to explain as the effect of the sun playing on shards of pyrite scattered over the region's mountainside). To honour the vision, the monk hollowed out a cave in the rocks, plastered the walls and painted them with scenes from the life of Buddha.

Over the next thousand years, almost five hundred caves were carved out of the soft stone and embellished with exquisite murals and sophisticated clay statues, giving rise to the celebrated Sanctuary of Mogao in Western China. These images, sculpted and painted by succeeding generations of pious artists, record the metamorphosis of the essentially abstract Tibetan and Chinese Buddhist iconography into a figurative religion that calls for the depiction of fabulous stories involving adventurous gods, ambitious kings, enlightened monks and questing heroes. In time, the sanctuary received various names, among them Mogaoku, or Caves of Unparallelled Height, and Qianfodong, or Site of a Thousand Buddhas.[184] Then, sometime in the eleventh century, probably to preserve them from the cupidity of foreign armies, a collection of over fifty thousand invaluable manuscripts and paintings was hidden away and sealed in one of the Mogao caves, transforming the site into the world's "largest and earliest paper archive and only Buddhist library of its time,"[185] which was to lie undisturbed for seven centuries.

But this honeycomb of caves at Mogao was not the only precious repository in the region. Not far from the sanctuary rose the ancient city of Dunhuang, founded in the fourth century B.C. and one of the most important central stopping places on the Great Silk Road, which ran from Luoyang on the Yellow River to the east, towards Samarkand and Baghdad to the west. A couple of centuries after its foundation, due to its strategic position on the edge of the Chinese Empire, Dunhuang became a garrison town coveted by many nations: the Tibetans, the Turkic Uigurs, the Khotanese, the Tanguts and eventually the Mongols, who conquered this eminently cosmopolitan area in the early thirteenth century, under the rule of Genghis Khan. An extraordinary mixture of cultures came together at this border between the two great deserts, gathering under one roof (or the several roofs of Dunhuang) the luxurious fashions of Persia and the formal styles of Hellenistic Asia, the multitudinous cultures of India and the conventions of Chinese crafts, the abstractions of Tibetan civilization and the representations of European figurative arts.

The Dunhuang Caves on the Great Eastern Silk Road.

A vertical fifth-century frieze from Dunhuang, decorated with dancing figures, seems to mimic the movements of a similar frieze discovered in Pompeii; a third-century haut relief in stone, illustrating the story of how Prince Siddhartha learned sixty-four different alphabets from his teacher, Visvamitra, shows the young boy sitting cross-legged with his writing implements in the same position and crowned with the same halo as the Christ Child carved in ivory on a German prayer-book cover from the tenth century, exhibited at the Musée de l'Oeuvre Notre Dame in Strasbourg; a sixth-century ceiling decoration from Dunhuang, representing three hares chasing each other in a circle, echoes that on the thirteenth-century floor tiles of Chester Cathedral in England; tapestries found many miles to the east of Khotan, an oasis visited by Marco Polo in 1274, show images of Roman gladiators; murals from a Buddhist temple in an eighth-century Tibetan fort near the desert of Lop Nor in China depict winged angels reminiscent of those in hundreds of medieval European altars.[186]

In an empire as vast as China, such cultural intermingling had long been known to be a consequence, good or bad, of expansionist policies, and it was clear to the Chinese that one of the conqueror's prerogatives was not to silence, but to take on and become enriched by, the achievements of the cultures it vanquished. An ancient Chinese chronicle tells how, after conquering the kingdom of Ch'in in 206 B.C., the Chinese leaders Hsiang Yu of Ch'u and Liu Pang of Han fought each other for supremacy. One night, when Hsiang Yu and his troops were besieged by Liu Pang, they heard the songs of their native Ch'u being sung in the enemy camp, "and they finally realized that the land of Ch'u was now completely in the hands of Liu Pang of Han."[187]

All these different peoples whose tastes and traditions influenced and transformed one another, whether they were passing through or settling for a time in those faraway regions, recorded their transactions and experiences—momentary or transcendent, practical or imaginative—in the regular course of their lives. Dunhuang thereby became, as well as a trading place for precious manuscripts, a dumping ground for every conceivable kind of doodle and scribble penned by the monks, pilgrims, soldiers and merchants who visited it over two thousand years: administrative papers and private documents, personal and public correspondence, holy writings and secular accountings, casual scrapbooks and ceremonial scrolls. Even after this section of the Silk Road became less frequented and Dunhuang fell out of favour the mass of detritus continued to accumulate, the remains of the daily lives of the people who lived here. For hundreds of years, both the hoard of manuscripts in

Mogao and the scraps and rag-ends left behind in the abandoned dwellings of Dunhuang lay forgotten under the desert sand.

In 1900 a British scholar with the improbable name of Marcus Aurelius (later reduced to Mark Aurel) Stein, born in Hungary and employed in the India Office, became curious about the stories that trickled through concerning a seemingly legendary region. He made his way over thousands of inhospitable kilometres of rock and sand in search of the forgotten sanctuary. In one of his published reports of the adventure, Stein named the area Serindia, echoing Pausanias's nomenclature.[188] Stein led four expeditions to Serindia, and in spite of little and belated assistance from the British authorities he amassed an extraordinary cache of manuscripts and objects.

To the government of China, at least, Stein's expeditions seemed like excuses for indiscriminate looting in order to fill the rooms of the British Museum. However, Stein collected not only costly manuscripts and works of art but also the odds and ends left behind as mere rubbish by the inhabitants of the desert cities, which he said, "though it could never tempt treasure-seekers of succeeding ages, has acquired for us exceptional value:"[189] a broken mousetrap or a shard from a shattered drinking-cup, a list of instructions on how to preserve grain and a humble apology for having gotten drunk at a party, the first draft of a Buddhist poem and a prayer for the safe recovery of a kidnapped child.

Not all the booty was unearthed by the expeditions. Thousands of the more valuable manuscripts that Stein brought back to England had been sold to him by a Daoist monk named Wang Yuanlu, who had already

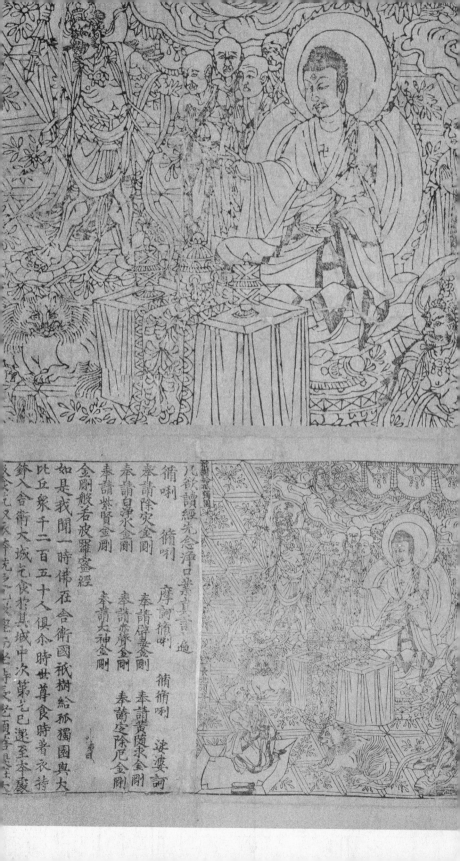

凡欲讀經完念淨口業真言

唵 修唎 修唎 摩訶修唎 修修唎 薩婆訶

奉請除災金剛
奉請辟毒金剛
奉請黃隨求金剛
奉請定除灾金剛

奉請白淨水金剛
奉請赤聲金剛
奉請大神金剛

奉請紫賢金剛

金剛般若波羅蜜經

如是我聞一時佛在舍衛國祇樹給孤獨園與大
比丘眾千二百五十人俱爾時世尊食時著衣持
鉢入舍衛大城乞食於其城中次第乞已還至本處

The magnificent Diamond Sutra.

given away many important pieces to secure the favour of local magistrates. Many of Stein's acquisitions were unique: the earliest surviving examples of Chinese painted scrolls, complete with their original silk ties; the earliest cosmological map in existence (which for the Chinese was also a diagram of political administration, since the emperor was believed to be the Celestial Commander); and the celebrated Diamond Sutra, the oldest known printed book in the world. Preserved today among the holdings of the British Museum, they constitute one of the rarest, most important collections of all time.

But a collection representing what? What do they have in common—these great works on philosophy and astronomy, theology and politics, carefully preserved in a sealed cave for a future reader, and the fragments of letters, lists and jottings found in the ruins of a tavern or in a bricked-up latrine? Unlike the Mauritanian libraries in the oasis cities of Chinguetti and Ouadane, kept by guardians who accepted their assignment as an ancestral duty, neither the treasures of Serindia nor its discarded leavings came into the hands of any expert authority except a late and remote outsider. Chance brought them together, but now, rescued from their entombment, these fragments have an evident coherence. What lies before us, in the halls of the British Museum and in the stacks of the British Library, may appear as only the booty of an ambitious explorer, a foundling collection of orphan writings, the stammering chronicle of a lost civilization, a cautionary tale for our empires today. Or we can see Stein's enterprise as a rescue mission. In its own time each of these pieces possessed a value and a function without any relation to the others. Brought together, they stand before us in joint witness, as a library of survivors, of actors in a long-vanished history.

THE LIBRARY

AS WORKSHOP

I will lodge where I have a mind.

Robert Louis Stevenson, *Lay Morals*

There's a notable difference, for me, between the large room in which I keep most of my books, and the smaller room in which I work. In the large room, the "library proper," I choose the volumes I need or want, I sit and read and make notes, I consult my encyclopedias. But in my study, the chosen books are those that I consider more immediate, more necessary, more intimate. Battered copies of both the *Pocket Oxford Dictionary* and the two-volume *Shorter Oxford,* the faithful and stout *Robert,* my *Pequeño Larousse Ilustrado* from school, *Roget's Thesaurus* in the 1962 version, before unholy hands revised and mangled it, Killy's *Literatur Lexicon,* Graves's *Greek Myths* in the Penguin edition. . . . These feel like extensions of myself, ready at arm's length, always helpful, known of old. Many times I have had to work in rooms without these familiar volumes, and felt their absence as a kind of blindness or lack of voice.

In my study I also require certain talismans that have washed onto my desk over the years, which I distractedly finger while I think of the next words to write. Renaissance scholars recommended keeping different objects in the study: musical and astronomical instruments to lend variety and harmony to the space, natural curiosities such as strangely shaped stones and coloured shells, and portraits of Saint Jerome, patron saint of readers. I follow their recommendation in part. Among the objects on my desk are a horse-shaped soapstone from Congonhas do Campo, a bone carved into a skull from Budapest, a pebble from the Sibyl's Cave near Cumae. If my library chronicles my life story, my study holds my identity.

The rooms in which writers (that subspecies of readers) surround themselves with the materials they need for their work acquire an animal quality, like that of a den or a nest, holding the shape of their bodies and offering a container to their thoughts. Here the writer can make his own bed among the books, be as monogamous or polygamous a reader as he wishes, choose an approved classic or an ignored newcomer, leave arguments unfinished, start on any page opened by chance, spend the night reading out loud so as to hear his own voice read back to him, in Virgil's famous words, under "the friendly silence of the soundless moon." The humanist teacher Battista Guarino, son of the celebrated humanist Guarino Veronese, insisted that readers should not peruse the page silently "or mumble under their breath, for it so often happens that someone who can't hear himself will skip over numerous verses as though he were somewhere else. Reading out loud is of no small benefit to the understanding, since of course what sounds like a voice from outside makes our ears spur the mind sharply to attention." According to Guarino, uttering the words even helps the reader's digestion, because it "increases heat and thins the blood, cleans out all the veins and opens the arteries, and allows no unnecessary moisture to stand motionless in those vessels which take in and digest food."[190] Digestion of words as well; I often read aloud to myself in my writing corner in the library, where no one can hear me, for the sake of better savouring the text, so as to make it all the more mine.

If the private space is the genus, then the study lodged inside that space is the species. During the Renaissance, ownership of a study was, for anyone who aspired to write, a sign of education and civilized taste. More than any other room in the house, a study was thought to possess a secret character of its own, which might persist long after that owner's death.[191] Composed of texts and talismans, icons and instruments of all sorts, a reader's or writer's study is something of a shrine, not to a deity but to an activity. The display of tools of the trade proclaims it a workshop; its order (or disorder) does not follow the requirements of an ordinary library, however private. The study is not a pared-down version of the larger structure—the library—which sometimes contains it. It has a different mission: it provides a practical space for self-reflection and conceit, for belief in the power of objects and reliance on the authority of a dictionary. The historian Jacob Burckhardt spoke of the Renaissance as "an awakening of individuality,"[192] but surely individuality had been awakened many times before, in older readers' studies, by men and women who created spaces in which their private selves could learn, grow, reflect and be reflected, in dialogue between the singular present and the endless generations past—spaces into which they withdrew from the bustle of social life. Sitting in the study of his seaside house in Antium, in the first century B.C., Cicero wrote to his intimate friend Atticus, "I amuse myself with books, of which I have a goodly store at Antium, or I count the waves—the weather is unsuitable for fishing mackerel."[193] Later he added, "Reading and writing bring me, not solace indeed, but distraction."[194] Distraction from the noise of the world. A place to think.

In 1929, Virginia Woolf published her now famous lectures on "Women and Fiction" under the title *A Room of One's Own,* and there she defined forever our need for a private space for reading and writing: "The whole of the mind must lie wide open if we are to get the sense that the writer is communicating his experience with perfect fullness. There must be freedom and there must be peace." And she added, "Not a wheel must grate, not a light glimmer. The curtains must be close drawn."[195] As if it were night.

The studios of celebrated writers are curious memorials. Rudyard Kipling's studies in his house in Vermont, the Naulakha, and at Rottingdean, in which most of the books deal with travel or industrial crafts, bears witness to his interest in the exact technical phrase and word; in Erasmus's room in Brussels, the light from the rhomboid windowpanes plays on volumes sent to him by those friends and colleagues for whom he liked to write; Friedrich Dürrenmatt's closed, white, rectangular

Rudyard Kipling in his study at his house in Vermont, the Naulakha.

library in Neuchâtel has a simple bookshelf of neat modern bindings wrapping itself around the room, like one of the circular labyrinths he crafted in his novels; Victor Hugo's cloth-lined and soft-carpeted mansion on the Place des Vosges in Paris seems haunted by manuscripts of his melodramatic stories and sketches of his ghostly landscapes; Arno Schmidt's small, ugly rooms in Bargfeld bei Celle, in Lower Saxony, are lined with ramshackle shelves that held inglorious English titles (such as the novels of Edward Bulwer-Lytton, whose texts Schmidt re-created in better German versions), and small boxes with snippets handwritten on bits of cardboard—miniature archives kept by Schmidt in thematic order, which he used to compose his masterpieces; thousands more studios and libraries around the world are preserved as memorials to their phantom owners, who might at any moment once again run an absent-minded hand over a familiar piece, sit in the customary chair, pick out a much-leafed book from among its fellows or open a volume to a certain page with cherished words. Deserted libraries hold the shades of the writers who worked within, and are haunted by their absence.

In Valladolid, readers of *Don Quixote* can stroll through the house occupied by Miguel de Cervantes from 1602 to 1605, the year in which the first part of the novel was published, and experience a voyeuristic thrill. The house has melodramatic associations: on the night of 27 June 1605, a certain Gaspar de Ezpeleta was walking home when, just outside this house, he was assaulted by a masked man and mortally wounded. Ezpeleta managed to cry out, bringing to his assistance a neighbour who in turn summoned Cervantes, and the two carried the dying man to the address of a well-known lady. The mayor of Valladolid, suspecting Cervantes (or one of his relatives) of being responsible for the attack, ordered that the writer and his family be imprisoned. They were released a few days later, after proving their innocence, but historians have long debated the question of Cervantes's involvement in the murder. The house, though carefully restored, has necessarily been furnished with bits and pieces that never were in Cervantes's possession. Only the study, on the second floor, contains a few objects that almost certainly belonged to him: not the "ebony and ivory" desk described in the will of his daughter, Isabel de Cervantes, but another, also mentioned in the document, "made of walnut, the largest one I possess," two paintings, one of Saint John and the other of the Virgin, a copper brazier, a chest for keeping papers and a single bookshelf holding some of the titles mentioned in his work. In this room he wrote several stories for his *Exemplary Novels,* and here he must have discussed with his friends the conception of his singular Quixote.[196]

In one of the first chapters of *Don Quixote,* when the barber and the priest have decided to purge the knight's library of the books that seem to have brought on his madness, the housekeeper insists that the room must first be sprinkled with holy water, "for there might be here one of those many wizards who inhabit these books, and he might cast a spell on us, to punish us for wanting to expel them from the world."[197] Like so many people who do not read, the housekeeper fears the power of the books she refuses to open. The same superstition holds true for most readers; the books we keep closest to hand are possessed by magic. The stories that unfold in the space of a writer's study, the objects chosen to watch over a desk, the books selected to sit on the shelves, all weave a web of echoes and reflections, of meanings and affections, that lend a visitor the illusion that something of the owner of this space lives on between these walls, even if the owner is no more.

Sometimes the shade of the writer and that of his library mingle long before his death. For many years, until he left to die in Geneva in 1986, Borges lived in Buenos Aires among books he could no longer see, since blindness had overtaken him in his early fifties. His small apartment was on the sixth floor of an unobtrusive building in the centre of town, around the corner from the Plaza San Martín. The door was always opened by Fani, the maid, who would lead his frequent visitors into a small entrance hall where, in the gloom, stood Borges's several walking sticks and canes, "patiently waiting," as he liked to say, "to be taken out for a stroll." Then, through a curtained doorway, one entered the living room, where the master would greet his guests with a weak, shy handshake. To the right, a table covered with a lace cloth and four straight-backed chairs furnished the dining room; to the left, under a window, stood a well-worn couch and two or three armchairs. Borges would sit on the couch and the visitor would be asked to take one of the armchairs facing him. His blind eyes would stare into a point in space as he spoke, his asthmatic voice echoing through the room full of the familiar things of his daily life: a small table on which he kept a silver mug and a *mate* that had belonged to his grandfather, a miniature writing desk dating from his mother's first communion, two white bookshelves set in the wall holding encyclopedias, and two low bookcases of dark wood. On the wall hung a painting by his sister, Norah Borges, depicting the Annunciation, and an engraving by Piranesi showing mysterious circular ruins. A short corridor to the far left led to the bedrooms: his mother's, full of old photographs, and his own, simple as a monk's cell, with an iron bedstead, two bookcases and a single chair. On the wall of his bedroom hung a wooden plate with the coats of arms of the various cantons of Switzerland, and a copy of Dürer's engraving *Knight, Death and the Devil*, which Borges had celebrated in two exquisite sonnets.

Considering that Borges called the universe a book, and said that he imagined paradise "in the shape of a library,"[198] his visitors expected a place copiously lined with books, shelves bursting at the seams, piles of print blocking the doorways and protruding from every crevice—a jungle of ink and paper. Instead, they'd discover this modest apartment where books occupied a discreet, orderly place. When the young Mario Vargas Llosa visited Borges sometime in the mid-fifties, he remarked on the spartan surroundings and asked why the master didn't live in a more bookish, more luxurious home. Borges took great offence at this remark. "Maybe that's how they do things in Lima," he said to the indiscreet Peruvian, "but here in Buenos Aires we don't like to show off."

These few bookcases, however, were Borges's pride. "I'll tell you a secret," he once explained. "I like to pretend I'm not blind, and I covet books like a man who can see. I even covet new encyclopedias, and imagine I can follow the course of rivers in their maps and find wonderful things in the various entries." He liked to tell how, as a child, he used to accompany his father to the National Library and, too timid to ask for a book, simply take one of the volumes of the Britannica from the open shelves and read whatever article opened itself to his eyes. Sometimes he would be lucky, as when he chose volume *De–Dr* and learned about the Druids, the Druzes and Dryden.[199] He never abandoned this custom of trusting himself to the ordered chance of encyclopedias, and he spent many hours leafing through (and having read to him) the volumes of the Garzanti, the Brockhaus, the Britannica or the Espasa-Calpe. Then, if there was a particularly appealing tidbit of information, he would ask his reader to record it, with the page number, at the back of the revelatory volume.

The two low bookcases in his living room held works by Stevenson, Chesterton, Henry James and Kipling, as well as J.W. Dunne's *An Experiment with Time,* several scientific romances by H.G. Wells, Wilkie Collins's *The Moonstone,* various novels by Eça de Queiroz in yellowing cardboard bindings, books by nineteenth-century Argentine writers. Here too were Joyce's *Ulysses* and *Finnegans Wake; Vies Imaginaires,* by Marcel Schwob; detective novels by John Dickson Carr, Milward Kennedy and Richard Hull; Mark Twain's *Life on the Mississippi,* Arnold Bennett's *Buried Alive;* a small paperback edition of David Garnett's *Lady into Fox* and *A Man in the Zoo,* with delicate woodblock illustrations; Spengler's *Der Untergang des Abendlandes;* the several tomes of Gibbon's *Decline and Fall;* various books on

mathematics and philosophy, including titles by Sweden-
borg and Schopenhauer; and his beloved *Wörterbuch der
Philosophie*, by Fritz Mauthner. Some of these books
had accompanied Borges since his adolescent days; others, mostly the ones in English and German, carried
labels from the Buenos Aires bookstores where they had
been bought, all now vanished: Mitchell's, Rodriguez,
Pygmalion.

The bookcases in the bedroom held volumes of
poetry and one of the largest collections of Anglo-
Saxon and Icelandic literature in Latin America. Here
Borges kept the books he needed to study what he
called "the harsh and laborious words/ That, with lips
now turned to dust,/ I mouthed in the days of
Northumbria and Mercia/ Before becoming Haslam or
Borges":[200] Skeat's *Etymological Dictionary*, an anno-
tated version of *The Battle of Maldon*, Richard Meyer's
Altgermanische Religionsgeschichte. The other bookcase
contained the poems of Enrique Banchs, of Heine, of
San Juan de la Cruz, and many commentaries on Dante.
Mysteriously absent from his bookshelves were Proust,
Racine, Goethe's *Faust*, Milton and the Greek tragedies
(all of which he had, of course, read and mentioned in
his writings).

Absent too were his own books. He would proudly
tell visitors who asked to see an early edition that he
didn't possess a single volume that carried (he would
say) "that eminently forgettable" name. The truth is that
he didn't need them. Though he pretended not to
remember, he could recite by heart poems learned many
decades earlier, and correct and alter in his memory his
own writings, usually to the stupefaction and delight of

his listeners. Shortly after his death, his widow, Maria Kodama, donated the majority of his books to a foundation in Buenos Aires bearing his name, and from time to time certain volumes are shown in exhibitions organized in his honour. Lying open in glass cases, stripped of their surroundings, honoured but unread—less purveyors of words than funerary objects, expelled from their home after his death—books seem to suffer the fate of the spouses and servants of those ancient kings whose households followed their master to the grave.

A study lends its owner, its privileged reader, what Seneca called *euthymia*, a Greek word which Seneca explained means "well-being of the soul," and which he translated as *"tranquillitas."*[201] Every study ultimately aspires to *euthymia*. *Euthymia*, memory without distraction, the intimacy of a reading time—a secret period in the communal day—that is what we seek in a private reading space. According to Blake,

> There is a Moment in each Day that Satan cannot find,
> Nor can his Watch Fiends find it, but the Industrious find
> This Moment & it multiply, & when it once is found
> It renovates every Moment of the Day if rightly placed.[202]

Though we primarily seek *euthymia* in these private moments, we can sometimes discover it in the communal space of a public library. In Mameluke Cairo, in the fifteenth century, though there were indeed scholars who worked in their own private rooms, readers of lesser means were encouraged to visit the public libraries of schools and mosques. Here, books were made available to those who could not afford to buy them; here, they could copy out the desired works for their own use, whether to learn texts by heart or study them at leisure. The thirteenth-century scholar Ibn Jama'a, though recommending that students purchase books whenever possible, thought it most important that they be "carried in the heart" and not merely kept on a shelf. Copying out texts helped one commit them to memory, thereby building (he thought) a sort of parallel library to the one of ink and paper. "The student should always have with him an inkwell, so as to be able to write down useful things he hears," Ibn Jama'a advised.[203] It was understood that the written text supported the text learned by heart, since "what is only memorized flies away, what is written down remains" (an Islamic version of the Latin *verba volant, scripta manent*).[204] According to Ibn Jama'a, the art of memory was akin to that of architecture, since by practising it a reader could build to his taste a private palace furnished with collected treasures, declaring ownership of the texts he had chosen in a deep and definitive way. To sharpen the skill of memorizing books, the use of honey, toothpicks and twenty-one raisins a day was recommended, while the consumption of coriander and eggplant was deemed deleterious. Ibn Jama'a also advised against "reading inscriptions on tombs, walking between camels haltered in a line, or flicking away lice,"[205] all activities that affected the keenness of memory.

At the end of the fifteenth century, to exercise his memory among the books he knew best, Niccolò Machiavelli preferred to read in his study at night—the time when he found it easiest to enjoy those qualities which for him most defined the relationship of a reader and his books:

intimacy and leisured thought. "When evening comes," he wrote, "I return home and go into my study. On the threshold I strip off my muddy, sweaty, workday clothes, and put on the robes of court and palace, and in this graver dress I enter the antique courts of the ancients and am welcomed by them, and there I taste the food that alone is mine, for which I was born. There I make bold to speak to them and ask the motives for their actions, and they, in their humanity, reply to me. And for the course of four hours I forget the world, remember no vexations, fear poverty no more, tremble no more at death: I pass into their world."[206]

THE LIBRARY

AS MIND

> . . . to give visible form to the psychic presence and to the movements
> of the soul.
>
> Aby Warburg, *Ausgewählte Schriften*

Like Machiavelli, I often sit among my books at night. While I prefer to write in the morning, at night I enjoy reading in the thick silence, when triangles of light from the reading lamps split my library shelves in two. Above, the high rows of books vanish into darkness; below sits the privileged section of the illuminated titles. This arbitrary division, which grants certain books a glowing presence and relegates others to the shadows, is superseded by another order, which owes its existence merely to what I can remember. My library has no catalogue; having placed the books on the shelves myself, I generally know their position by recalling the library's layout, and areas of light or darkness make little difference to my exploring. The remembered order follows a pattern in my mind, the shape and division of the library, rather as a stargazer connects in narrative patterns the pinpoints of the stars; but the library in turn reflects the configuration of my mind, its distant astrologer. The deliberate yet random order of the shelves, the choice of subject matters, the intimate history of each book's survival, the traces of certain times and certain places left between the pages, all point to a particular reader. A keen observer might be able to tell who I am from a tattered copy of the poems of Blas de Otero, the number of volumes by Robert Louis Stevenson, the large section devoted to detective stories, the minuscule section devoted to literary theory, the fact that there is much Plato and very little Aristotle on my shelves. Every library is autobiographical.

In the Cathedral of Sainte Cécile of Albi, in the south of France, a late-fifteenth-century fresco depicts a scene from the Last Judgment. Under an unfurled scroll, the recalled souls march towards their fate, each naked and solemnly carrying on the breast an open book. In this troop of resurrected readers, the Book of Life has been divided and reissued as a series of individual volumes, open,[207] as the Apocalypse has it, so that the dead may be "judged out of those things which were written in the books."[208] The idea persists even today: our books will bear witness for or against us, our books reflect who we are and who we have been, our books hold the share of pages granted to us from the Book of Life. By the books we call ours we will be judged.

What makes a library a reflection of its owner is not merely the choice of the titles themselves, but the mesh of associations implied in the choice. Our experience builds on experience, our memory on other memories. Our books build on other books that change or enrich them, that grant them a chronology apart from that of literary dictionaries. I'm now, after all this time, incapable

The Last Judgement fresco at Sainte Cecile Cathedral in Albi.

of tracing all these connections myself. I forget, or don't even know, in what way many of these books relate to one another. If I advance in one direction—Margaret Laurence's African stories conjure up in my memory Isak Dinesen's *Out of Africa,* which in turn makes me think of her *Seven Gothic Tales,* which leads me back to Edgardo Cozarinsky (who introduced me to Dinesen's work) and his book on Borges and film, and further back to the novels of Rose Macaulay, which Cozarinsky and I discussed one afternoon long ago in Buenos Aires, both of us surprised that someone else knew about them— then I miss the other strands of this complicated web, and wonder how, like a spider, I was able to string the seemingly immeasurable distance, for example, from Ovid's *Tristia* to the poems of 'Abd al-Rahman, exiled to North

Africa from his home in Spain. It is not only a matter of fortuitous connections. Books are transformed by the sequence in which they are read. *Don Quixote* read after *Kim* and *Don Quixote* read after *Huckleberry Finn* are two different books, both coloured by the reader's experience of journeys, friendship and adventures. Each of these kaleidoscope volumes never ceases to change; each new reading lends it yet another twist, a different pattern. Perhaps every library is ultimately inconceivable, because, like the mind, it reflects upon itself, multiplying geometrically with each new reflection. And yet, from a library of solid books we expect a rigour that we forgive in the library of the mind.

Such fluid mental libraries are not (or were not) uncommon; in Islam they are exemplary. Even though the Koran was written down very early, most ancient Arab literature was for a long time entrusted to the recollection of its readers. For instance, after the death in 815 of the great poet Abu Nuwas, no copy of his work was found; the poet had learned by heart all his poems, and in order to set them down on paper the scribes had to resort to the memory of those who had listened to the master. Precision of recall was deemed all-important, and throughout the Islamic Middle Ages, it was considered more valuable to learn by listening to books read out loud than by private study, because the text then entered the body through the mind and not merely through the eyes. Authors published not so much by transcribing their work themselves as by dictating it to their assistants, and students learned by hearing those texts read out to them or by reading them to a teacher. Because of the Islamic belief that only oral transmission was truly legitimate, memory (not its physical representation in the solid world of books and manuscripts, though these were important enough to be treasured in schools and mosques) was deemed to be the great repository of a library.[209] Up to a point, "library" and "memory" were synonymous.

And yet, however careful our reading, remembered texts often undergo curious changes; they fragment, shrivel up or grow unpredictably long. In my mental library, *The Tempest* is reduced to a few immortal lines, while a brief novel such as Juan Rulfo's *Pedro Páramo* occupies my entire Mexican imaginary landscape. A couple of sentences by George Orwell in the essay "Shooting an Elephant" expand in my memory to several pages of description and reflection that I think I can actually see in my mind, printed on the page; of the lengthy medieval romance *The Devoured Heart,* all I can remember is the title.

Neither the solid library on my shelves nor the shifting one of memory holds absolute power for long. Over time, the labyrinths of my two libraries mysteriously intermingle. And often, through what psychologists call the perseverance of memory (the mental phenomenon by which a certain idea is perceived as true even after it has proven false), the library of the mind ends by overriding the library of paper and ink.

Is it possible to set up a library that imitates this whimsical, associative order, one that might seem to an uninformed observer a random distribution of books, but that in fact follows a logical if deeply personal organization? I can think of at least one example.

One day in 1920, the philosopher Ernst Cassirer, recently appointed to the chair of philosophy at Hamburg's New University and working at the time on the first volume of his groundbreaking *Philosophy of Symbolic Forms,* asked to visit the famous Warburg Library, established thirty years earlier by Aby Warburg. Following Warburg's conception of the universe, books on philosophy were set next to those on astrology, magic and folklore, and art compendiums rubbed covers with works of literature and religion, while manuals on language were placed next to volumes of theology, poetry and art. Cassirer was taken through the uniquely organized collection by the assistant director, Fritz Saxl, and at the end of the tour he turned to his host and said, "I'll never come back here. If I returned to this labyrinth, I'd end up by losing my way."[210]

Years later, Cassirer explained his panic: "[Warburg's] library isn't simply a collection of books but a catalogue of problems. And it isn't the thematic fields of the library that provoked in me this overwhelming impression, but rather the library's very organizing principle, a principle far more important than the mere extension of the subjects covered. Here, indeed, the history of art, the history of religion and myth, the history of linguistics and culture were not only placed side by side but linked one to the other, and all of them linked in turn to a single ideal centre."[211] After Warburg's death in 1929, Cassirer compared the shelves of the library's reading room, built to follow the elliptical shape of the walls, to "the breath of a magician." For Cassirer, Warburg's books, arranged according to the intricacies of his thought, were, like the books of Prospero, the stronghold of his life's force.

Aby Warburg was born in Hamburg on 13 June 1866, the eldest son of a Jewish banker. Photographs show him as a short, shy-looking man with powerful dark eyes. In a questionnaire he once imagined for his own amusement, he described himself as "a small gentleman with a black moustache who sometimes tells stories in dialect."[212] Unable to reconcile himself to his father's demands to embrace both Jewish orthodoxy and the family banking business, he suffered from long bouts of anxiety and melancholia. To find relief, he sought experience of the world in books, and became deeply interested in the early philosophies of Greek and Rome, in the cultures of the Renaissance, in Native American civilizations and in Buddhist religion. He seemed unable to accept the constraints of any one discipline or school of thought. An eclectic curiosity dominated all his undertakings.

His passion for books and images began in his child-hood. Among the earliest intellectual experiences he could remember was seeing, at the age of six, the striking illustrations of Balzac's *Petites misères de la vie conjugale*, depicting melodramatic family scenes in which weeping women, angry men, screaming children and amused servants acted out the misfortunes of bourgeois married life. The boy became obsessed by them, and they vividly haunted his dreams. A couple of years later, he started devouring books "full of stories about Red Indians." These images and adventures offered him, he was later to recall, "a means of withdrawing from a depressing reality in which I was quite helpless." Unable to voice his anger and frustration, what Warburg called the emotion of pain, he sought and found "an outlet in fantasies of romantic cruelty. This was my inoculation against *active* cruelty."[213] His siblings remembered him always surrounded by books, reading every scrap of paper he came across—even the family encyclopedia, which he perused from the first to the last volume.

Not only reading but collecting books became for Warburg a vital need. On his thirteenth birthday, determined to follow neither his father's career nor his family's religion, the voracious adolescent made his younger brother Max the offer of his birthright: he would exchange his privilege, as the eldest son, of entering the family firm, for the promise that Max would buy him all the books he ever wanted. Max, aged twelve, agreed. From then on, the many books purchased with funds supplied by the faithful Max became the core of Warburg's library.

Warburg's collecting passion was never entirely haphazard. On the contrary; from very early on, his reading seems to have been directed towards certain very specific questions. Most of us, looking back, find it astonishing to recognize in our first books inklings of an interest that did not become apparent until much later, which nevertheless apparently stirred us long before we could put our interest into words. The emotions of Warburg's childhood books finally found an explanation in Gotthold Ephraim Lessing's *Laokoon*, a classic text that he read for the first time when he entered Bonn University at the age of twenty.[214] Lessing's *Laokoon* became for him a magical touchstone. "One must be young," the aged Goethe had written almost sixty years earlier, "to understand the influence that Lessing's *Laokoon* had on us, tearing us away from the passivity of contemplation and opening up free realms of thought. The *ut pictura poesis* [the classical comparison between the aesthetics of painting and those of poetry], so long misunderstood, was all of a sudden brushed away; their summits seemed very different to us, and yet they seemed very close in their foundations."[215] In Lessing's work the young Warburg recognized not only the power of an argument that attempted to explore the different creative systems of images and words, but above all the notion that each age recaptures for its own reasons an aspect of tradition upon which it builds its own symbology and meaning, what he was to call "the survival of antiquity, a problem of a purely historical nature."[216] The question that began to take shape for Warburg was how our oldest symbols are renewed at different ages, and how their reincarnations link and reverberate in each other. One of the most resonant words in his intellectual development was *Kompatibilität*, compatibility[217]— experience by association—so it's not surprising that he chose to explain his own library with a definition borrowed from the critic Ewald Hering. For Warburg his library was memory, but "memory as organized matter."[218]

The library that Warburg began to assemble in his adolescence, which in 1909 he transferred to his new house on the Heilwigstrasse in Hamburg, was above all a personal one, and it followed a uniquely idiosyncratic cataloguing system. During the late eighteenth and early nineteenth centuries, a controversy raged in Germany about the best method of organizing a library. The opposing parties argued, on the one hand, for a hierarchical order of subjects to guide the reader from one field of knowledge to another, and on the other, for an order based on the size of a volume and its date of acquisition. (The latter, incidentally, was a system that had been employed successfully in certain medieval libraries.)[219] For Warburg, neither method was satisfactory. He demanded from his collection a fluidity and vivacity that neither enclosure by subject nor restrictions of chronology allowed him. Fritz Saxl noted in 1943 how Warburg had reacted to the idea of such mechanical cataloguing, which, in an age of increased book production, was rapidly replacing the "much more scholarly familiarity which is gained by browsing." According to Saxl, "Warburg recognized the danger" and spoke of the "law of the good neighbour." The book with which one was familiar was not, in most cases, the book one needed. It was the unknown neighbour on the shelf that contained the vital information, even though one might not guess this from its title. "The overriding idea was that all the books together—each containing its larger or smaller bit of information and being supplemented by its neighbours—should by their titles guide the student to perceive the essential forces of the human mind and its history. Books were for Warburg more than instruments of research. Assembled and grouped, they expressed the thought of mankind in its constant and in its changing aspects."[220]

Not only books. Warburg had a remarkable memory for images, and was able to weave complicated tapestries of iconographical connections which he then attempted to expand upon in fragmentary essays. While poring through antiquarian catalogues, he would jot down on small cards the titles that caught his attention, accompanied by dense commentaries in what he called his "thick eel-gruel style,"[221] filing them in separate boxes according to a complicated (and variable) system. Those who knew him spoke of the "instinct" that guided him in compiling important bibliographies on whatever subject interested him at the time, an instinct that led him to rearrange (and keep rearranging) the books on the shelves following the lines of thought he was at any given moment pursuing. As Warburg imagined it, a library was above all an accumulation of associations, each association breeding a new image or text to be associated, until the associations returned the reader to the first page. For Warburg, every library was circular.

Warburg dedicated his library, with its oval reading room (which he called *die kulturwissenschaftliche Bibliothek Warburg*, the Warburg Library of Cultural Science), to the Greek goddess of memory, Mnemosyne, mother of the Muses. For Warburg the history of humankind was an ongoing, constantly changing attempt to give tongue and features to archaic experiences, less individual than generic, embedded in social memory. Like many scholars of his generation, he had been influenced by the theories of the German neurologist Richard Semon, who had argued for a physiological theory of emotions.[222] According to Semon, memory is the quality that distinguishes living from dead matter. Any event affecting living matter leaves a trace (what Semon calls an engram) that can be animated when we remember. For Warburg these engrams were in fact pure symbols alive at the core of every culture, and what interested him was why a given period (the Renaissance, for example, or the Enlightenment) would be so affected by certain of these symbols, or by certain aspects of them, that they would shape the voice and style of its literature and art. Because of its haunting power, Warburg wonderfully described this active memory as "a ghost story for adults."[223]

And the library itself? What was it like to stand in the midst of what Cassirer had compared to Prospero's stronghold? Most libraries give an impression of systematic order, of an organization made manifest by themes or numbers or alphabetical sequences. Warburg's library shows no such system. When I visited the reconstructed reading room in Hamburg (which today holds only a small part of his volumes) and inspected the rounded shelves in the oval central chamber, the feeling I had was bewilderment; it was like standing in the middle of a foreign city whose signposts doubtlessly meant something but whose sense I couldn't fathom. The shelves suggested to the eye an uninterrupted association of titles, not a linear order with a beginning and an end. Intellectually it was possible for me to find reasons for the proximity of any two titles, but those reasons could be so varied or could seem so far-fetched that I could not relate them to any traditional sequence—such as M following L, or 2999 preceding 3000. Warburg's system was closer to that of poetic composition. Reading the verse "Bright is the ring of words" on a page offers an immediate and complete comprehension of the poet's vision. The reader requires no explanation; the line conveys a full and instantaneous revelation about the act of reading, through the words and the elicited music. But if the poet were explicitly to lay before us all the connecting byways and meanderings springing from his ineffable intuition as to the nature of poetry—if he tried to make all the leads and connections visible to us—such comprehension would elude us. So it is with Warburg's library.

But Warburg would not allow these connections to remain invisible, nor would he consider them except as constantly changing, so he constructed his library as a space uninterrupted by sharp angles, in which they could retain endless mobility. In a sense, his library was an attempt to disclose, in all their rawness, the bare nerves of his thought, and to allow room for his ideas to migrate and mutate and mate. If most libraries of his time resembled an entomologist's display case of pinned and labelled specimens, Warburg's revealed itself to the visitor as a child's glass-fronted ant farm.

In the spring of 1914, bending to his colleagues' pressure, Warburg decided to open his library to scholars and scholarly research, instituting as well a system of grants that would enable students to come to Hamburg and work. Fourteen years earlier he had warily mentioned the idea to his brother Max; now he returned to the vast project, and discussed its possibilities with Fritz Saxl. He did so with great reluctance because, he admitted, he loathed losing possession of the private intellectual realm he had so laboriously created. And yet he realized that this opening up of the library was the necessary next step in his attempt to chart the intricate symbolic heritage of humankind, "the afterlife of the ancient world."[224]

But the First World War put a temporary end to these plans. In the midst of the bleakness and confusion of the time, Warburg, who had suffered intermittently from anxiety and depression since his childhood, began to intuit a bleak concordance between his mental state and the state of the world. "Like a seismograph, his sensitive nerves had already recorded the underground tremors to which others remained utterly deaf," wrote one of his contemporaries.[225] Warburg now saw his search for connections between our earliest symbolic representations of irrational impulses and fears, and later artistic manifestations of those symbols, as a tension reflected in his own mental struggles. He had wanted to believe that science would eventually, by chronicling the metamorphoses of our phobic reflexes, find rationally apprehensible explanations for our primordial emotional experiences. Instead, he realized, science had constructed as the latest avatar an even more advanced machinery of war, with its mustard gas and deadly trenches.

In one of his fragments (to which he had appended the exorcism "You live and do me no harm"[226]) he wrote the following: "We are in the age of Faust, in which the modern scientist endeavours—between magic practice and mathematics—to conquer the realm of reflective reason through an increased awareness of the distance between the self and the external world."[227] The end of the war in 1918 brought him little relief. Two years later the distance seemed, in his eyes, to have vanished almost completely.

In 1920, facing the prospect of opening his library to a scholarly public, and unable to sustain the mental anguish any more, Warburg entered the famous clinic of the Swiss doctors Otto and Ludwig Binswanger in Kreuzlingen, where Friedrich Nietzsche had been treated thirty years earlier.[228] He remained there until 1924. "Why," he asked then, "does fate consign a creative human being to the realm of eternal unrest, leaving it up to him to choose where his intellectual upbringing will take place: whether in hell, purgatory or paradise?"[229]

His time at the clinic was one of slow recovery and attempts at reassembly, as he tried to put together his scattered mind, fragmented as it was into thousands of images and piecemeal notes. "God is in the details," he liked repeating. And yet he felt—like Rousseau, who had said, "I die in details"—that he could no longer gather the many strands of image and thought he had once pursued. But under Dr. Binswanger's care he began to feel whole again, and in 1923 he asked whether the authorities would release him if he could prove his mental stability. He suggested speaking to the clinic's patients, and on April 23 he delivered a lecture on native serpent rituals he had witnessed in North America as a young man. In a journal note he made at the time, he remarked that he saw himself as Perseus, slayer of the serpent-headed Medusa, who avoided staring directly into the poisonous monster's eyes by looking at her reflection in his shield. He also noted that, in the Middle Ages, Perseus had been debased from hero to mere fortune-teller, to be rescued only later, during the Renaissance, as a symbol of heroic humanity.[230]

When Warburg left the clinic in 1924, he discovered that Saxl, in agreement with Warburg's family, had finally transformed the library into the projected research centre.

The change, however much he had foreseen it, troubled him greatly and made him feel diminished; "Warburg redux," he signed one of his letters at the time. And yet the transformation also seemed to fill him with "an almost awe-inspiring energy," and he set himself to work once again, under these new conditions, amidst his beloved books.

It would be obvious to any visitor walking into Warburg's library that, from its very conception, his creation was essentially a visual one. The shape of the shelves, the associated titles they housed, the pictures and photographs that littered the rooms, all spoke of his concern with the physical representation of ideas and symbols. The sources of his questions were images; books allowed him to reflect on these images, and provided words to bridge the silence between them. Memory, that key word in Warburg's vocabulary, meant above all the memory of images.

Warburg's unfinished and unfinishable project was the great iconographic sequence he called Mnemosyne, a vast collection of images that charted, across a tapestry of connections, the many trails the scholar had been following. But how to display these images? How to place them in front of him so that they could be studied in sequence, but a sequence that could be varied according to new ideas and newly perceived connections? The solution to this problem came from Saxl. Upon Warburg's return to Hamburg, Saxl met him with large wooden panels, like standing blackboards, across which he had stretched black hessian. Warburg's images could be fixed with pins on the cloth, and easily removed whenever he wanted to alter their position. These giant displays, "pages" of an endless book of variable sequence, became the core of all Warburg's activities in the last years of his life. Since he could change both the panels and the images on them at will, they became the physical illustration of his realm of thought and his library, to which he appended streams of notes and comments. "These images and words are intended as help for those who come after me in their attempt to achieve clarity," he wrote, "and thus to overcome the tragic tension between instinctive magic and discursive logic. They are the confessions of an (incurable) schizoid, deposited in the archives of mental healers."[231] In fact, Saxl's panels—a book of giant shifting pages—restored to Warburg, up to a point, his lost private space; they were a private domain that helped him recover some of his mental health.

Aby Warburg died in 1929, at the age of sixty-three. Three years after his death, a couple of volumes of his collected works appeared in Germany; they were the last to be published in his homeland for a long time. Fragmented and wonderfully far-ranging, his writings are yet another version of his library, another representation of the intricacies of his thought, another map of his extraordinary mind. He wanted his intuition to conclude in scientific laws; he would have liked to believe that the thrill and terror of art and literature were steps towards understanding cause and function. And yet, again and again, he returned to the notion of memory as desire, and desire itself as knowledge. In one of his fragments he writes "that the work of art is something hostile moving towards the beholder."[232] With his library

One of Warburg's "Mnemosyne" panels.

he attempted to create a space in which that hostility would not be tamed (something he realized could not be done without destruction) but lovingly reflected back, with curiosity, respect and awe, a mirror of his curious, intelligent mind.

In 1933, following the appointment of Hitler as Chancellor of the Reich, the Warburg library and staff emigrated to England. Six hundred boxes of books plus furniture and equipment were shipped across the sea to London. I like to imagine the many barges crossing the water, laden with the volumes assembled over the years, a fragmented portrait of their owner—a reader now dead, but present in this dismantled representation of his library about to be reshaped in a foreign land. The books were first accommodated in an office building in Millbank; three years later, the University of London agreed to house the collection but not rebuild the oval shelves. On 28 November 1944, the Warburg Institute was finally incorporated in the university, where it still functions today. Fifty-one years later, a copy of Warburg's house was built in Hamburg on the site of his old home on the Heilwigstrasse, and an attempt was made, based on original photographs, to reproduce the shelving and the display of part of his collection, so that anyone who visits the house and stands for a moment in the reading room can feel as if Warburg's mind is still at work among his memorable and changing shelves.

THE LIBRARY

AS ISLAND

An old man is always a Crusoe.

François Mauriac, *Nouveaux mémoires intérieurs*

More than three hundred years before the Warburg library crossed the sea to England, another, more modest library was shipwrecked on the coast of a desert island somewhere in the South Pacific. On one of the early days of October of the year 1659, Robinson Crusoe returned to the mangled remains of his craft and managed to bring ashore a number of tools and various kinds of food, as well as "several things of less value" such as pens, ink, paper and a small collection of books. Of these books, a few were in Portuguese, a couple were "Popish prayer-books" and three were "very good Bibles." His "dreadful deliverance" had left him terrified of death through starvation, but once the tools and the food had met his material needs he was ready to seek entertainment from the ship's meagre store of books. Robinson Crusoe was the founder—if a reluctant founder—of a new society. And Daniel Defoe, his author, thought it necessary

that at the beginning of a new society there should be books.

We might be tempted to guess what these "several Portuguese books" were. Probably a copy of Camões's *Lusiads*, a fitting book in a ship's collection; perhaps the sermons of the illustrious Antonio Vieira, including the wonderful "Sermon of Saint Anthony to the Fishes," in which Crusoe might have read a defence of the brothers of the savage Friday; most certainly the *Peregrination* of Fernão Mendes Pinto, which tells of strange voyages through the still mysterious Orient and which the omnivorous Defoe knew well. We can't tell precisely what those books were, because in spite of keeping a diary in which he dutifully recorded the changes of weather and mood, Crusoe never wrote any more about the books. Perhaps, true to the English conviction that English is the only language a gentleman requires, he was unable to read Portuguese. Whatever the reason, he seems very soon to have forgotten the books entirely, and when he leaves the island almost thirty years later, on 11 June 1687, and makes a detailed list of his possessions, he doesn't breathe a word about those anonymous volumes.

He does tell us, however, of his uses of the Bible. It colours each of his actions, it dictates the meaning of his sufferings, it is the instrument through which he will try, Prospero-like, to make a useful servant out of Friday. Crusoe writes, "I explained to [Friday], as well as I could, why our blessed Redeemer took not on Him the nature of angels but the seed of Abraham, and how for that reason the fallen angels had no share in the redemption; that he came only to the lost sheep of the House of Israel, and the like." And he adds, with disarming frankness, "I had, God knows, more sincerity than knowledge in all the methods I took for this poor creature's instruction."

For Crusoe the book is not only an instrument of instruction but also one of divination. Some time later, sunk in despair, trying to understand his pitiful condition, he opens the Bible and finds this sentence: "I will never, never leave thee, nor forsake thee," and immediately it seems to him that these words are meant for his eyes especially. On that faraway coast, starting over with a few odds and ends from society's ruins—seeds, guns and the Word of God—he constructs a new world at whose centre the Holy Bible shines its fierce and ancient light.

We can live in a society founded on the book and yet not read, or we can live in a society where the book is merely an accessory and be, in the deepest, truest sense, a reader. As a society the Greeks, for instance, cared little for books, and yet individually they were assiduous readers.[233] Aristotle, whose books (as we know them today) were probably lecture notes taken down by his students, read voraciously, and his own library was the first in ancient Greece of which there is any certain information.[234] Socrates—who despised books because he thought they were a threat to our gift of memory, and never deigned to leave a written word—chose to read the speech of the orator Lycias, not to hear it recited by the enthusiastic Phaedrus.[235] Crusoe would perhaps have elected to have the text recited to him, if he'd been given the choice. Even though this representative of a book-centred Judeo-Christian society "read daily the Word of God," as he tells us himself, Crusoe was not a keen reader of the Bible, his Book of Power (to borrow Luther's phrase). He consulted it daily—as he would have consulted the Internet had it existed, and allowed himself to be guided by it. But he did not make the Word his, as Saint Augustine insisted we must do, "incarnating" the written text.[236] He merely accepted society's reading of it. Had Crusoe been shipwrecked at the end of our millennium, it is easy to imagine him rescuing from the ship not the Book of Power but a PowerBook.

What distinguishes Crusoe from Defoe, that avid reader, since they are both members of the society of the book? What distinguishes someone for whom a book is powerful or prestigious, but who can be content with no books or with only one single emblematic volume, from a reader of books individually chosen and now personally meaningful? There is an unbridgeable chasm between the book that tradition has declared a classic and the book (the same book) that we have made ours through instinct, emotion and understanding: suffered through it, rejoiced in it, translated it into our experience and (notwithstanding the layers of readings with which a book comes into our hands) essentially become its first discoverers, an experience as astonishing and unexpected as finding Friday's footprint on the sand. "The songs of Homer," declared Goethe, "have the power to deliver us, if only for brief moments, from the fearsome load with which tradition has weighed us down over many thousands of years."[237] To be the first to enter Circe's cave, the first to hear Ulysses call himself Nobody, is every reader's secret wish, granted over and over, generation after generation, to those who open the *Odyssey* for the first time. This modest *jus primae noctis*, or "first-night rights," assures for the books we call classics their only useful immortality.

There are two ways of reading the much-quoted verse of Ecclesiastes, "Of making many books there is no end."[238] We can read it as an echo of the words that follow—"and much study is a weariness of the flesh"—and we can shrug at the impossible task of reaching the end of our library; or we can read it as a jubilation, a prayer of thanks for the bounty of God, so that the connecting "and" reads as "but": "but much study is a weariness of the flesh." Crusoe chooses the first reading; Aristotle (and his descendants down to Northrop Frye) the second. Beginning some lost afternoon in Mesopotamia, countless readers have persevered in picking their way through "many books," in spite of the "weariness of the flesh." Every reader has found charms by which to secure possession of a page that, by magic, becomes as if never read before, fresh and immaculate. Libraries are the vaults and treasure chests of those charms.

These two kinds of readers are, of course, not the only possible ones. At the other extreme from Crusoe—the man whose library consists of one venerated Book and a few other books he doesn't read—sits the reader for whom every book in his library is open to reprimand, the reader who believes that any interpretive reading must be erroneous. Discipline, not pleasure, dictates such readers' craft, and they sometimes find occupations in the seats of academia, or the customs office.

One evening of 1939, in Buenos Aires, Borges and two of his friends, the writers Adolfo Bioy Casares and Silvina Ocampo, decided to immortalize this punctilious censor. The three were extraordinarily eclectic readers. In Bioy and Silvina's library (a large, decrepit hall in a nineteenth-century apartment overlooking one of the loveliest parks in the city) they talked about books, put together anthologies, attempted translations into Spanish, defended with passion their personal choices and mocked with equal passion the authors they disliked. They complemented one another: Borges preferred the epic genre and the philosophical fantastic story; Bioy the psychological novel and social satire; Silvina, lyrical poetry and the literature of the absurd. Together, their reading covered every style and every genre.

Sometimes they played at making up stories. One of these inventions (which was never finished) concerned a young literary enthusiast who seeks out the work of an older writer who, before his death, acquired a reputation for unsurpassed refinement and stylistic perfection. Unable to find more than a few unappealing texts, the enthusiast travels to the writer's home and, among the dead man's papers, discovers a curious list of "Things to avoid in literature":[239]

~ psychological curiosities and paradoxes: murders through kindness, suicides through contentment;

~ surprising interpretations of certain books and characters: the misogyny of Don Juan, etc.;

~ twin protagonists too obviously dissimilar: Don Quixote and Sancho, Sherlock Holmes and Watson;

~ novels with identical twin characters, like *Bouvard and Pécuchet*. If the author invents a trait for one, he is forced to invent an equivalent trait for the other;

~ characters depicted through their peculiarities, as in Dickens;

~ anything new or astonishing. Civilized readers are not amused by the discourtesy of a surprise;

~ idle games with time and space: Faulkner, Borges, etc.;

~ the discovery in a novel that the real hero is the prairie, the jungle, the sea, the rain, the stock market;

~ poems, situations, characters with which the reader might—God forbid!—identify;

~ phrases that might become proverbs or quotations; they are incompatible with a coherent book;

~ characters likely to become myths;

~ chaotic enumeration;

~ a rich vocabulary. Synonyms. *Le mot juste*. Any attempt at precision;

~ vivid descriptions, worlds full of rich physical details, as in Faulkner;

~ background, ambiance, atmosphere. Tropical heat, drunkenness, the voice on the radio, phrases repeated like a refrain;

~ meteorological beginnings and endings. Pathetic fallacies. *"Le vent se lève! Il faut tenter de vivre!"*;

~ any metaphors. Particularly visual metaphors. Even more particularly, metaphors drawn from agriculture, seamanship, banking. As in Proust;

~ anthropomorphism;

~ books that parallel other books. *Ulysses* and the *Odyssey*;

~ books that pretend to be menus, photo albums, road maps, concert programs;

~ anything that might inspire illustrations. Anything that might inspire a film;

~ the extraneous: domestic scenes in detective novels. Dramatic scenes in philosophical dialogues;

~ the expected. Pathos and erotic scenes in love stories. Puzzles and crimes in detective stories. Ghosts in supernatural stories;

~ vanity, modesty, pederasty, no pederasty, suicide.

At the end of this reader's demands lies, of course, the absence of any literature.

Happily, most readers fall between these two drastic extremes. Most of us neither shun books in veneration of literature, nor shun literature in veneration of books. Our craft is more modest. We pick our way down endless library shelves, choosing this or that volume for no discernible reason: because of a cover, a title, a name, because of something someone said or didn't say, because of a hunch, a whim, a mistake, because we think we may find in this book a particular tale or character or detail, because we believe it was written for us, because we believe it was written for everyone except us and we want to find out why we have been excluded, because we want to learn, or laugh, or lose ourselves in oblivion.

Libraries are not, never will be, used by everyone. In Mesopotamia as in Greece, in Buenos Aires as in Toronto, readers and non-readers have existed side by side, and the non-readers have always constituted the majority. Whether in the exclusive scriptoria of Sumer and medieval Europe, in popular eighteenth-century London or in populist twenty-first-century Paris, the number of those for whom reading books is of the essence is very small. What varies is not the proportions of these two groups of humanity, but the way in which different societies regard the book and the art of reading. And here the distinction between the book enthroned and the book read comes again into play.

If a visitor from the past arrived today in our civilized cities, one of the aspects that might surprise this ancient Gulliver would certainly be our reading habits. What would he see? He would see huge commercial temples in which books are sold in their thousands, immense edifices in which the published word is divided and arranged in tidy categories for the guided consumption of the faithful. He would see libraries with readers milling about in the stacks as they have done for centuries. He would see them exploring the virtual collections into which some of the books have been mutated, leading the fragile existence of electronic ghosts. Outside, too, the time-traveller would find a host of readers: on park benches, in the subway, on buses and trams and trains, in apartments and houses, everywhere. Our visitor could be excused if he supposed that ours was a literate society.

On the contrary. Our society accepts the book as a given, but the act of reading—once considered useful and important, as well as potentially dangerous and subversive—is now condescendingly accepted as a pastime, a slow pastime that lacks efficiency and does not contribute to the common good. As our visitor would eventually realize, in our society reading is nothing but an ancillary act, and the great repository of our memory and experience, the library, is considered less a living entity than an inconvenient storage room.

During the student revolts that shook the world in the late 1960s, one of the slogans shouted at the lecturers at the University of Heidelberg was *Hier wird nicht zitiert!*, "No quoting here!" The students were demanding original thought; they were forgetting that to quote is to continue a conversation from the past in order to give context to the present. To quote is to make use of the Library of Babel; to quote is to reflect on what has been said before, and unless we do that, we speak in a vacuum where no human voice can make a sound. "To write history is to cite it," declared Walter Benjamin.[240] To write the past, converse with history—this was the humanist ideal that Benjamin was echoing, an ideal which Nicholas de Cusa first put forward as early as 1440. In his *On Learned Ignorance* de Cusa suggested that the earth was not, perhaps, the centre of the universe, and that outer space might be infinite rather than bounded by divine decree, and he proposed the creation of a semi-utopian society that, like the universal library, would contain all humankind, one in which politics and religion would have ceased to be disruptive forces.[241] It is interesting to note that, for the humanists, a correlation existed between the suspicion of unbounded space that belongs to no one, and the knowledge of a wealthy past that belongs to all.

This is, of course, the very reverse of the definition of the World Wide Web. The Web defines itself as a space that belongs to all, and it precludes a sense of the past. There are no nationalities on the Web (except, of course, for the fact that its lingua franca is a watered-down version of English), and there is no censorship (except that governments are finding ways to ban access to certain sites). The world's tiniest book (the New Testament engraved on a five-millimetre-square tablet[242]) or the oldest multiple-page codex (six bound sheets of twenty-four–carat gold in the Etruscan language, dating from the fifth century B.C.[243]) possesses qualities that cannot be perceived merely through the words it contains but must be appreciated in its full and distinct physical presence. On the Web, where all texts are equal and alike in form, they become nothing but phantom text and photographic image.

The past (the tradition that leads to our electronic present) is, for the Web user, irrelevant, since all that counts is what is currently displayed. Compared to a book that betrays its age in its physical aspect, a text called up on the screen has no history. Electronic space is frontierless. Sites—that is to say, specific, self-defined homelands—are founded on it but neither limit nor possess it, like water on water. The Web is quasi-instantaneous; it occupies no time except the nightmare of a constant present. All surface and no volume, all present and no past, the Web aspires to be (advertises itself as) every user's home, in which communication is possible with every other user at the speed of thought. That is its main characteristic: speed. The Venerable Bede, lamenting the quickness and brevity of our life on earth, compared it to the passage of a bird through a well-lit dining hall, entering from the darkness at one end and exiting through the darkness at the other;[244] our society would interpret Bede's lament as an act of boasting.

Since electronic technology is present in all our fields of leisure and labour, we think of it as all-reaching, and speak of it as if it were to replace every other technology, including the technology of books. Our future paperless society, defined by Bill Gates in a paper book,[245] is a society without history, since everything on the Web is instantly contemporary; for writers, for example, thanks to our word processors, there is no archive of our notes, hesitations, developments and drafts. Walter Benjamin noted, shortly before the rise of Nazism, that "Mankind, which in Homer's time was an object of contemplation for the Olympian gods, now is one for itself. Its self-alienation has reached such a degree that it can experience its own destruction as an aesthetic pleasure of the first order."[246] To this self-alienation we have now added the alienation of our own ideas, and enjoy watching the destruction of our own past. We no longer record the evolution of our intellectual creations. To a future observer, it will appear that our ideas were born fully developed, like Athena from her father's brow—except that, since our historical vocabulary will be forgotten, the cliché will mean nothing.

On 18 January 1949, an American by the name of James T. Mangan filed a charter with the Cook County recorder of Deeds, and under the state of Illinois attorney's authority claimed ownership of the whole of space. After giving his vast territory the name of Celestia, Mr. Mangan notified all countries on earth of his claim, warned them not to attempt any trips to the moon and petitioned the United Nations for membership.[247] Mr. Mangan's ambitious enterprise has now, in a more practical sense, been taken over by multinational corporations. Their methods have been extraordinarily effective. By offering electronic users the appearance of a world controlled from their keyboard, a world in which everything can be "accessed" and everything can be had, as in fairy tales, by a simple tap of the finger, multinational companies have ensured that, on the one hand, users will not protest against being turned into consumers, since they are supposedly "in control" of cyberspace; and that, on the other hand, they will be prevented from learning anything profound, whether about themselves, their immediate surroundings or the rest of the world. Commenting in 2004 on the usefulness of the Web as a creative tool, the celebrated American comic-strip artist Will Eisner explained that, when he first discovered this electronic medium, he believed it to be an almost magical source of new artistic inventions, but that of late it had become "merely a supermarket to which consumers come to look for the cheapest possible product."[248]

This sleight of hand is achieved, every time a reader locks onto the Web, by stressing velocity over reflection and brevity over complexity, preferring snippets of news and bytes of facts over lengthy discussions and elaborate dossiers, and by diluting informed opinion with reams of inane babble, ineffectual advice, inaccurate facts and trivial information, made attractive with brand names and manipulated statistics.

But the Web is an instrument. It is not to blame for our superficial concern with the world in which we live. Its virtue is in the brevity and multiplicity of its information; it cannot also provide us with concentration and depth. The electronic media can assist us (do in fact assist us) in a myriad of practical ways, but not in all, and can't be held responsible for that which they are not meant to do. The Web will not be the container of our cosmopolitan past, like a book, because it is not a book and will never be a book, in spite of the endless gadgets and guises invented to force it into that role. Nor can it be in any useful sense a universal library, in spite of such ambitious programs as the Google project and the earlier Project Gutenberg (PG), which has, since 1971, placed some ten thousand texts on the Web—many of which are duplicates, and many more unreliable, having been hastily scanned and badly checked for typographical errors. In 2004 the English critic Paul Duguid remarked, "A brief, critical encounter suggests . . . that while in many ways PG does resemble—and improve on—conventional libraries, it also resembles a church jumble-sale bookstall, where gems and duds are blessed alike by the vicar because all have been donated."[249]

Neither will the Web lend us bed and board in our passage through this world, because it is neither a resting place nor a home, neither Circe's cave nor Ithaca. We alone, and not our technologies, are responsible for our losses, and we alone are to blame when we deliberately choose oblivion over recollection. We are, however, adroit at making excuses and dreaming up reasons for our poor choices.

The Abnaki people of North America believed that a special group of deities, the Oonagamessok, presided over the making of petroglyphs, and they explained the gradual disappearance of these rock engravings by saying that the gods were angry because of the lack of attention accorded them since the arrival of the whites.[250] The petroglyphs of our common past are fading not because of the arrival of a new technology but because we are no longer moved to read them. We are losing our common vocabulary, built over thousands and thousands of years to help and delight and instruct us, for the sake of what we take to be the new technology's virtues. The world, as Crusoe discovered, is always large enough to accommodate one more marvel. Being a cosmopolitan today may mean being eclectic, refusing to exclude one technology for the sake of another. Our tendency to build walls is useful only to provide a starting point for self-definition, walls that contain the bed in which we are born, in which we dream, we breed and we die; but outside the walls lies Siddhartha's realization that all human beings grow old, all are prone to nightmare and disease, and all must ultimately come to the same implacable end. Books endlessly repeat that one same story.

Among the libraries' new incarnations are some that dispense with (or cannot afford) new technologies. In 1990 the Colombian Ministry of Culture set up an organization of itinerant libraries that would take books to the farthest corners of the country.[251] While library-buses had been in place since 1982 in the districts surrounding Bogotá, the government deemed it important to reach the inhabitants of the more distant rural regions. For this purpose, large green carrier bags with capacious pockets, that could easily be folded into convenient packages, were devised to transport books on donkeys' backs up into the jungle and the sierra. Here the books are left for several weeks in the hands of a teacher or village elder who becomes, de facto, the librarian in charge. The bags are unfolded and hung from a post or a tree, allowing the local population to browse and choose. Sometimes the librarian reads aloud to those who have not learned to read for themselves; occasionally a member of a family who has attended school reads to the others. "That way," explained one of the villagers in an interview, "we can know what we don't know and pass it on to others." After the allotted period, a new batch is sent to replace the previous one. Most of the books are technical works, agricultural handbooks and manuals on water filtration, collections of sewing patterns and veterinary guides, but a few novels and other literary works are included. According to one librarian, the books are always safely accounted for. "I know of only one instance in which a book was not returned," she told me. "We had taken, along with the usual practical titles, a Spanish translation of the *Iliad*. When the time came to exchange it, the villagers refused to give it back. We decided to make them a present of it, but we asked them why they wanted to keep that particular title. They explained that Homer's story exactly reflected their own: it told of a wartorn country in which mad gods wilfully decide the fate of humans who never know exactly what the fighting is about, or when they will be killed."[252]

As those remote Colombian readers know, our existence flows, like an impossible river, in two directions: from the endless mass of names, places, creatures, stars, books, rituals, memories, illuminations and stones we call the world to the face that stares at us every morning from the depth of a mirror; and from that face, from that body which surrounds a centre we cannot see, from that which

One of the "donkey-libraries" of the Colombian rural areas.

names us when we say "I," to everything that is Other, outside, beyond. A sense of who we are individually, coupled with a sense of being citizens, collectively, of an inconceivable universe, lends something like meaning to our life—a meaning put into words by the books in our libraries.

It is likely that libraries will carry on and survive, as long as we persist in lending words to the world that surrounds us, and storing them for future readers. So much has been named, so much will continue to be named, that in spite of our foolishness we will not give up this small miracle that allows us the ghost of an understanding. Books may not change our suffering, books may not protect us from evil, books may not tell us what is good or what is beautiful, and they will certainly not shield us from the common fate of the grave. But books grant us myriad possibilities: the possibility of change, the possibility of illumination. It may be that there is no book, however well written, that can remove an ounce of pain from the tragedy of Iraq or Rwanda, but it may also be that there is no book, however foully written, that does not allow an epiphany for its destined reader. Robinson Crusoe explains, "It may not be amiss for all people who shall meet my story to make this just observation from it, viz., how frequently in the course of our lives, the evil which in itself we seek most to shun, and which, when we are fallen into it, is the most dreadful to us, is oftentimes the very same means or door of our deliverance, by which alone we can be raised again." This, of course, is not Crusoe speaking, but Defoe—the reader of so many books.

Histories, chronologies and almanacs offer us the illusion of progress, even though, over and over again, we are given proof that there is no such thing. There is transformation and there is passage, but whether for better or for worse merely depends on the context and the observer. As readers, we have gone from learning a precious craft whose secret was held by a jealous few, to taking for granted a skill that has become subordinate to principles of mindless financial profit or mechanical efficiency, a skill for which governments care almost nothing. We have gone from one scale of values to the other many times, and will no doubt do so again. We can't be spared this erratic course, which seems to be an intrinsic part of our human nature, but we can at least sway with the knowledge of our swaying, and with the conviction that at one point or another our skill will once again be recognized as of the essence. The library of Robinson Crusoe—made up of just the Good Book— was not merely an idol or a prop but his new society's essential tool, his way of lending order to the universe.

The Apostle Paul (the only apostle not to have known Jesus face to face) would boldly say to those he encountered, men and women seeking the Scriptures, "Do you seek a proof of Christ speaking in me?," knowing that since he had read the Word, the Word was now lodged inside him, even if he had not met the Author; that he had become the Book, the Word made flesh, through that little bit of the divine that the craft of reading allows to all those who seek to learn the secrets held by a page. This is the wisdom of the Essene sect, the devout people who gave us, so many centuries ago, the Dead Sea scrolls: "We know that the body is corruptible and the stuff of which it is made impermanent. But we also know that the soul [and I, the scrolls' future reader, will interject, "the book,"] is immortal and imperishable."

THE LIBRARY

AS SURVIVAL

"I lived off art, I lived off love,
I never harmed a living soul. . . .
Why then, Lord,
Why do You reward me thus?"

Puccini, *Tosca*, Act II

Like the Dead Sea scrolls, like every book that has come down to us from the hands of distant readers, each of my books holds the history of its survival. From fire, water, the passage of time, neglectful readers and the hand of the censor, each of my books has escaped to tell me its story.

A few years ago, in a stand at the Berlin flea market, I found a thin black book bound in hard cloth covers that bore no inscription whatsoever. The title page, in fine Gothic lettering, declared it to be a *Gebet-Ordnung für den Jugendgottesdienst in der jüdißchen Gemeinde zu Berlin (Sabbath-Nachmittag)* [Order of Prayer for Youth Service in the Jewish Community of Berlin (Sabbath-Evening)]. Among the prayers is included one "for our king, Wilhelm II, Kaiser of the German Realm" and his "Empress and Queen Auguste-Victoria." This was the eighth edition, printed by Julius Gittenfeld in Berlin in 1908, and had been bought at the bookstore of C. Boas

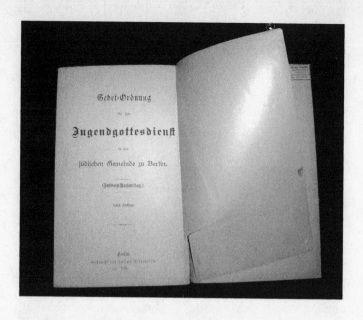

The German prayer book printed in Berlin in 1908.

Nachf. on Neue Friedrichstraße 69, "at the corner of Klosterstraße," a corner that no longer exists. There was no indication of the name of the owner.

A year before the book was printed, Germany had refused the armament limitations proposed by the Hague Peace Conference; a few months later, the expropriation law decreed by Reichskanzler and Preußischer Ministerpräsident Fürst Bernhard von Bülow authorized further German settlements in Poland; in spite of hardly ever being used against Polish landowners, this law granted Germany early territorial rights that in turn, in June 1940, allowed the establishment of a concentration camp in Auschwitz. The original owner of the *Gebet-Ordnung* probably bought or was given the book when he was thirteen years old, the age at which he would have his bar mitzvah and be permitted to join in synagogue prayers. If he survived the First World War, he would have been thirty-eight on the birth of the Third Reich in 1933; if he stayed on in Berlin, it is likely that he was deported, like so many other Berlin Jews, to Poland.[253] Perhaps he had time to give the prayer book to someone before being taken away; perhaps he hid it, or left it behind with other books he had collected.

After the Nazis began their looting and destruction of the Jewish libraries, the librarian in charge of the Sholem Aleichem Library in Biala Podlaska decided to save the books by carting away, day after day, as many as he and a colleague could manage, even though he believed that very soon "there would be no readers left." After two weeks the holdings had been moved to a secret attic, where they were discovered by the historian Tuvia Borzykowski long after the war ended. Writing about the librarian's action, Borzykowski remarked that it was carried out "without any consideration as to whether anyone would ever need the saved books":[254] it was an act of rescuing memory per se. The universe, the ancient cabbalists believed, is not contingent on our reading it; only on the possibility of our reading it.

With the emblematic book-burning in a square on Unter den Linden, opposite the University of Berlin, on the evening of 10 May, 1933, books became a specific target of the Nazis. Less than five months after Hitler became chancellor, the new propaganda minister of the Reich, Dr. Joseph Goebbels, declared that the public burning of books by authors such as Heinrich Mann, Stefan Zweig, Freud, Zola, Proust, Gide, Helen Keller and H.G. Wells allowed "the soul of the German people again to express itself. These flames not only illuminate the final end of an old era; they also light up the new."[255] The new era proscribed the sale or circulation of thousands of books, in either shops or libraries, as well as the publishing of new ones. Volumes commonly kept on sitting-room shelves because they were prestigious or entertaining became suddenly dangerous. Private holdings of the indexed books were prohibited; many books were confiscated and destroyed. Hundreds of Jewish libraries throughout Europe were burnt down, both personal collections and public treasure-houses. A Nazi correspondent gleefully reported the destruction of the famous library of the Lublin Yeshiva in 1939:

> For us it was a matter of special pride to destroy the Talmudic Academy, which was known as the greatest in Poland. . . . We threw the huge talmudic library out of the building and carried the books to the market place, where we set fire to them. The fire lasted twenty hours. The Lublin Jews assembled around and wept bitterly, almost silencing us with their cries. We summoned the military band, and with joyful shouts the soldiers drowned out the sounds of the Jewish cries.[256]

At the same time, the Nazis decided to spare a number of books for commercial and archival purposes. In 1938 Alfred Rosenberg, one of the principal Nazi theoreticians, proposed that Jewish collections, including both secular and religious literature, should be preserved in an institute set up to study "the Jewish question." Two years later, the Institut zur Erforschung der Judenfrage was opened in Frankfurt am Main. To procure the necessary material, Hitler himself authorized Rosenberg to create a task force of expert German librarians, the notorious ERR, Einsatzstab Reichsleiter Rosenberg.[257] Among the confiscated collections incorporated to the institute were those of the rabbinical seminaries of Breslau and Vienna, the Hebraica and Judaica departments of the Frankfurt Municipal Library, the Collegio Rabbinico in Rome, the Societas Spinoziana in The Hague and the Spinoza Home in Rijnsburg, the Dutch publishing companies Querido, Pegazus and Fischer-Berman,[258] the International Institute of Social History in Amsterdam, Beth Maidrash Etz Hayim, the Israelitic seminary of Amsterdam, the Portuguese Israelitic seminary and the Rosenthaliana, Rabbi Moshe Pessah in Volos, the Strashun Library in Vilna (the grandson of the founder committed suicide when ordered to assist with the cataloguing), libraries in Hungary (a parallel institute on "the Jewish question" was set up in Budapest), libraries in Denmark and Norway and dozens of libraries in Poland (especially the great library of the Warsaw synagogue and of the Institute for Jewish Studies). From these vast hoards, Rosenberg's henchmen selected the books to be sent to his institute; all others were destroyed. In February 1943 the institute issued the following directives for the selection of library material: "all writings which deal with the history, culture, and nature of Judaism, as well as books written by Jewish authors in languages other than Hebrew and Yiddish, must be shipped to Frankfurt." But "books in Hebrew script (Hebrew or Yiddish) of recent date, later than the year 1800, may be turned to pulp; this applies also to prayer books, *Memorbücher*, and other religious works in the German language."[259] Regarding the many Torah scrolls, it was suggested that "perhaps the leather can be put to use for bookbinding." Miraculously, my prayer book escaped.

Seven months after these directives were given, in September 1943, the Nazis set up a "family camp" as an extension of the Auschwitz precinct, in the birch forest of Birkenau, which included a separate block, "number 31," built especially for children. It was designed to serve as proof to the world that Jews deported to the east were not being killed. In fact, they were allowed to live six months before being sent on to the same fate as the other deported victims. Eventually, having served its purpose as propaganda, the "family camp" was permanently closed.[260]

While it lasted, Block 31 housed up to five hundred children together with several prisoners appointed "counsellors," and in spite of the severe surveillance it possessed, against all expectations, a clandestine children's library. The library was minuscule; it consisted of eight books, which included H.G. Wells's *A Short History of the World*, a Russian school textbook and an analytical geometry text. Once or twice an inmate from another camp managed to smuggle in a new book, so that the number of holdings rose to nine or ten. At the end of each day, the books, together with other valuables such as medicines and bits of food, would be entrusted to one of the older girls, whose responsibility it was to hide them in a different place every night. Paradoxically, books that were banned throughout the Reich (those by H.G. Wells, for instance) were sometimes available in concentration camp libraries.

Although eight or ten books made up the physical collection of the Birkenau children's library, there were others that circulated through word of mouth alone. Whenever they could escape surveillance, the counsellors would recite to the children books they had themselves learned by heart in earlier days, taking turns so that different counsellors "read" to different children every time; this rotation was known as "exchanging books in the library."[261]

It is almost impossible to imagine that under the unbearable conditions imposed by the Nazis, intellectual life could still continue. The historian Yitzhak Schipper,

Liberation of the survivors of the Birkenau Concentration Camp.

who was writing a book on the Khazars while he was an inmate of the Warsaw ghetto, was asked how he did his work without being able to sit and research in the appropriate libraries. "To write history," he answered, "you need a head, not an ass."[262]

There was even a continuation of the common, everyday routines of reading. This persistence adds to both the wonder and the horror: that in such nightmarish circumstances men and women would still read about Hugo's Jean Valjean and Tolstoy's Natasha, would fill in request cards and pay fines for late returns, would discuss the merits of a modern author or follow once again the cadenced verses of Heine. Reading and its rituals became acts of resistance; as the Italian psychologist Andrea Devoto noted, "everything could be treated as resistance because everything was prohibited."[263]

In the concentration camp of Bergen-Belsen, a copy of Thomas Mann's *The Magic Mountain* was passed around among the inmates. One boy remembered the time he was allotted to hold the book in his hands as "one of the highlights of the day, when someone passed it to me. I went into a corner to be at peace and then I had an hour to read it."[264] Another young Polish victim, recalling the days of fear and discouragement, had this to say: "The book was my best friend, it never betrayed me; it comforted me in my despair; it told me that I was not alone."[265]

"Any victim demands allegiance," wrote Graham Greene,[266] who believed it was the writer's task to champion victims, to restore their visibility, to set up warnings that, by means of an inspired craft, will act as touchstones for something approaching understanding. The authors of the books on my shelves cannot have known who would read them, but the stories they tell foresee or imply or witness experiences that may not yet have taken place.

Because the victim's voice is all-important, oppressors often attempt to silence their victims: by literally cutting out their tongues, as in the case of the raped Philomela in Ovid, and Lavinia in *Titus Andronicus*, or by secreting them away, as the king does with Segismundo in Calderón's *Life Is a Dream*, or as Mr. Rochester does to his mad wife in *Jane Eyre*, or by simply denying their stories, as in the professorial addendum in Margaret Atwood's *The Handmaid's Tale*. In real life, victims are "disappeared," locked up in a ghetto, sent to prison or a torture camp, denied credibility. The literature on my shelves tells over and over again the victim's story, from Job to Desdemona, from Goethe's Gretchen to Dante's Francesca, not as mirror (the German surgeon Johann Paul Kremer warned in his Auschwitz diary, "By comparison, Dante's inferno seems almost a comedy"[267]) but as metaphor. Most of these stories would have been found in the library of any educated German in the 1930s. What lessons were learned from those books is another matter.

In Western culture, the archetypal victim is the Trojan princess Polyxena. The daughter of Priam and Hecuba, she was supposed to marry Achilles but her brother Hector opposed the union. Achilles stole into the temple of Apollo to catch sight of her, but was discovered there and murdered. According to Ovid, after the destruction of Troy the spirit of Achilles appeared to the victorious Greeks as they were about to embark, and demanded that the princess be sacrificed to him. Accordingly, she was dragged to Achilles' tomb and killed by Achilles' son Neoptolemus. Polyxena is perfect for the victim's role: innocent of cause, innocent of blame, innocent of benefiting others with her death, a blank page haunting the reader with unanswered questions. Arguments, however specious, were made by the Greeks to find reasons for the ghost's request, to justify compliance with the sacrifice, to excuse the blade that Achilles' son drove into her bared breast. But no argument can convince us that Polyxena's death was merited. The essence of her victimhood—as of all victimhood—is injustice.

My library witnesses the injustice suffered by Polyxena, and all fictional phantoms who lend voice to countless ghosts who were once solid flesh. It does not clamour for revenge, another constant subject of our literatures. It argues that the strictures that define us as a social group must be constructive or cautionary, not wilfully destructive, if they are to have any sane collective meaning—if the injury to a victim is to be seen as an injury to society as a whole, in recognition of our common humanity. Justice, as the English dictum has it, must not only be done, it must be seen to be done. Justice must not seek a private sense of satisfaction, but must publicly lend strength to society's self-healing impulse to learn. If justice takes place, there may be hope, even in the face of a seemingly capricious divinity.

A Hasidic legend collected by Martin Buber tells of a man who took God to trial. In Vienna, a decree was issued that would make the difficult life of the Jews of Polish Galicia even harder. The man argued that God should not turn his people into victims, but should allow them to toil for him in freedom. A tribunal of rabbis agreed to consider the man's arguments, and considered, as was proper, that both plaintiff and defendant retire during their deliberations. "The plaintiff will wait outside; we cannot ask You, Lord of the Universe, to withdraw, since your glory is omnipresent. But we will not allow You to influence us." The rabbis deliberated in silence and with their eyes closed. Later that evening, they called the man and told him their verdict: his argument was just. At that very same hour, the decree was cancelled.[268]

In Polyxena's world, the outcome is less happy. God, the gods, the Devil, nature, the social system, the world, the *primum mobile*, refuses to acknowledge guilt or responsibility. My library repeats again and again the same question: Who makes Job endure so much pain and loss? Who is to blame for Winnie's sinking in Beckett's *Happy Days?* Who relentlessly destroys the life of Gervaise Macquart in Zola's *L'assommoir?* Who victimizes the protagonists of Rohinton Mistry's *A Fine Balance?*

Throughout history, those confronted with the unbearable account of the horrors they have committed— torturers, murderers, merciless wielders of power, shamelessly obedient bureaucrats—seldom answer the question "why?" Their impassive faces reject any admission of guilt, reflect nothing but a refusal to move from the past of their deeds into the consequences. Yet the books on my shelves can help me imagine their future. According to Victor Hugo, hell takes on different shapes for its different inhabitants: for Cain it has the face of Abel, for Nero that of Agrippina.[269] For Macbeth, hell bears the face of Banquo; for Medea, that of her children. Romain

Gary dreamt of a certain Nazi officer condemned to the constant presence of the ghost of a murdered Jewish clown.[270]

If time flows endlessly, as the mysterious connections between my books suggest, repeating its themes and discoveries throughout the centuries, then every misdeed, every treason, every evil act will eventually find its true consequences. After the story has stopped, just beyond the threshold of my library, Carthage will rise again from the strewn Roman salt. Don Juan will confront the anguish of Doña Elvira. Brutus will look again on Caesar's ghost, and every torturer will have to beg his victim's pardon in order to complete time's inevitable circle.

My library allows me this unrealizable hope. But for the victims, of course, no reasons, literary or other, can excuse or expiate the deeds of their torturers. Nick Caistor, in his introduction to the English edition of *Nunca más*, the report on the "disappeared" during the Argentinian military dictatorship, reminds us that the stories that ultimately reach us are but the reports of the survivors. "One can only speculate," says Caistor, "as to what accounts of atrocity the thousands of dead took with them to their unmarked graves."[271]

It is difficult to understand how people continue to carry out the human gestures of everyday life when life itself has become inhuman; how, in the midst of starving and sickness, beatings and slaughter, men and women persist in civilized rituals of courtesy and kindness, inventing stratagems of survival for the sake of a speck of something loved, for one book rescued out of thousands, one reader out of tens of thousands, for a voice that will echo until the end of time the words of Job's servant:

"And I only am escaped alone to tell thee." Throughout history, the victor's library stands as an emblem of power, repository of the official version, but the version that haunts us is the other, the version in the library of ashes. The victim's library, abandoned or destroyed, keeps on asking, "How were such acts possible?" My prayer book belongs to that questioning library.

After the European crusaders, following a forty-day siege, took the city of Jerusalem on 15 July, 1099, slaughtering the Muslim men, women and children and burning alive the entire Jewish community inside the locked synagogue, a handful of Arabs who had managed to escape arrived in Damascus, bringing with them the Koran of 'Uthman, one of the oldest existing copies of the holy book. They believed that their fate had been foretold in its pages (since God's word must necessarily hold all past, present and future events), and that, if only they had been able to read the text clearly, they would have known the outcome of their own narrative.[272] History was, for these readers, nothing but "the unfolding of God's will for the world."[273] As our libraries teach us, books can sometimes help us phrase our questions, but they do not necessarily enable us to decipher the answers. Through reported voices and imagined stories, books merely allow us to remember what we have never suffered and have never known. The suffering itself belongs only to the victims. Every reader is, in this sense, an outsider.

Emerging from hell, travelling against Lethe's current towards recollection, Dante carries with him the sounds of the suffering souls, but also the knowledge

that those souls are being punished for their own avowed sins.[274] The souls whose voices resound in our present are, unlike Dante's damned, blameless. They were tortured and killed for no other reason than their existence, and maybe not even that. Evil requires no reason. How can we contain, between the covers of a book, a useful representation of something that, in its very essence, refuses to be contained, whether in Mann's *The Magic Mountain* or in an ordinary prayer book? How can we, as readers, hope to hold in our hands the circle of the world and time, when the world will always exceed the margins of a page, and all we can witness is the moment defined by a paragraph or a verse, "choosing," as Blake said, "forms of worship from poetic tales"? And so we return to the question of whether a book, any book, can serve its impossible purpose.

Perhaps. One day in June 1944, Jacob Edelstein, former elder of the Theresienstadt ghetto, who had been taken to Birkenau, was in his barracks, wrapped in his ritual shawl, saying the morning prayers he had learned long ago from a book no doubt similar to my

Gebet-Ordnung. He had only just begun when SS Lieutenant Franz Hoessler entered the barracks to take Edelstein away. A fellow prisoner, Yossl Rosensaft, recalled the scene a year later:

Suddenly the door burst open and Hoessler strutted in, accompanied by three SS men. He called out Jacob's name. Jacob did not move. Hoessler screamed: "I am waiting for you, hurry up!" Jacob turned round very slowly, faced Hoessler and said: "Of my last moments on this earth, allotted to me by the Almighty, I am the master, not you." Whereupon he turned back to face the wall and finished his prayers. He then folded his prayer shawl unhurriedly, handed it to one of the inmates and said to Hoessler: "I am now ready."[275]

THE LIBRARY

AS OBLIVION

> What has been lost cannot be destroyed or diminished.
>
> Petrarch, *On His Own Ignorance*

If Night is the child of Chaos, then Lethe or Oblivion is its granddaughter, born of the terrible union between Night and Discord. In the sixth book of the *Aeneid*, Virgil imagines Lethe as a river whose waters allow the souls on their way to the underworld to forget their former selves, so that they can be born again.[276] Lethe allows us oblivion of our former experience and happiness, but also of our prejudices and sorrows.

My library consists half of books I remember and half of books I have forgotten. Now that my memory is not as keen as it used to be, pages fade as I attempt to conjure them up. Some vanish from my experience entirely, unrecalled and invisible. Others haunt me temptingly with a title or an image, or a few words out of context. What novel begins with the words "One spring evening of 1890"? Where did I read that King Solomon used a looking-glass to discover whether the Queen of Sheba had hairy legs? Who wrote that peculiar book *Flight into*

Darkness, from which I remember only the description of a blind corridor full of birds flapping their wings? In what story did I read the phrase "the lumber room of his library"? What volume showed a burning candle on the cover, with thick crayons on cream-coloured paper? Somewhere in my library are the answers to these questions, but I have forgotten where.

Visitors often ask if I've read all my books; my usual answer is that I've certainly opened every one of them. The fact is that a library, whatever its size, need not be read in its entirety to be useful; every reader profits from a fair balance between knowledge and ignorance, recall and oblivion. In 1930 Robert Musil imagined a devoted librarian who, working in Vienna's Imperial Library, knows every single title in that gigantic assembly. "Do you want to know how I've been able to familiarize myself with every one of these books?" he asks an astonished visitor. "Nothing prevents me from telling you: it is because I read none of them!" And he adds, "The secret of every good librarian is never to read anything of all the literature with which he is entrusted, except the titles and the tables of contents. He who puts his nose inside the book itself is lost to the library! . . . Never will he be able to possess a view of the whole!" Hearing these words, Musil tells us, the visitor wants to do one of two things—either burst into tears or light a cigarette—but he knows that within the library walls both options are denied him.[277]

I have no feeling of guilt regarding the books I have not read and perhaps will never read; I know that my books have unlimited patience. They will wait for me till the end of my days. They don't require that I pretend to know them all, nor do they urge me to become one of the "professional book-handlers" imagined by Flann O'Brien, who greedily collect books but do not read them, and who could (says O'Brien) earn their living "handling" books for a modest fee, making them look read, annotating the margins with forged comments and inscriptions, and even inserting theatre programs and other ephemera as bookmarks between the virgin leaves.[278]

Edward Gibbon, commenting on the voluminous library and crowded harem of the Roman emperor Gordian the Younger in the third century A.D., noted approvingly, "Twenty-two acknowledged concubines, and a library of sixty-two thousand volumes attested the variety of his inclinations; and from the productions which he left behind him, it appears that both the one and the other were designed for use rather than for ostentation."[279] Of course, no one except a mad prodigy would think of reading through a sixty-two-thousand-volume library, page after page, from Abbott to Zwingli, committing every book to memory, even if such a feat were possible. Gordian must have employed what Samuel Johnson, sixteen centuries later, called the cursory mode of reading. Johnson himself read with no method or discipline, sometimes leaving books uncut and following the text only where the pages fell open. "I do not suppose," he said, "that what is in the pages that are closed is worse than what is in the open pages." He never felt the obligation to read a book to the end or to start at the first page. "If a man begins to read in the middle of a book, and feels an inclination to go on, let him not quit it to go to the beginning. He may perhaps not feel again the inclination." He thought it "strange advice" to urge someone to finish a book once started. "You may as well resolve that whatever men you happen to get acquainted with, you are to keep to them for life," he argued. Nor would he necessarily seek out specific titles, but simply open whatever books he might come upon. Luck, he felt, was as good a counsellor as scholarship.

Johnson's obsessive biographer, James Boswell, mentions that when Johnson was a boy, "having imagined that his brother had hid some apples behind a large folio upon an upper shelf in his father's shop, he climbed up to search for them. There were no apples; but the large folio proved to be Petrarch, whom he had seen mentioned, in some preface, as one of the restorers of learning. His curiosity having been thus excited, he sat down with avidity, and read a great part of the book." I am all too familiar with such happy encounters.

The forgotten volumes of my library lead a tacit, unobtrusive existence. And yet, their very quality of having been forgotten allows me, sometimes, to rediscover a certain story, a certain poem, as if it were utterly new. I open a book I think I have never opened before and come upon a splendid line that I tell myself I mustn't forget, and then I close the book and see, on an endpaper, that my wiser, younger self marked that particular passage when he first discovered it at the age of twelve or thirteen. Lethe does not restore my innocence, but it allows me to be once more the boy who didn't know who had murdered Roger Ackroyd, or who wept over the fate of Anna Karenina. I begin again at the first words, aware that I can't truly begin again; I feel bereft of an experience that I know I've already had, and that I must acquire once more, like a second skin. In ancient Greece, the snake was Lethe's symbol.

But there are libraries in which oblivion (or the attempt at oblivion) is sought precisely in order to discourage rediscovery. The already-mentioned censored libraries, the officious bureaucratic libraries, the scholarly libraries intent on documenting only that which academia considers to be true—all these belong to a dark and skulking breed. In an amusing book on the values of oblivion, the German scholar Harald Weinrich notes that a certain scientific frame of mind works along the lines of deliberate exclusion, so that, for instance, the library of scientific publications from which the Nobel Prize committee chooses its recipients is limited by the following four rules of enforced forgetting:

I. That which has been published in a language other than English . . . forget it.

II. That which has been published in a style different from that of the rewarded article . . . forget it.

III. That which has not been published in one of the prestigious magazines X, Y or Z . . . forget it.

IV. That which was published more than fifty years ago . . . forget it.[280]

If reading is a craft that allows us to remember the common experience of humankind, it follows that totalitarian governments will try to suppress the memory held by the page. Under such circumstances, the reader's struggle is against oblivion. After the bombing of Kabul in 2001, Shah Muhammad, a librarian–cum–bookseller who had survived various regimes of intolerance, described his experience to a journalist.[281] He had opened his store thirty years earlier and had somehow managed to elude the executioners. His inspiration to resist for the sake of his books, he said, came from a verse by Firdausi, the celebrated tenth-century Persian poet, in *The Book of Kings:* "When facing a great danger, act sometimes as the wolf does, sometimes as the sheep." Meekly Shah Muhammad bound his books in red during the dogmatic Communist regime, and pasted strips of paper over the images of living things during the iconoclastic reign of the Taliban. "But the communists burned my books. . . .

The Afghan bookseller Shah Muhammad Rais in Kabul.

And then the Taliban burned my books again." Finally, during the last raid on his shop, while the police were piling his books on the pyre, Shah Muhammad abandoned his meek behaviour and went to see the minister of Culture. "You destroy my books," he told him, "maybe you'll destroy me, but there is something you'll never destroy." The minister asked what that might be. "The history of Afghanistan," Shah Muhammad answered. Miraculously, he was spared.

In the United States, attempts to curtail the reading of the black population date from the earliest days of slavery. In order to prevent slaves from rebelling, it was essential that they remain illiterate. If slaves learned to read, it was argued, they would become informed of political, philosophical and religious arguments in favour of abolition, and rise against their masters. Therefore, slaves who learned to read, even the Bible, were often punished with death; it was assumed that, while conversion of the slaves was "convenient,"[282] knowledge of the Scriptures was to be acquired only through the eyes of their white masters. The black teacher Booker T. Washington noted that in his childhood "the great ambition of the older people was to try to learn to read the Bible before they died. With this end in view, men and women who were fifty and seventy-five years old, would be found in night-schools."[283]

Not all whites believed that slaves learning to read would necessarily lead to an uprising; there were those who thought that, if they learned to read the Bible, they would become, on the contrary, meek and obedient

servants. Even after the American Bible Society began to distribute Bibles to freed slaves in the late 1860s, there were those among free-thinking white educators who believed that education must serve not as a means to intellectual freedom, but "as an essential tool to moderate the threat arising from 'an inferior, dangerous addition to the republic.'"[284]

In the American South, libraries were not open to the black population until the early twentieth century. The first one recorded was the Cossitt Library in Memphis, Tennessee, which agreed to provide the LeMoyne Institute, a school for black children, with a librarian and a collection of books.[285] In the Northern states, where public libraries had opened their doors to black readers a few years earlier, the fear of treading forbidden territory was still present as late as the 1950s. The young James Baldwin remembered standing at the corner of Fifth Avenue and Forty-second Street, admiring "the stone lions that guarded the great main building of the Public Library." The building seemed to him so vast that he had never yet dared enter it; he was terrified of losing himself in a maze of corridors and marble steps, and never finding the books he wanted. "And then everyone," he

wrote, as if observing himself from the distance of many years, "all the white people inside, would know that he was not used to great buildings, or to so many books, and they would look at him with pity."[286]

Oblivion can be forced on libraries in many ways—by the happenstances of war, or of displacement. In 1945, shortly before the end of the Second World War, a Russian officer discovered in an abandoned German train station a number of open crates overflowing with Russian books and papers that the Nazis had looted. This, according to the writer Ilya Ehrenburg, was all that was left of the celebrated Turgeniev Library, which the author of *Fathers and Sons* had founded in Paris in 1875 for the benefit of émigré students, and which the novelist Nina Berberova called "the greatest Russian library in exile."[287] And even those volumes have today vanished.

The Yiddish poet Rachel Korn, who spent most of her life, as she described it, "shipwrecked in Canada," said that, after being exiled from her village in East Galicia, she felt like someone "being forced to leave your belongings on a sinking ship." But she resisted what seemed to her "enforced oblivion." "When you have been forced to leave your country," she said, "every library is lost, except the ones you remember. And even those, you have to reread in your mind, over and over again, so that the pages don't keep falling out." Her daughter explained how, shortly after their arrival in Montreal, Korn had obliged her, every night, to go through the poems by Pushkin, by Akhmatova, by Mandelstam, that she had learned by heart, as if they were bedtime prayers. "Sometimes she corrected us and sometimes I corrected her." Those remembered texts were the only library that counted for her in exile.[288]

Sometimes a library is wilfully allowed to vanish. In April 2003, the Anglo-American army stood by while the National Archives, the Archaeological Museum and the National Library of Baghdad were ransacked and looted. In a few hours, much of the earliest recorded history of humankind was lost to oblivion. The first surviving examples of writing, dating from six thousand years ago; medieval chronicles that had escaped the pillage of Saddam Hussein's henchmen; numerous volumes of the exquisite collection of Korans kept at the Ministry of Religious Endowment—all disappeared, probably forever.[289] Lost are the manuscripts lovingly penned by the illustrious Arab calligraphers, for

The looting of the National Library and State Archives of Baghdad.

whom the beauty of the script had to mirror the beauty
of the contents. Vanished are collections of tales like
those of the *Arabian Nights,* which the tenth-century
Iraqi book dealer Ibn al-Nadim called evening stories
because one was not supposed to waste the hours of the
day reading trivial entertainment.[290] The official documents that chronicled Baghdad's Ottoman rulers have
joined the ashes of their masters. Gone, finally, are the
books that survived the Mongol conquest of 1258, when
the invading army threw the contents of the libraries into
the Tigris to build a bridge of paper that turned the
waters black with ink.[291] No one will ever again follow
the years of correspondence that meticulously described
dangerous voyages from the past and wonderful cities
caught in time. And no one will again consult, in these
particular copies, great reference works such as *Dawn for*

the Night-Blind, by the fourteenth-century Egyptian scholar al-Qalqashandi, who, in one of the fourteen volumes, explained in detail how each of the letters of Arabic script should be formed, since he believed that what was written would never be forgotten.[292]

Though a good number of objects were returned to Iraq in the months following the looting, by the end of 2004 a large proportion of the stolen books, documents and artifacts had not been recovered, in spite of the efforts of Interpol, UNESCO, ICOM (International Council of Museums) and several cultural agencies around the world. And many irreplaceable texts and objects were destroyed. "In all, what was recovered makes up less than 50 percent of what was stolen," declared Dr. Donny George, director of the Baghdad Archeological Museum. "More than half of the looted material is still missing, which is a great loss for Iraq and for all of humanity."[293]

Luciano Canfora has argued the importance of documenting not only the history of the disappearance of libraries and books, but the history of the awareness of their disappearance.[294] He points out, for example, that in the first century B.C. Diodorus Siculus, commenting on the Greek philosopher Theopompus's chronicles of the campaigns of Philip of Macedon, noted that the entire book consisted of fifty-eight volumes of which "unfortunately, five are no longer to be found." Canfora explains that since Diodorus lived most of his life in Sicily, in regretting the loss of Theopompus's five volumes he meant that they were absent from the local collections, probably from the historical library of Taormina. Eight

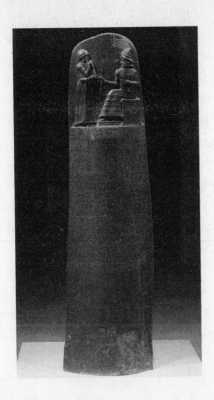

Stele with the Code of Hammurabi.

centuries after Diodorus, however, the Byzantine patri-
cian Photius, compiler of an encyclopedic bibliography
under the title *Bibliotheka,* or *Library,* remarked, "We
have read the *Chronicles* of Theopompus, of which only
fifty-three volumes have survived." The loss noticed
by Diodorus was still true for Photius; that is to say, the
awareness of the absence had become part of the work's
own history, counterbalancing, in some small measure,
the oblivion to which the lost volumes had been
condemned.

Trust in the survival of the word, like the urge to forget what words attempt to record, is as old as the first clay tablets stolen from the Baghdad Museum. To hold and transmit memory, to learn through the experience of others, to share knowledge of the world and of ourselves, are some of the powers (and dangers) that books confer upon us, and the reasons why we both treasure and fear them. Four thousand years ago, our ancestors in Mesopotamia already knew this. The Code of Hammurabi—a collection of laws inscribed on a tall, dark stone stele by King Hammurabi of Babylonia in the eighteenth century B.C., and preserved today in the Louvre Museum—offers us, in its epilogue, an enlightened example of what the written word can mean to the common man.

> In order to prevent the powerful from oppressing the weak, in order to give justice to the orphans and widows . . . I have inscribed on my stele my precious words . . . If a man is sufficiently wise to maintain order in the land, may he heed the words I have written on this stele. . . . Let the oppressed citizen have the inscriptions read out. . . . The stele will illuminate his case for him. And as he will understand what to expect [from the words of the law], his heart will be set at ease.[295]

THE LIBRARY

AS IMAGINATION

> "It is as easy to dream up a book as it is difficult to put it on paper."
>
> Balzac, *Le cabinet des antiques*

There are two big sophora trees in my garden, just outside my library windows. During the summer, when friends are visiting, we sit and talk under them, sometimes during the day but usually at night. Inside the library, my books distract us from conversation and we are inclined to silence. But outside, under the stars, talk becomes less inhibited, wider ranging, strangely more stimulating. There is something about sitting outside in the dark that seems conducive to unfettered conversation. Darkness promotes speech. Light is silent—or, as Henry Fielding explains in *Amelia*, "*Tace*, madam, is Latin for a candle."[296]

Tradition tells us that words, not light, came first out of the primordial darkness. According to a Talmudic legend, when God sat down to create the world, the twenty-two letters of the alphabet descended from his terrible and august crown and begged him to effect his creation through them. God consented. He allowed the alphabet to give birth to the heavens and the earth in darkness, and then to bring forth the first ray of light from the earth's core, so that it might pierce the Holy Land and illuminate the entire universe.[297] Light, what we take to be light, Sir Thomas Browne tells us, is only the shadow of God, in whose blinding radiance words are no longer possible.[298] God's backside was enough to dazzle Moses, who had to wait until he had returned to the darkness of the Sinai in order to read to his people their Lord's commandments. Saint John, with praiseworthy economy, summed up the relationship between letters, light and darkness in one famous line: "In the beginning was the Word."

Saint John's sentence describes the reader's experience. As anyone reading in a library knows, the words on the page call out for light. Darkness, words and light form a virtuous circle. Words bring light into being, and then mourn its passing. In the light we read, in the dark we talk. Urging his father not to allow himself to die, Dylan Thomas pressed now famous words on the old man: "Rage, rage against the dying of the light."[299] And Othello too, in agony, confuses the light of candles with the light of life, and sees them as one and the same: "Put out the light," he says, "and then put out the light."[300] Words call for light in order to be read, but light seems to oppose the spoken word. When Thomas Jefferson introduced the Argand lamp to New England in the mid-eighteenth century, it was observed that the conversation at dinner tables once lit by candlelight ceased to be as brilliant as before, because those who excelled in talking now took to their rooms to read.[301] "I have too much light," says the Buddha, refusing to say another word.[302]

In one other practical sense, words create light. The Mesopotamian who wished to continue his reading when night had fallen, the Roman who intended to pursue his documents after dinner, the monk in his cell and the scholar in his study after evening prayers, the courtier retiring to his bedchamber and the lady to her boudoir, the child hiding beneath the blankets to read after curfew—all set up the light necessary to illuminate their task. In the Archaeological Museum of Madrid stands an oil lamp from Pompeii by whose light Pliny the Elder may have read his last book, before setting off to die in the eruption of A.D. 79. Somewhere in Stratford, Ontario, is a solitary candleholder that dates back (its owner boasts) to Shakespeare's time; it may once have held a candle whose brief life Macbeth saw as a reflection of his own. The lamps that guided Dante's exiled reading in Ravenna and Racine's cloistered reading in Port-Royal, Stendhal's in Rome and De Quincey's in London, all were born of words calling out from between their covers; all were light assisting the birth of light.

In the light, we read the inventions of others; in the darkness, we invent our own stories. Many times, under my two trees, I have sat with friends and described books that were never written. We have stuffed libraries with tales we never felt compelled to set down on paper. "To imagine the plot of a novel is a happy task," Borges once said. "To actually write it is an exaggeration."[303] He enjoyed filling the spaces of the library he could not see with stories he never bothered to write, but for which he sometimes deigned to compose a preface, summary or review. Even as a young man, he said, the knowledge of his impending blindness had encouraged him in the habit of imagining complex volumes that would never take printed form. Borges had inherited from his father the disease that gradually, implacably weakened his sight, and the doctor had forbidden him to read in dim light. One day, on a train journey, he became so engrossed by a detective novel that he carried on reading, page after page, in the fading dusk. Shortly before his destination, the train entered a tunnel. When it emerged, Borges could no longer see anything except a coloured haze, the "darkness visible" that Milton thought was hell. In that darkness Borges lived for the rest of his life, remembering or imagining stories, rebuilding in his mind the National Library of Buenos Aires or his own restricted library at home. In the light of the first half of his life, he wrote and read silently; in the gloom of the second, he dictated and had others read to him.

In 1955, shortly after the military coup that overthrew the dictatorship of General Perón, Borges was offered the post of director of the National Library. The idea had come from Victoria Ocampo, the formidable editor of *Sur* magazine and Borges's friend for many years. Borges thought it "a wild scheme" to appoint a blind man as librarian, but then recalled that, oddly enough, two of the previous directors had also been blind: José Mármol and Paul Groussac. When the possibility of the appointment was put forward, Borges's mother suggested that they take a walk to the library and look at the building, but Borges felt superstitious and refused. "Not until I get the job,"[304] he said. A few days later, he was appointed. To celebrate the occasion, he wrote a poem about "the

Jorge Luis Borges at his desk in the Buenos Aires National Library.

splendid irony of God" that had simultaneously granted him "books and the night."[305]

Borges worked at the National Library for eighteen years, until his retirement, and he enjoyed his post so much that he celebrated almost every one of his birthdays there. In his wood-panelled office, under a high ceiling studded with painted fleurs-de-lys and golden stars, he would sit for hours at a small table, his back towards the room's centrepiece—a magnificent, huge round desk, a copy of one that had belonged to the Prime Minister of France, Georges Clemenceau, that Borges felt was far too ostentatious. Here he dictated his poems and fictions, had books read to him by willing secretaries, received friends, students and journalists, and held study groups of Anglo-Saxon. The tedious, bureaucratic library work was left to his assistant director, the scholar José Edmundo Clemente.

Many of Borges's published stories and essays mention books that he invented without bothering to write them out. Among these are the many romances by the fictional Herbert Quain (the subject of an essaylike fiction), who varies one single plot in geometrical progression until the number of plots becomes infinite; the marvellous detective novel *The Approach to Al-Mu'tasim,* by "the Bombay lawyer Mir Bahadur Ali," supposedly reviewed by the very real Philip Guedalla and Cecil Roberts, and published by the equally real Victor Gollancz in London, with an introduction by Dorothy L. Sayers, under the revised title *The Conversation with the Man Called Al-Mu'tasim: A Game with Shifting Mirrors;* the eleventh volume of the *First Encyclopaedia of Tlön,* which Herbert Ashe received, shortly before his death, in a sealed and registered parcel from Brazil; the play *The Enemies,* which Jaromir Hladik left unfinished but was allowed to complete in his mind in a long, God-granted instant before his execution; and the octavo volume of infinite pages, bearing the words "Holy Writ" and "Bombay" on its spine, that (Borges tells us) he held in his hands shortly before retiring from his post as director of the National Library.[306]

The collecting of imaginary books is an ancient occupation. In 1532 there appeared in France a book signed by the apocryphal scholar Alcofribas Nasier (an anagram of François Rabelais) entitled *The horrible and frightening*

The Giant Gargantua created by François Rabelais.

deeds and accomplishments of the much renowned Pantagruel, King of the Dipsods, son of the great giant Gargantua.[307] In the seventh chapter of the second book, the young Pantagruel, having studied "very well" at Orléans, resolves to visit Paris and its university. It is, however, not the learned institution but the Abbey of St. Victor that holds his attention, for there he finds "a very stately and magnifick" library full of the most wonderful books. The catalogue that Rabelais copies for us is five pages long, and includes such marvels as:

The Codpiece of the Law

The Pomegranate of Vice

The mustard-pot of Penance

The Trevet of good thoughts

The Snatchfare of the Curats

The Spectacles of Pilgrims bound for Rome

The Fured Cat of the Sollicitors and Atturneys

The said Authors Apologie against those who alledge that the
    Popes mule doth eat but at set times

The bald arse or peel'd breech of the widows

The hotchpot of Hypocrites

The bumsquibcracker of Apothecaries

In a letter of advice sent to his son from Utopia, Gargantua encourages Pantagruel to make good use of his skills "by which we may in a mortal estate attain to a kinde of immortality." "All the world is full of knowing men," he writes, "of most learned Schoolmasters, and vast Libraries: and it appears to me as a truth, that neither in *Plato's* time, nor *Cicero's,* nor *Papinian's,* there was ever such conveniency for studying, as we see at this day there is. . . . I see robbers, hangmen, freebooters, tapsters, ostlers, and such like, of the very rubbish of the people, more learned now, than the Doctors and Preachers were in my time." The library that Rabelais invents is perhaps the first "imaginary library" in literature. It mocks (in the tradition of his admired Erasmus and Thomas More) the scholarly and monastic world, but, more important, allows the reader the fun of imagining the arguments and plots behind the rollicking titles. On another of his Gargantuan abbeys, that of Thelême, Rabelais inscribed the motto *Fays ce que voudra* (Do As You Please). On his library at St. Victor he might have written *Lys ce que voudra* (Read As You Please). I've written those words over one of the doors of my own library.

Rabelais was born in 1483 or 1484, near the town of Chinon, not far from where I now live. His house was called La Devinière, or The Soothsayer's House; its original name had been Les Cravandières, after *cravant*, meaning "wild goose" in the Touraine dialect. Since geese were used to predict the future, the house's name was changed to honour the birds' magical gift.[308] The house, the landscape around it, the towns and monuments even as far as the thin eleventh-century tower of Marmande that I can see from the end of my garden, became the setting for his gigantic saga. The success of *Pantagruel* (over four thousand copies sold in the first few months) made Rabelais decide to continue the adventures of his giants. Two years later he published *The Very Horrific Life of the Great Gargantua, Father of Pantagruel,* and several other volumes of the saga. In 1543 the Church banned Rabelais' books, and published an official edict condemning his work.

Rabelais could read Latin, Greek, Italian, Hebrew, Arabic and several dialects of French; he had studied theology, law, medicine, architecture, botany, archaeology and astronomy; he enriched the French language with more than eight hundred words and dozens of idioms, many of which are still used in Acadian Canada.[309] His imaginary library is the fruit of a mind too active to stop and record its thoughts, and his Gargantuan epic is a hodgepodge of episodes that allows the reader almost any choice of sequence, meaning, tone and even argument. It is as if, for Rabelais, the inventor of a narrative is not obliged to bring coherence, logic or resolution to the text. That (as Diderot would later make clear) is the task of the reader, the mark of his freedom. The ancient scholastic libraries took for granted the truth of the traditional commentaries on the classics; Rabelais, like his fellow humanists, questioned the assumption that authority equalled intelligence. "Knowledge without conscience," says Gargantua to his son, "is but the ruin of the soul."

The historian Lucien Febvre, in a study of the religious beliefs in Rabelais' time, attempted to describe the

Rabelais' House in Chinon, France.

writer in sixteenth-century terms. "What was Rabelais like mentally? Something of a buffoon . . . boozing his fill and in the evening writing obscenities? Or perhaps a learned physician, a humanist scholar who filled his prodigious memory with beautiful passages from the ancients . . . ? Or, better yet, a great philosopher, acclaimed as such by the likes of Theodore Beza and Louis Le Caron?" Febvre asks, and concludes, "Our ancestors were more fortunate than we are. They did not choose between two images. They accepted them both at the same time, the respectable one along with the other."[310]

Rabelais was able to maintain simultaneously both a questioning spirit, and faith in what he saw as the established truth. He needed to probe the assertions of fools, and to judge for himself the weight of truisms. The books he read as a scholar, full of the wisdom of the ancients, must have been balanced in his mind by the questions left unanswered and the treatises never written. His own library of parchment and paper was grounded by his imaginary library of forgotten or neglected subjects of study and reflection. We know what books (real books) he carried in his "portable library," a chestful that accompanied him throughout the twenty years of his wanderings in Europe. The list—which left him in constant peril of the Inquisition—included Hippocrates' *Aphorisms,* the works of Plato, Seneca and Lucian, Erasmus's *In Praise of Folly* and More's *Utopia,* and even a dangerous recently published Polish book, the *De revolutionibus* of Copernicus.[311] The books he invented for Pantagruel are their irreverent but tacit gloss.

The critic Mikhail Bahktin has pointed out that Rabelais' imaginary books have their antecedent in the parodic liturgies and comic gospels of earlier centuries. "The medieval parody," he says, "intends to describe only the negative or imperfect aspects of religion, ecclesiastical organization and scholarly science. For these parodists, everything, without exception, is humorous; laughter is as universal as seriousness, and encompasses the whole of the universe, history, society and conception of the world. Theirs is an all-embracing vision of the world."[312]

Rabelais' *Gargantua* was succeeded by a number of imitations in the following century. Most popular among these were a series of catalogues of imaginary libraries published (largely as political satires) in England during the Civil War, such as the *Bibliotheca Parliamenti* of 1653, attributed to Sir John Birkenhead, which included such irreverent titles as *Theopoeia, a discourse shewing to us mortals, that Cromwel may be reckoned amongst the gods, since he hath put off all humanity.*[313] In that same year Sir Thomas Urquhart published the first English translation of *Gargantua and Pantagruel,* and the learned Sir Thomas Browne composed, in imitation of Rabelais, a tract he called *Musaeum Clausum,* or, *Bibliotheca abscondita: containing some remarkable Books, Antiquities, Pictures and Rarities of several kinds, scarce or never seen by any man now living.* In this "Closed Museum or Hidden Library" are many strange volumes and curious objects: among them an unknown poem written in Greek by Ovid during his exile in Tomis, a letter from Cicero describing the Isle of Britain, a relation of Hannibal's march from Spain to Italy, a treatise on dreams by King Mithridates, an eight-year-old girl's miraculous collection of writings in Hebrew, Greek and Latin, and a Spanish translation of the works of Confucius. Among pictures of "rare objects" Sir Thomas lists "An handsome Piece of Deformity expressed in a notable hard Face" and "An Elephant dancing upon the Ropes with a *Negro* Dwarf upon his Back."[314] The clear intention is to mock the popular beliefs of the day, but the result is slightly stilted and far less humorous than its model. Even imaginary libraries can sink under the prestige and pompousness of academia.

In one instance both the library space and the book titles were visible, yet the books represented were imaginary. At Gad's Hill (the house he dreamed of as a child, which he managed to buy twelve years before his death in 1870), Charles Dickens assembled a copious library. A door in the wall was hidden behind a panel lined with several rows of false book spines. On these spines Dickens playfully inscribed the titles of apocryphal works of all sorts: Volumes I to XIX of Hansard's *Guide*

A wood-carving by Gwen Raverat depicting Sir Thomas Browne inspired by Death.

to *Refreshing Sleep,* Shelley's *Oysters, Modern Warfare* by General Tom Thumb (a famous Victorian circus dwarf), a handbook by the notoriously henpecked Socrates on the subject of wedlock, and a ten-volume *Catalogue of Statues to the Duke of Wellington.*[315]

Colette, in one of the books of memoirs with which she delighted in scandalizing her readers in the thirties and forties, tells the story of imaginary catalogues compiled by her friend Paul Masson—a ex–colonial magistrate who worked at the Bibliothèque Nationale, and an eccentric who ended his life by standing on the edge of the Rhine, stuffing cotton wool soaked in ether up his nose and, after losing consciousness, drowning in barely a foot of water. According to Colette, Masson would visit her at her seaside villa and pull from his pockets

Charles Dickens in his library in Gad's Hill.

a portable desktop, a fountain pen and a small pack of blank cards. "What are you doing?" she asked him one day. "I'm working," he answered. "I'm working at my job. I've been appointed to the catalogue section of the Bibliothèque Nationale. I'm making an inventory of titles." "Oh, can you do that from memory?" she marvelled. "From memory? What would be the merit? I'm doing better. I've realized that the Nationale is poor in Latin and Italian books from the fifteenth century," he explained. "Until chance and erudition fill the gaps, I am listing the titles of extremely interesting works that *should* have been written. . . . At least these titles may save the prestige of the catalogue. . . ." "But if the books don't exist . . . ?" "Well," Masson answered with a frivolous gesture, "I can't be expected to do *everything!*"[316]

Libraries of imaginary books delight us because they allow us the pleasure of creation without the effort of research and writing. But they are also doubly disturbing—first because they cannot be collected, and secondly because they cannot be read. These promising treasures must remain closed to all readers. Every one of them can claim the title Kipling gives to the never-to-be-written tale of the young bank clerk Charlie Mears, "The Finest Story in the World."[317] And yet the hunt for such imaginary books, though necessarily fruitless, remains compelling. What devotee of horror stories has not dreamt of coming upon a copy of the *Necronomicon*,[318] the demonic manual invented by H.P. Lovecraft in his dark Cthulhu saga? According to Lovecraft, the *Al Azif* (to give it its original title) was written by Abdul Alhazred *c.* 730 in Damascus. In 950 it was translated into Greek under the title *Necronomicon* by Theodorus Philetas, but the sole copy was burnt by the Patriarch Michael in 1050. In 1228 Olaus translated the original (now lost) into Latin.[319] A copy of the Latin work is supposedly kept in the library of Miskatonic University in Arkham, "one well known for certain forbidden manuscripts and books gradually accumulated over a period of centuries and begun in colonial times." Other than the *Necronomicon*, these forbidden works include "the *Unaussprechlichen Kulten* of von Junzt, the Comte d'Erlette's *Cultes des Goules*, Ludvig Prinn's *De Vermiis Mysteriis*, the *R'lyeh Text*, the *Seven Cryptical Books of Hsan*, the *Dhol Chants*, the *Liber Ivoris*, the *Celaeno Fragments*, and many other, similar texts, some of which exist only in fragmentary form, scattered over the globe."[320]

Not all imaginary libraries contain imaginary books. The library that the barber and the priest condemn to the flames in the first part of *Don Quixote;* Mr. Casaubon's scholarly library in George Eliot's *Middlemarch;* Des Esseintes's languorous library in Huysmans' *A rebours;* the murderous monastic library in Umberto Eco's *The Name of the Rose* . . . all these are merely wishful. Given money enough and time, such dream libraries could find a solid reality. The library that Captain Nemo shows

Professor Aronnax in *Twenty Thousand Leagues under the Sea* (with the exception of two books by Aronnax himself, of which only one is given a title, *Les grands fonds sous-marins*) is one that any wealthy French literary gentleman of the mid-nineteenth century might have acquired. "Here are," says Captain Nemo, "the major works of the ancient and modern masters, that is to say, all the most beautiful creations of humanity in the realms of history, poetry, fiction and science, from Homer to Victor Hugo, from Xenophon to Michelet, from Rabelais to Madame Sand."[321] All real books.

Like their brethren of solid wood and paper, not all imaginary libraries are composed only of books. Captain Nemo's treasure trove is enriched by two further collections, one of paintings and one of "curiosities," according to the custom of European scholars of his time. The duke's wilderness library in *As You Like It*, made up of "tongues in trees, books in the running brooks, sermons in stones, and good in every thing,"[322] requires no volumes of paper and ink. Pinocchio, in the nineteenth chapter of Collodi's novel, tries to imagine what he might do if he had a hundred thousand coins and were a wealthy gentleman, and wishes for a beautiful palace with a library "crammed full with candied fruit, cakes, panettoni, almond biscuits and wafers stuffed with cream."[323]

The distinction between libraries that have no material existence, and those with books and papers that we can hold in our hand, is sometimes strangely blurred. There exist real libraries with solid volumes that seem imaginary, because they are born from what Coleridge famously called the voluntary suspension of disbelief.

Captain Nemo's library, an illustration from the first edition of Twenty Thousand Leagues Under the Sea.

Among them stands the Father Christmas Library in the Provincial Archives of Oulu, Northern Finland, whose other, more conventional holdings go back to the sixteenth century. Since 1950 the Finnish Post's "Santa Claus Postal Service" has been in charge of replying to about six hundred thousand letters received yearly from more than one hundred and eighty countries. Until 1996 the letters were destroyed after being answered, but since 1998 an agreement between the Finnish Postal Services and the provincial authorities has allowed the Oulu Archives to select and preserve a number of the letters received every December, mainly, but not exclusively, from children. Oulu was chosen because, according to Finnish tradition, Father Christmas lives on Korvantunturi, or Ear Mountain, located in that district.[324]

Other libraries deserve to be imaginary for more whimsical reasons—such as the Doulos Evangelical Library, housed in the oldest-serving ocean liner, which tours the world with a cargo of half a million books and a staff of three hundred people; and the minuscule library of Geneytouse, in southwestern France, perhaps the smallest library in the world, lodged in a hut of nine square metres, without water, heating or electricity, founded by Etienne Dumont Saint-Priest, a local farmer passionate about literature and music, who had long dreamt of offering his village a place to read and exchange books.

But not all our libraries come from dreams; some belong to the realm of nightmares. In the spring of 1945, a group of American soldiers of the 101st Airborne Division discovered, hidden in a salt mine near Berchtesgaden, the remains of the library of Adolf Hitler, "haphazardly stashed in schnapps crates with the Reich Chancellery address on them."[325] Of the grotesque collection, only twelve hundred, bearing either the Führer's bookplate or his name, were deemed worth preserving in the Library of Congress in Washington, on the third floor of the Jefferson Building. According to the journalist Timothy W. Ryback, these spoils of war have been curiously overlooked by historians of the Third Reich. Hitler's original library has been estimated at sixteen thousand volumes, of which about seven thousand were on military history, over a thousand were essays on the arts, almost a thousand were works of popular fiction, several more were tracts of Christian spirituality and a few were pornographic stories. Only a handful of classic novels were included: *Gulliver's Travels*, *Robinson Crusoe*, *Uncle Tom's Cabin* and *Don Quixote*, as well as most of the adventure stories by Hitler's favourite author, Karl May. Among the volumes

Hitler's personal bookplate.

kept in the Library of Congress are a French vegetarian cookbook inscribed by its author, Maïa Charpentier, to *Monsieur Hitler, végétarien,* and a 1932 treatise on chemical warfare explaining the uses of prussic acid, later commercialized as Zyklon B. It is difficult to think of constructing, with any hideous accuracy, a portrait of this library's owner. Let there be libraries that the imagination condemns simply because of the reputation of their reader.

We lend libraries the qualities of our hopes and nightmares; we believe we understand libraries conjured up from the shadows; we think of books that we feel should exist for our pleasure, and undertake the task of inventing them unconcerned about any threat of inaccuracy or foolishness, any terror of writer's cramp or writer's block, any constraints of time and space. The books dreamt up through the ages by raconteurs thus unencumbered compose a much vaster library than those resulting from the invention of the printing press—perhaps because the realm of imaginary books allows for the possibility of one book, as yet unwritten, that escapes all the blunders and imperfections to which we know we are condemned. In the dark, under my two trees, my friends and I have shamelessly added to the catalogues of Alexandria entire shelves full of perfect volumes that disappeared without trace by morning.

THE LIBRARY

AS IDENTITY

.

My library was dukedom enough.

William Shakespeare, *The Tempest*

I keep a list of books that I feel are missing from my
library and that I hope one day to buy, and another,
more wishful than useful, of books I'd like to have but
I don't even know exist. In this second list are *A
Universal History of Ghosts*, *A Description of Life in the
Libraries of Greece and Rome*, a third Dorothy L. Sayers
detective novel completed by Jill Paton Walsh,
Chesterton on Shakespeare, a *Summary of Averroës on
Aristotle*, a literary cookbook that draws its recipes
from fictional descriptions of food, a translation of
Calderón's *Life Is a Dream* by Anne Michaels (whose
style, I feel, would suit Calderón's admirably), a
History of Gossip, the *True and Uncensored Memoirs of a
Publishing Life* by Louise Dennys, a well-researched,
well-written biography of Borges, an account of what
exactly happened during Cervantes's captivity in
Algiers, an as-yet-unpublished novel by Joseph Conrad,
the diary of Kafka's Milena.

We can imagine the books we'd like to read, even if they have not yet been written, and we can imagine libraries full of books we would like to possess, even if they are well beyond our reach, because we enjoy dreaming up a library that reflects every one of our interests and every one of our foibles—a library that, in its variety and complexity, fully reflects the reader we are. It is therefore not unreasonable to suppose that, in a similar fashion, the identity of a society, or a national identity, can be mirrored by a library, by an assembly of titles that, practically and symbolically, serves as our collective definition.

It was probably Petrarch who first imagined that a public library should be funded by the state.[326] In 1326, after the death of his father, he abandoned his legal studies and entered the Church as a means of pursuing a career in literature, which eventually culminated in his being crowned poet laureate on the Campidoglio in Rome in 1341. During the following years he divided his time between Italy and the south of France, writing and collecting books, and acquiring an unparalleled scholarly reputation. In 1353, tired of the squabbles at the papal court at Avignon, Petrarch settled for a time in Milan, then in Padua and finally in Venice. Here he was welcomed by the chancellor of the republic, who in 1362 obtained for him a palazzo on the Riva degli Schiavoni in return for the bequest of his by now celebrated library.[327] Petrarch agreed on condition that his books be "perfectly preserved . . . in some fire- and rain-proof location to be assigned for this purpose." Though he modestly stated that his books were neither numerous nor very valuable, he expressed the hope that "this glorious city will add other books at public expense, and that also private individuals . . . will follow the example. . . . In this fashion it might easily be possible to establish a large and famous library, equal to those of antiquity."[328] His wish was granted several times over. Instead of one national library, Italy boasts eight, two of which (those in Florence and in Rome) act jointly as the central library of the nation.

In Britain, the notion of a national library was late in developing. After the dispersal of the libraries following the dissolution of the monasteries ordered by Henry VIII, in 1556 the mathematician and astrologer John Dee, himself the owner of a remarkable collection of books, suggested to Henry's daughter Queen Mary the establishment of a national library that might collect the manuscripts and books "of ancient writers." The proposal was ignored, though repeated during the following reign of Elizabeth I by the Society of Antiquaries. A third plan was presented to her successor, James I, who showed himself agreeable to the idea but died before it could be put into practice. His son, Charles I, had no interest in the matter, despite the fact that royal librarians were routinely appointed during his reign to look after the haphazard royal collections, though with little inclination or success.

Then in 1694, during the reign of William III, the classical scholar Richard Bentley was appointed to the post of keeper of the royal books. Shocked by the sorry state of the library, Bentley published, three years later, *A proposal for building a Royal Library and establishing it by Act of Parliament,* in which he suggested that a new edifice should be erected in St. James's Park for the specific purpose of housing books, and that it should receive an annual grant from Parliament. Though his urging received no answer, Bentley's devotion to the nation's books never ceased. In 1731, when a fire broke out one night in the Cotton Collection (which contained, in addition to the already mentioned Lindisfarne Gospels, two of the earliest manuscripts of the New Testament, the Codex Sinaiticus of the mid-fourth century and the Codex Alexandrinus of the early fifth century), the royal librarian was seen running out into the street "in wig and night-dress, with the Codex Alexandrinus under his arm."[329]

As a result of Bentley's proposal, in 1739 Parliament acquired the magnificent books and objects left by Sir Hans Sloane on his death, and later, in 1753, Montagu House in Bloomsbury, to store them. The house had been designed by an architect from Marseilles in the so-called French style, after the first Montagu House had burnt down in 1686, only a few years after its construction, and possessed many rooms suitable for the display of Sloane's treasures, as well as several acres of fine gardens for visitors to stroll in.[330] A few years later, George II donated his royal book collection to the library—which was by then called the British Museum. On 15 January 1759, the British Library at the Museum opened its impressive doors. At the king's request, the contents were made available to the general public. "Tho' chiefly designed for the use of learned and studious men, both native and foreigners, in their researches into several parts of knowledge, yet being a national establishment . . . the advantages accruing from it should be rendered as general as possible."

Portrait of Sir Antonio Panizzi.

During its early years, however, the librarians' main task was not to compile catalogues and seek new titles, but to guide visitors around the museum's collections.[331]

The hero of the British Library saga is the Italian-born Antonio Panizzi, mentioned previously with regard to the shape of the Reading Room. Threatened with arrest in Italy for being a member of the secret *carbonari*, who opposed Napoleonic rule, the twenty-five-year-old revolutionary had fled to the safety of England. After a brief period as a teacher of Italian, he was named assistant librarian at the British Museum in 1831. A year later he became a British citizen, changing his name to Anthony.

Like his compatriot Petrarch, Panizzi felt that it was the state's responsibility to fund a national library for the benefit of everyone. "I want," he said in a report dated 14 July, 1836, "a poor student to have the same means of indulging his learned curiosity, of following his rational pursuits, of consulting the same authorities, of fathoming the most intricate inquiry, as the richest man in the Kingdom, as far as books go, and I contend that Government is bound to give him the most liberal and unlimited assistance in this respect."[332] In 1856 Panizzi ascended to the post of principal librarian, and through his keen intellectual gifts and his administrative abilities he transformed the institution into one of the world's greatest cultural centres.[333]

To achieve his goal, Panizzi planned and started the library's catalogue; he enforced the 1842 Copyright Act, which required that a copy of every book printed in Great Britain be deposited in the library; he successfully lobbied for an increase in government funds; and by insisting that the staff be recognized as civil servants he greatly bettered the librarians' working conditions, which must have been infernal. The biographer and essayist Edmund Gosse, a good friend of Swinburne, Stevenson and Henry James, was employed in the library in the late 1860s as "one of the humblest of mankind, a Junior Assistant in the Printed Books Department." He described his working space, shortly before Panizzi's improvements, as an overheated, "singularly horrible underground cage, made of steel bars, called the Den . . . a place such as no responsible being is allowed to live in nowadays, where the transcribers on the British Museum staff were immured in a half-light."[334]

Panizzi (Gosse depicted him as a "dark little old Italian, sitting like a spider in a web of books")[335] wanted the British Museum library to be one of the finest, best-run libraries in the world, but above all he wanted the "web of books" to be the stronghold of British cultural and political identity. He outlined his vision in the clearest possible terms:

> 1st. The attention of the Keeper of the emphatically British library ought to be directed most particularly to British works and to works

relating to the British Empire; its religious, political and literary as well as scientific history; its laws, institutions, descriptions, commerce, arts, etc. The rarer and more expensive a work of this description is, the more reasonable efforts ought to be made to secure it for the library. 2ndly. The old and rare, as well as the critical editions of ancient classics, ought never to be sought for in vain in this collection; nor ought good comments, as also the best translations into modern languages be wanting.

3rdly. With respect to foreign literature, arts and sciences, the library ought to possess the best editions of standard works for critical purposes or for use. The public have, moreover, a right to find in their national library heavy, as well as expensive, foreign works, such as literary journals, transactions of societies, large collections, historical or otherwise, complete series of newspapers, and collections of law and their best interpreters.[336].

Panizzi saw the British national library as a portrait of the national soul. Foreign literature and cultural material were to be collected (he posted agents for this purpose in Germany and in the United States), but mainly for comparison and reference, or to complete a collection. What mattered to Panizzi was that every aspect of British life and thought be represented, so that the library could become a showcase of the nation itself. He was clear as to what a national library should stand for; less obvious was, to his mind, the manner in which it should be used. Since even a national library's capacity to accommodate readers is limited, should such an institution be only one of last resort? Thomas Carlyle complained that every Tom, Dick and Harry used the library for purposes totally unconnected with scholarship and study. "I believe," he wrote, "there are several people in a state of imbecility who come to read in the British Museum. I have been informed that there are several in that state who are sent there by their friends to pass away the time."[337]

Panizzi wanted the library always to be available to every "poor student" wishing to indulge "his learned curiosity." For practical reasons, however, should a national library be available only to those readers (students or otherwise) who have failed to find the books they need in other public libraries? Should it provide ordinary services to the common reader, or should it function solely as an archive of last resort, holding that which, because of its rarity or uniqueness, cannot be distributed more broadly? Up to 2004 the British Library delivered reader's cards only to those who could prove that the books they were looking for were not available elsewhere, and even then, only to researchers who could provide evidence of their status through letters of reference. Commenting on the "accessibility" program that eliminated this requirement that one be a "researcher," in September 2005 a reader unwittingly echoed Carlyle's complaint: "Every day the library is filled with, among others, people sleeping, students doing their homework, bright young things writing film scripts—in fact, doing almost anything except consulting the library's books."[338]

The ultimate function of a national library is still in question. Today, electronic technology can open a national library to most readers in their own homes, and even provide cross-library services; not only is the reading space extended well beyond the library's walls, but the books themselves mingle with and complement the holdings of other libraries. For example: I wish to consult a book on the intriguing subject of mermaid mythology, *Les Sirènes* by Georges Kastner, published in Paris in 1858. I discover that the large municipal library of Poitiers does not possess a copy. My librarian kindly offers to search for the nearest library that might hold one, and discovers (thanks to the electronic cataloguing system) that the only copy in France is at the Bibliothèque Nationale. Because of its rarity, the book cannot be lent out, but it can be photocopied. The Poitiers library can request that a complete, bound photocopy be made which will enter their holdings, so that I am able to borrow it. The system, though not perfect, allows me access to some of the rarest books in the national holdings—and even beyond, in the stacks of other countries bound by inter-library agreements.

Since *Les Sirènes* is an old book and not covered by the laws of copyright, it could have been scanned and entered into one of the virtual library systems, so that I could download and print it myself or, for a fee, commission a printing from a server. This seemingly new system echoes one established centuries ago by medieval universities, in which a text recommended by a teacher could be copied by scribes who set up shop outside the university walls and sold their services to the students. In order to preserve, as far as possible, the accuracy of classical texts, university authorities devised an ingenious method. Carefully checked manuscripts were lent to "stationers" who, for a fixed tariff or tax, sent them out to be copied, either to obtain texts to sell themselves, or to rent to students too poor to commission copies, who were therefore forced to do the work themselves. The original text (an *exemplar*) did not go out as a single book, but in sections (*peciae*) that were returned to the stationer after being copied; he could then rent them out once again. When the first printing presses were installed, university authorities considered them nothing more than a useful means of producing copies with a little more speed and accuracy.[339]

Lebanon is a country that boasts at least a dozen different religions and cultures. Its national library is a recent acquisition, dating only to 1921, when Viscount Philippe de Tarazi, a Lebanese historian and bibliophile, donated his collection to the state with the precise instructions that it become "the core of what should become the Great Library of Beyrouth." De Tarazi's donation comprised twenty thousand printed volumes, a number of precious manuscripts and the first issues of national newspapers. Three years later, in order to augment the collection, a government decree established a legal deposit system (requiring that a copy of every book printed in the country be submitted), and staffed the library with eight clerks under the jurisdiction of the Ministry of Education. During the civil war that ravaged the country from the mid-1970s to the mid-1990s, the National Library was many times bombed and looted. In 1979, after four years of fighting, the government closed the facilities and stored the surviving manuscripts and documents in the vaults of the National Archives. Modern printed books were stored in a separate building between 1982 and 1983, but this site was also heavily bombed, and the books spared by gunfire were damaged by rainwater and insect infestation. At last, after the war ended, and with the assistance of a group of experts from the French Bibliothèque Nationale, plans were drawn up in 1994 to re-establish the surviving collections in a new site.

Visiting Lebanon's rescued books is a melancholy experience. It is obvious that Lebanon still requires much assistance to disinfect, restore, catalogue and put away its collection. The works are stacked in modern rooms in a customs building too near the sea to prevent dampness. A handful of clerks and volunteers page through the piles of print and place the books on shelves; an expert eye will determine which are worth restoring and which must be discarded. In another building, a librarian specializing in ancient texts sifts through the Oriental manuscripts, some dating from the ninth century, in order to grade the severity of the deterioration, marking each piece with a coloured label, from red (the worst condition) to white (requiring minor repairs). But it is obvious that neither the staff nor the funding suffices for the enormous task.

But there is a hopeful side. A now vacant building that used to house the Faculty of Law of the Lebanese University in Beyrouth has been designated the home of the new National Library, and should soon be open to the public. In her report on the project, read out in May 2004, Professor Maud Stéphan-Hachem, advisor to the minister of Culture, pointed out that the library might in fact "help reconcile a plural reality," reweaving all of Lebanon's cultural strands.

The project of a national library for Lebanon has always been defended, supported and favoured by all our intellectual bibliophiles, but up to now each one of them appropriated the project for

The books of the Lebanon National Library in precarious storage.

himself, lending it his own dreams and his own personal vision of our much embattled culture. It could however become a project of the whole of our society, a public project in which the entire state must have a hand, especially because of its eminently political dimension. It should not be reduced to a mere saving of books, or to the rebuilding of an institution modelled on other such libraries in the world. It is a political project of Lebanese reconciliation, preserving the memory both of the recognition of others, effected concretely through inventories and recordings, and of the recognition of the value of their works.[340]

Can a library reflect a plurality of identities? My own library—set up in a small French village to which it has no visible connection, and made up of fragmentary libraries collected in Argentina, England, Italy, France, Tahiti and Canada during the course of a peripatetic life—proclaims a number of changing identities. I am, in a sense, the library's only citizen, and can therefore claim common bonds with its holdings. And yet many friends have felt that the identity of this ragbag library was at least partly theirs as well. It may be that, because of its kaleidoscopic quality, any library, however personal, offers to whoever explores it a reflection of what he or she seeks, a tantalizing wisp of intuition of who we are as readers, a glimpse into the secret aspects of the self.

Immigrants sometimes gravitate to libraries to learn more about their country of adoption, not only its history and geography and literature, its dates and maps and national poems, but also a general understanding of how the country thinks and organizes itself, how it divides and catalogues the world—a world that includes the immigrant's past. Queens Borough Public Library in New York is the busiest library in the United States, circulating over fifteen million books, tapes and videos a year—mainly to an immigrant population, since nearly half the residents of Queens speak a language other than English at home, and more than a third were born in a foreign country. The librarians speak Russian, Hindi, Chinese, Korean, Gujarati and Spanish, and can explain to their new readers how to get a driver's licence or navigate the Internet and learn English. The most sought-after titles are translations of American potboilers into the immigrants' own languages.[341] Queens may not be the cultural repository that Panizzi had in mind for a nation, but it has become one of many libraries that hold up a mirror to the pluralistic, vertiginous, challenging identity of the country and the times.

THE LIBRARY

AS HOME

Beyond the national library of any nation lies a library greater than all, because it contains each and every one of them: an inconceivably vast and ideal library of all the books ever written, and of those that exist only as possibilities, as volumes still to come. This colossal accumulation of libraries overshadows any single collection of books and yet is implied in every one of their volumes. My edition of the *Odyssey*, "translated into English prose by T.E. Shaw" (better known as Lawrence of Arabia), echoes back to Alexandria and to the rigorous commentaries of Aristarchus, as well as forward to the generous library of *Odyssey*s assembled by George Steiner in Geneva, and to the various pocket editions of Homer an anonymous reader in Montevideo sent to help rebuild the Library of Sarajevo. Each of these readers reads a different *Odyssey*, and their readings extend the adventures of Ulysses well beyond the Fortunate Isles, into infinity.

For me, among all of Ulysses' stories none is as moving as his homecoming. The Sirens, the Cyclops, the sorceress and her spells are prodigious wonders, but the old man who weeps at the sight of the remembered shore and the dog who dies of a broken heart at the feet of his remembered master seem truer and more compelling than the marvels. Nine-tenths of the poem consist of surprise; the end is recognition.

What is this homecoming? It can be argued that we perceive the world in one of two ways—as a foreign land or as home—and that our libraries reflect both these opposing views. As we wander among our books, picking at random a volume from the shelves and leafing through it, the pages either astound us by their difference from our own experience or comfort us with their similitude. The greed of Agamemnon or the meekness of Kim's Lama are to me utterly foreign; Alice's bewilderment or Sinbad's curiosity reflect again and again my own emotions. Every reader is either a pausing wanderer or a traveller returned.

It's late at night. It's raining heavily. I can't sleep. I wander into my library, take a book off its shelf and read. In a faraway castle of broken walls, where the shadows were many and a cold wind breathed through the cracks of the battlements and casements, there lived a count of many years and great renown. His knowledge of the world came mainly from books, and he was certain of his place in history. This aristocratic man claimed the right to be proud because

in our veins flows the blood of many brave races who fought as the lion fights, for lordship. Here, in the whirlpool of European races, the Ugric tribe bore down from Iceland the fighting spirit which Thor and Wodin gave them, which their Berserkers displayed to such fell intent on the seaboards of Europe, aye, and of Asia and Africa, too, till the peoples thought that the were-wolves themselves had come. . . . When was redeemed that great shame of my nation, the shame of Cassova [Kosovo], when the flags of the Wallach and the Magyar went down beneath the Crescent; who was it but one of my own race who as Voivode crossed the Danube and beat the Turk on his own ground! This was a Dracula indeed![342]

A seventeenth-century portrait of Vlad Dracul or Vladislaus Dracula, recently discovered in the Würtenberg State Library, Germany.

Count Dracula's seat is in Transylvania. This is his *umbilicus mundi,* the navel of his world, the landscape that feeds his imagination, if not his body, since as time goes by it becomes difficult for him to find fresh blood in his native mountains, and he is forced to seek material nourishment abroad. "I long to go through the crowded streets of your mighty London," says the count, "to be in the midst of the whirl and rush of humanity, to share its life, its change, its death, and all that makes it what it is."[343] But wherever Dracula travels, he cannot be wholly parted from his home. The books on his dusty shelves chronicle his ancient story; all other libraries hold no interest for him. His castle with its ancestral library is his only real home, and he must always have with him a boxful (or coffinful) of the native earth in which he is so deeply rooted. Like Antaeus, he must touch his mother earth or die.

I put Bram Stoker's novel away and reach for a second book, a few shelves above it. It tells the story of another traveller, one whose monstrous features the book hints at but never quite reflects. Like Count Dracula, this wanderer is also a lonely gentleman resolved that no one shall be his master, but unlike the count, he has no illusions about his aristocracy. He has no home, no roots, no ancestry. "I possessed no money, no friends, no kind of property,"[344] he tells us. He moves through the world like an exile from nowhere; he is a citizen of the cosmos because he is a citizen of no place. "I am content to suffer alone, while my sufferings shall endure,"[345] he says in resignation. He teaches himself through books, collecting in his memory a curious and eclectic library. His first readings are vicarious;

he listens to a family of peasants read out loud, some-what implausibly, a philosophical meditation on universal history, C.-F. Volney's *Ruins of Empires*. "Through this work," he explains, "I obtained a cursory knowledge of history, and a view of the several empires at present existing in the world; it gave me an insight into the manners, governments, and religions of the different nations of the earth." He wonders how human beings can be "at once so powerful, so virtuous, and magnificent, yet so vicious and base?" For this he has no answer, but even though he feels he is "not even of the same nature as man,"[346] he nevertheless loves humankind and wishes to belong to the human realm. A lost suitcase full of clothes and books provides him with a few other readings: Milton's *Paradise Lost*, Plutarch's *Lives* and Goethe's *Sorrows of Young Werther*. From *Werther* he learns "despondency and gloom," from Plutarch "high thoughts." But *Paradise Lost* moves him with a sense of wonder. "As I read," he says, "I applied much personally to my own feelings and condition. I found myself similar, yet at the same time strangely unlike the beings concerning whom I read, and to whose conversation I was a listener. I sympathized with, and partly understood them, but I was unformed in mind; I was dependent on none, and related to none."[347] In spite of finding glimmers of his own story in the story of the fallen Adam, this bewildered reader finds that, however much he reads, human libraries do not account for him. Notwithstanding his eagerness to be part of the universal audience, this citizen of the world will be hounded from the world, will be scorned as a foreigner in every sense, as a creature beyond the pale of every society. Miserable, feared and hated, he will cause the death of his own maker, and finally Dr. Frankenstein's monster will lose himself forever in the ice of the North Pole, inside the frozen blank page known as Canada, the dumping ground of so many of the world's fantasies.

Frankenstein's monster is both the utter foreigner and the perfect world citizen; he is alien in every way, a horror to look upon, and yet made up of all manner of human pieces. Learning like a child for the first time the nature of the world and of himself, he is the archetypal *lector virgo,* the curious being willing to be taught by the open page, a visitor to the library of the world carrying no prejudices or experience to colour his reading. When the monster enters the blind hermit's cottage, he pronounces these words: "Pardon the intrusion. . . . I am a traveller in want of a little rest." A traveller for whom there are no borders, no nationalities, no limitations of space, because he belongs nowhere, the monster must even excuse himself for entering a world into which he has not willingly come, promoted from darkness, in the words of Milton's Adam.[348] I find the phrase "Pardon the intrusion" unbearably moving.

For Frankenstein's monster, the world as described in books is monothematic; all volumes are from the same library. Though he travels from place to place— Switzerland, the Orkneys, Germany, Russia, England and the wilds of Tartary—he sees not the particularities but the common traits of these societies. For him, the world is almost featureless. He deals in abstracts, even though he learns details from various books of history. "I read of men concerned in public affairs governing or

Illustration by Chevalier for the 1831 edition of Mary Shelley's
Frankenstein *or* The Modern Prometheus.

massacring their species. I felt the greatest ardour for
virtue arise within me, and abhorrence for vice, as far as
I understood the signification of these terms, relative as
they were, as I applied them, to pleasure and pain
alone."[349] And yet these lessons will prove fruitless.
Human libraries, the monster will learn, contain for him
only alien literature.

At home in a single place and at home in the world are
two notions that can both be experienced as negative.
Count Dracula trusts only his private library. He prides

himself on being *boyar* (belonging to the Russian nobility), and can scornfully list a number of nationalities he is not. Frankenstein's monster, having no library of his own, looks for his reflection in every book he encounters, and yet never succeeds in recognizing his own story in those "foreign" pages.

And yet the possibility of a greater and deeper experience was always there for either of them. Seneca, echoing Stoic notions from four hundred years earlier, denied that the only books that should matter to us are those of our contemporaries and fellow citizens. According to Seneca, we can pick from any library whatever books we wish to call ours; each reader, he tells us, can invent his own past. He observed that the common assumption—that our parents are not of our choosing—is in fact untrue; we have the power to select our own ancestry. "Here are families with noble endowments," he writes, pointing at his bookshelf. "Choose whichever you wish to belong to. Your adoption will give you not only the name but actually the property, and this you need not guard in a mean or niggardly spirit: the more people you share it with, the greater it will become. . . . This is the sole means of prolonging your mortality, rather than transforming it into immortality." Whoever realizes this, says Seneca, "is exempt from the limitations of humanity; all ages are at his service as at the service of a god. Has time gone by? He holds it fast in recollection. Is time now present? He makes use of it. Is it still to come? He anticipates it. The amalgamation of all time into one, makes his life long."[350] For Seneca, it was not the notion of superiority that mattered (Plutarch made fun of those who considered the moon of Athens superior to the moon of Corinth[351]) but that of communality, the sharing among all human beings of one common reason under one divine logos. As a consequence, he widened the circle of the self to embrace not only family and friends but also enemies and slaves, as well as barbarians or foreigners, and ultimately the whole of humanity.

Centuries later, Dante was to apply this definition to himself: "As fish have water, I have the world as my home."[352] He added that though he loved his native Florence to the point of suffering exile for her cause, he could truthfully say, after reading many poets and prose writers, that the earth was full of other places more noble and more beautiful. His vigorous belief in a cosmopolitan library allowed Dante to affirm an independent national identity, yet to see the world as his patrimony and fountainhead. For the cosmopolitan reader a homeland is not in space, fractured by political frontiers, but in time, which has no borders. This was why Erasmus, two centuries after Dante, praised Aldus Manutius, the great Venetian printer, for providing readers with a "library without walls," in the shape of his octavo volumes of the classics.[353]

The cosmopolitan library also lies at the core of Jewish culture. For the Jews, born within an oral tradition, it is paradoxically the Book—the revealed word of God— that stands at the centre of their intellectual and religious experience. For them, the Bible is itself a library, the most complete and reliable library of all, everlasting and all-encompassing, rooted in time and therefore possessed of a constant existence past, present and future. Its words carry more weight than the futile scourges of age and human change, so that even after the destruction of the Second Temple, in A.D. 70, the rabbinical scholars of the Diaspora would discuss in their distant synagogues, as instructed by the Book, the physical rules of conduct to be observed within a building that no longer had a physical being.[354] To believe that the library holds a truth greater than that of the time and place in which we stand: this is the intellectual or spiritual allegiance that Seneca was arguing for. This too was the argument held by the Arab scholars of the Middle Ages, for whom libraries existed both "in time, making present the past Greek and Arab ages as exemplary cultural models, and in space, gathering what was dispersed and bringing near what was far away. . . . They rendered visible the invisible, and were concerned with possessing the world."[355]

Jean Jacques Rousseau was of two minds about this ecumenical sentiment. In *Émile* he argued that the words *patrie* (fatherland) and *citoyen* (citizen) should be deleted from every modern language. But he also insisted, "Distrust those cosmopolitans who seek in the depths of their books the duties they scorn to perform at home. This kind of philosopher professes love for the Tartars, in order to be excused from loving his neighbours."[356] Sometime in the mid-seventeenth century, the poet Thomas Traherne penned what we can read today as a premature answer to Rousseau, in a manuscript that remained unpublished for two hundred and fifty years, until it was discovered by chance in a London bookstall and bought for a few pence by a curious collector. Traherne wrote, "You will never enjoy the world aright, till the sea itself floweth in your veins, till you are clothed with the heavens, and crowned with the stars: and perceive yourself to be the sole heir of the whole world, and more than so, because men are in it who are every one sole heirs as well as you."[357]

The notion of a cosmopolitan past was with us for many centuries, perhaps until the pre-Raphaelites introduced the idea of anachronism, a barrier separating what belonged to our present from what belonged to ages gone by. For Sir Thomas Browne or for Erasmus, Plato and Aristotle were fellow debaters. Platonic and Aristotelian ideas were renewed in the minds of Montaigne and Petrarch, and the dialogue was continued throughout the generations, not on a vertical timeline but on a horizontal plane, along the same circular path to knowledge. "Whatever meant reality to our ancestors persists, and is hidden in every kind of art," says the Emperor Augustus in Hermann Broch's *The Death of Virgil.*[358]

"For as though there were a Metempsuchosis," wrote Sir Thomas Browne in 1642, "and the soul of one man passed into another, opinions do find, after certain Revolutions, men and minds like those that first begat them. To see our selves again, we need not look for Plato's year: every man is not only himself; there hath been many Diogenes, and as many Timons, though but few of that name: men are liv'd over again, the world is now as it was in Ages past; there was none then, but there hath been some one since that parallels him, and is, as it were, his revived self."[359] For Browne the past is made contemporary through our reading and thinking; the past is a bookshelf open to all, an infinite source of that which then becomes ours by worthy appropriation. There are no copyright laws here, no legal boundaries, no picket fences with the sign "Private, Keep Out."

Closer to our time, the philosopher Richard Rorty drew the following conclusion from Browne's cosmopolitan vision of history. "The best a prophet or a demiurge can hope for is to say once again what has often been said, but to say it just a little bit better."[360] The past is the cosmopolitan's mother country, the universal fatherland, an endless library. In it (so thought Sir Thomas Browne) lies our hope for an endurable future.

At about the same time as Browne was writing these words in his *Religio Medici*, Gabriel Naudé, in his *Advice for Setting Up a Library*, was rejoicing in the riches a library could afford:

> For if it is possible to enjoy in this world a certain sovereign good, a certain perfect and accomplished happiness, I believe that there is none more desirable than the dialogue and the fruitful and pleasant entertainment that a wise man might receive from such a Library, and that it is not so strange a thing to possess Books, *ut illi sint coenationum ornamenta, quam ut studiorum instrumenta*. Since he can rightfully call himself because of it a cosmopolitan or citizen of the whole world, he can know everything, see everything and ignore nothing; in brief, since he is absolute master of this contentment, he can use it as he pleases, take it when he wants to, converse with it as much as he likes, and without obstacles, without labours and without effort he can be instructed and know all the most precise characteristics of *Everything that is, that was and that may be/ On earth, in the sea, in the uttermost hiding-places of the Heavens.*[361]

CONCLUSION

We have always wanted to remember more, and we will continue, I believe, to weave webs to catch words in the hope that somehow, in the sheer quantity of accumulated utterances, in a book or on a screen, there will be a sound, a phrase, a spelled-out thought that will carry the weight of an answer. Every new technology has advantages over the previous one, but necessarily lacks some of its predecessor's attributes. Familiarity, which no doubt breeds contempt, breeds also comfort; that which is unfamiliar breeds distrust. My grandmother, born in the Russian countryside at the end of the nineteenth century, was afraid of using that new invention called the telephone when it was first introduced to her neighbourhood in Buenos Aires, because, she said, it didn't allow her to see the face of the person she was speaking to. "It makes me think of ghosts," she explained.

Electronic text that requires no page can amicably accompany the page that requires no electricity; they need not exclude each other in an effort to serve us best. Human imagination is not monogamous nor does it need to be, and new instruments will soon sit next to the PowerBooks that now sit next to our books in the multi-media library. If the Library of Alexandria was the emblem of our ambition of omniscience, the Web is the emblem of our ambition of omnipresence; the library that contained everything has become the library that contains anything. Alexandria modestly saw itself as the centre of a circle bound by the knowable world; the Web, like the definition of God first imagined in the twelfth century,[362] sees itself as a circle whose centre is everywhere and whose circumference is nowhere.

And yet the new sense of infinity created by the Web has not diminished the old sense of infinity inspired by the ancient libraries; it has merely lent it a sort of tangible intangibility. There may come a new technique of collecting information next to which the Web will seem to us habitual and homely in its vastness, like the aged buildings that once lodged the national libraries in Paris and Buenos Aires, Beyrouth and Salamanca, London and Seoul.

Solid libraries of wood and paper, or libraries of ghostly flickering screens, stand as proof of our resilient belief in a timeless, far-reaching order that we dimly intuit or perceive. During the Czech insurrection against the Nazis in May 1945, when Russian troops were entering Prague, the librarian Elena Sikorskaja, Vladimir Nabokov's sister, realized that the German officers now attempting to retreat had not returned several of the books they had borrowed from the library she worked in. She and a colleague decided to reclaim the truant volumes, and set out on a rescue mission through the streets down which the Russian trucks were victoriously bundling. "We reached the house of a German pilot who returned the books quite calmly," she wrote to her brother a few months later. "But by now they would let no one cross the main road, and everywhere there were Germans with machine guns,"[363] she complained. In the midst of the confusion and chaos, it seemed important to her that the library's pathetic attempt at order should, as far as possible, be preserved.

However appealing we may find the dream of a knowable universe made of paper and a meaningful cosmos made of words, a library, even one colossal in its proportions or ambitious and infinite in its scope, can never offer us a "real" world, in the sense in which the daily world of suffering and happiness is real. It offers us instead a negotiable image of that real world which (in the words of the French critic Jean Roudaut) "kindly allows us to conceive it,"[364] as well as the *possibility* of experience, knowledge and memory of something intuited through a tale or guessed at through a poetic or philosophical reflection.

Saint John, in a moment of confusion, tells us not to love the world or the things that are in the world because "all that is in the world, the lust of the flesh, and the lust of the eyes, and the pride of life, is not of the Father, but is of the world."[365] This injunction is at best a paradox. Our humble and astonishing inheritance is the world and only the world, whose existence we constantly test (and prove) by telling ourselves stories about it. The suspicion that we and the world are made in the image of something wonderfully and chaotically coherent far beyond our grasp, of which we are also part; the hope that our exploded cosmos and we, its stardust, have an ineffable meaning and method; the delight in retelling the old metaphor of the world as a book we read and in which we too are read; the conceit that what we can know of reality is an imagination made of language—all this finds its material manifestation in that self-portrait we call a library. And our love for it, and our lust to see more of it, and our pride in its accomplishments as we wander through shelves full of books that promise more and more delights, are among our happiest, most moving proofs of possessing, in spite of all the miseries and sorrows of this life, a more intimate, consolatory, perhaps redeeming faith in a method behind the madness than any jealous deity could wish upon us.

In her novel *The Blue Flower*, Penelope Fitzgerald says, "If a story begins with finding, it must end with searching."[366] The story of my library certainly began with finding: finding my books, finding the place in which to lodge them, finding the quiet in the space lit under the darkness outside. But if the story must end with searching, the question has to be: searching for what? Northrop Frye once observed that, had he been present at the birth of Christ, he did not think he would have heard the angels singing. "The reason why I think so is that I do not hear them now, and there is no reason to suppose that they have stopped."[367] Therefore, I am not searching for revelation of any kind, since anything said to me is necessarily limited by what I'm capable of hearing and understanding. Not for knowledge beyond what, in some secret way, I already know. Not for illumination, to which I can't reasonably aspire. Not for experience, since ultimately I can only become aware of what is already in me. For what, then, do I search, at the end of my library's story?

Consolation, perhaps. Perhaps consolation.

ACKNOWLEDGMENTS

Those who read, those who
      tell us what they read,
Those who noisily turn
      the pages of their books,
Those who have power over
      red and black ink,
      and over pictures,
Those are the ones who lead us,
      guide us, show us the way.

                            Aztec Codex from 1524,
                                Vatican Archives

While writing this book, I have contracted many debts. In the alphabetical order dear to libraries, my thanks:

To my friends and colleagues Enis Batur, Anders Björnsson, Antoine Boulad, Roberto Calasso, Juan Gustavo Cobo Borda, Viviane Flament, Dieter Hein, Chris Herschdorfer, Patricia Jaunet, Marie Korey, Richard Landon, Lilia Moritz Schwarcz, Hubert Nyssen, Felicidad Orquín, Lucie Pabel and Gottwalt Pankow, Dominique Papon, Fabrice Pataut, Arturo Ramoneda, Sylviane Sambord, Alberto Ruy Sánchez, Maud Stéphan-Hachem, Jean-Luc Terradillos.

To the staff of the London Library and of the Médiathèque de Poitiers, and to Anne-Catherine Sutermeister and Silvia Kimmeier of the Bibliothèque Cantonale et Universitaire de Lausanne.

To my agents, Michèle Lapautre in Paris, Guillermo Schavelzon in Barcelona, Ruth Weibel in Zurich,

Bruce Westwood and Nicole Winstanley and the staff at Westwood Creative Artists in Toronto.

To Gena Gorrell, whose critical, unrelenting, meticulous reading cleared the book of a vast number of errors and fatuities. To Deirdre Molina, for her painstaking care in following the book from manuscript to print. To C.S. Richardson, for another splendid book design. To Liba Berry, for the excellent proofread. To Michelle MacAleese, for her thorough photo research. To Barney Gilmore, for the comprehensive index.

To my editors, Rosellina Arquinto, Hans-Jürgen Balmes, Valeria Ciompi, Carmen Criado, Haye Koningsveld, Luiz Schwarcz, Marie-Catherine Vacher and, first and foremost, overriding the laws of the alphabet, Louise Dennys.

Finally, I'm deeply grateful to the S. Fischer Stiftung in Berlin and to the Simon Guggenheim Foundation in New York for their financial assistance over the past years, without which this book would no doubt be still languishing in the future.

Notes

FOREWORD

1. Robert Louis Stevenson, "Pulvis et Umbra," II, in *Across the Plains* (London: Chatto & Windus, 1892).

2. Northrop Frye, Notebook 3:128, in *Northrop Frye Unbuttoned: Wit and Wisdom from the Notebooks and Diaries*, selected by Robert D. Denham (Toronto: Anansi, 2004).

3. Francesco Petrarca, "On His Own Ignorance and That of Many Others," in *Invectives*, ed. David Marsh (Cambridge, MA, and London: Harvard University Press, 2003).

THE LIBRARY AS MYTH

4. M. le Comte de Mondion, "Mondion, le chateau—la paroisse, 1096–1908," in *Bulletins de la Société des Antiquaires de l'Ouest* (Poitiers, second quarter of 1909).

5. R.L. Stevenson (in collaboration with Mrs. Stevenson), "The Dynamiter," in *More New Arabian Nights* (London: Longmans, Green & Co., 1885).

6. Walter Benjamin, "Unpacking My Library," in *Illuminations*,

ed. Hannah Arendt, trans. Harry Zohn (New York: Harcourt Brace & World, 1968).

7. Lucan, *The Civil War (Pharsalia)*, ed. J.D. Duff, IX:973 (Cambridge, MA: Harvard University Press; London: William Heinemann, 1988).

8. *Essais de Montaigne*, ed. Amaury-Duval (Paris: Chassériau, 1820).

9. Ibid.

10. Samuel Taylor Coleridge, *Literary Remains*, II:206, ed. Henry Nelson Coleridge (New York: Harper, 1853).

11. Virginia Woolf, "Hours in a Library," in *The Essays of Virginia Woolf, Volume ii, 1912–1918*, ed. Andrew McNeillie (London: The Hogarth Press, 1987).

12. Genesis 11:5–7.

13. Louis Ginzberg, *The Legends of the Jews*, Vol. I (Baltimore & London: Johns Hopkins University Press, 1998).

14. Strabo, *Geography*, Book XIII, quoted by Luciano Canfora, "Aristote, 'fondateur' de la Bibliothèque d'Alexandrie," in *La nouvelle Bibliothèque d'Alexandrie*, ed. Fabrice Pataut (Paris: Buchet/Chastel, 2003).

15. Pliny the Elder, *Natural History*, translated by and with an introduction by John Healy (London: Penguin, 1991); Book XII, 69–70.

16. Luciano Canfora, *La biblioteca scomparsa* (Palermo: Sellerio Editore, 1987).

17. Charles A. Goodrum & Helen W. Dalrymple, *Guide to the Library of Congress*, rev. edition (Washington: Library of Congress, 1988).

18. Christoph Kapeller, "L'architecture de la nouvelle Bibliothèque d'Alexandrie," in Pataut, *La nouvelle Bibliothèque d'Alexandrie*.

19. Hipólito Escolar Sobrino, *La biblioteca de Alejandría* (Madrid: Gredos, 2001).

20. Mustafa El-Abbadi, *La antigua biblioteca de Alejandría: Vida y destino*, trans. José Luis García-Villalba Sotos (Madrid: UNESCO, 1994).

21. Strabo, *Geography*, Book XVII.

22. Franz Kafka, *Die Erzählungen: Originalfassung* (Frankfurt am Main: S. Fischer Verlag, 2000).

23. See Saint Augustine, *The City of God*, trans. Henry Bettenson, Book XXI:9 (Harmondsworth, Middlesex: Penguin, 1984).

24. Escolar Sobrino, *La biblioteca de Alejandría.*

25. Quoted in Canfora, *La biblioteca scomparsa.*

26. Geo. Haven Putnam, A.M., *Books and Their Makers during the Middle Ages*, Vol. I (reprint) (New York: Hillary House, 1962).

27. *"Le monde est fait pour aboutir à un beau livre,"* Stéphane Mallarmé, in "Réponses à des enquêtes, Sur l'évolution littéraire," in *Proses diverses* (Paris: Gallimard, 1869).

28. Joseph Brodsky, "In a Room and a Half," in *Less Than One* (New York: Farrar, Straus & Giroux, 1986).

29. I discuss this project in my chapter "Peter Eisenman: The Image As Memory," in *Reading Pictures* (Toronto: Alfred A. Knopf, 2000).

30. Quoted in Escolar Sobrino, *La biblioteca de Alejandría.*

31. Quoted in Roberto Calasso, *I quarantanove gradini* (Milano: Adelphi, 1991).

32. These references are from Canfora, *La biblioteca scomparsa.*

33. *"Polvo serán, mas polvo enamorado,"* Francisco de Quevedo, in "Amor constante meas allá de la muerte," in *Antología poética* (selected by, and with a prologue by, Jorge Luis Borges) (Madrid: Alianza Editorial, 1982).

THE LIBRARY AS ORDER

34. Pepys bequeathed to Magdalene College, Cambridge, exactly three thousand numbered volumes, beginning with the smallest and ending with the largest.

35. Pliny the Younger, *Letters I–X*, ed. R.A.B. Mynors, II:17:8 (Oxford: Oxford University Press, 1963).

36. "*Sa chambre de douleur était un arc-en-ciel . . . réservant à l'oeil et au souvenir des surprises et des bonheurs attendus,*" Michel Melot, in *La sagesse du bibliothécaire* (Paris: L'oeil neuf éditions, 2004).

37. Georges Perec, in *Penser/Classer* (Paris: Hachette, 1985).

38. Benjamin, "Unpacking My Library."

39. John Wells, *Rude Words: A Discursive History of the London Library* (Macmillan: London, 1991).

40. Terry Belanger, *Lunacy and the Arrangement of Books* (New Castle, DE: Oak Knoll Books, 1985).

41. G.K. Chesterton, "Lunacy and Letters," in *On Lying in Bed and Other Essays,* selected by Alberto Manguel (Calgary: Bayeux Arts, 2000).

42. Jean-Pierre Drège, *Les bibliothèques en Chine au temps des manuscrits* (Paris: École française d'Extrême-Orient, 1991).

43. W.F. Mayers, "Bibliography of the Chinese Imperial Collection of Literature," *China Review,* Vol. VI, no. 4 (London, 1879).

44. Michel Foucault, *Les mots et les choses* (Paris: Gallimard, 1966). Foucault considers this kind of eclectic list a "distortion of classification that prevents us from conceiving it [the classification]" ("*cette distorsion du classement qui nous empêche de le penser* ").

45. Wolfgang Bauer, "The Encyclopaedia in China," *Cahiers d'histoire mondiale,* Vol. IX, no. 3 (Paris, 1966).

46. Sergei A. Shuiskii, "Khallikan," in *Dictionary of the Middle Ages,* ed. Joseph R. Strayer, Vol. 7 (New York: Charles Scribner's Sons, 1986).

47. El-Abbadi, *La Antigua biblioteca de Alejandría.*

48. Dorothy May Norris, *A History of Cataloguing and Cataloguing Methods: 1100–1850, with an Introductory Survey of Ancient Times* (London: Grafton & Co., 1939).

49. Houari Touati, *L'armoire à sagesse: Bibliothèques et collections en Islam* (Paris: Aubier, 2003).

50. Diogenes Laertius, *Lives of Eminent Philosophers,* trans. R.D.

Hicks, Vol. I:57 (Cambridge, MA, and London: Harvard University Press, 1972).

51. Youssef Eche, *Les bibliothèques arabes publiques et semi-publiques en Mésopotamie, en Syrie et en Egypte au Moyen-âge* (Damascus: Institut français de Damas, 1967).

52. Touati, *L'armoire à sagesse*.

53. Bayard Dodge, *The Fihrist of al-Nadim: A Tenth-Century Survey of Muslim Culture* (New York: Columbia University Press, 1970).

54. D. Mallet, "La bibliothèque d'Avicenne," in *Studia Islamica*, Vol. 83, 1996. Quoted in Touati, *L'armoire à sagesse*.

55. Suetonius, "Julius Caesar," in *The Twelve Caesars*, trans. Robert Graves, rev. ed. (London: Penguin, 1989).

56. Lionel Casson, *Libraries in the Ancient World* (New Haven and London: Yale University Press, 2001).

57. T. Birt, *Die Buchrolle in der Kunst* (Leipzig, 1907).

58. Samuel Pepys, *The Diary of Samuel Pepys, M.A. F.R.S.*, ed. Henry B. Wheatley F.S.A. (19 December, 1666), (London: George Bell & Sons, 1899).

59. Melvil Dewey, "Decimal Classification Beginning," in *Library Journal* 45 (2/15/20). Quoted in Wayne A. Wiegand, *Irrepressible Reformer: A Biography of Melvil Dewey* (Chicago and London: American Library Association, 1996).

60. The latest revision of Dewey's system, the XXI edition of 1998, has altered some of these classifications, so that now, while 200 is still attributed to Religion and 260 to Christian theology, 264 is reserved for Public Worship, and God can be found under three different headings: 211 (Concepts of God), 212 (Existence and Attributes) and 231 (Trinity and Divine Nature). See Lois Mai Chan, John P. Comaromi, Mohinder P. Satija, *Classification décimale de Dewey: guide pratique* (Montréal: Editions ASTED, 1995).

61. Dewey's reading notebook entries, quoted in Wiegand, *Irrepressible Reformer*.

62. Wiegand, *Irrepressible Reformer*.

63. Charles Dickens, *Our Mutual Friend*.

64. Dewey's reading notebook entries, quoted in Wiegand, *Irrepressible Reformer*.

65. The Spanish method of granting priority to the father's surname, e.g., García, doesn't work if the author is known by his second surname.

66. Henry Green, *Pack My Bag: A Self-Portrait* (London: The Hogarth Press, 1940).

THE LIBRARY AS SPACE

67. Jules Verne, *Vingt mille lieues sous les mers* (Paris: Hetzel, 1870). This same passage, in a similar context, is quoted by Perec in *Penser/Classer*. I am grateful to Cyril de Pins for pointing it out to me.

68. Belanger, *Lunacy and the Arrangement of Books*.

69. A.N.L. Munby, *Some Caricatures of Book-Collectors: An Essay* (London: privately printed, 1948); quoted in Belanger, *Lunacy and the Arrangement of Books*.

70. Lewis Carroll, *Sylvie and Bruno* (1889), in *The Complete Works of Lewis Carroll* (London: The Nonesuch Press, 1922).

71. Emanuele Tesauro, *Il cannocchiale aristotelico* (1670) (Savigliano: Editrice artistica Piemontese, 2000).

72. Anthony Grafton, "Une bibliothèque humaniste: Ferrare," in *Le pouvoir des bibliothèques: La mémoire des livres en Occident,* under the direction of Marc Baratin and Christian Jacob (Paris: Albin Michel, 1996).

73. Quoted in Grafton, "Une bibliothèque humaniste: Ferrare."

74. Ibid.

75. Robert D. McFadden, "Recluse buried by paper avalanche," in *The International Herald Tribune* (Paris, 31 December, 2003).

76. See Nicholson Baker, "The Author vs. the Library," *The New Yorker* (New York, 14 October, 1996).

77. Goodrum & Dalrymple, *Guide to the Library of Congress.*

78. Nicholson Baker, *Double Fold: Libraries and the Assault on Paper* (New York: Random House, 2001).

79. Quoted in Baker, *Double Fold,* p. 257.

80. Robin McKie and Vanessa Thorpe, "Digital Domesday Book," in *The Observer* (London, 3 March, 2002).

81. Katie Hafner, "Memories on Computers May Be Lost to Time," in *The International Herald Tribune* (Paris, 28 November, 2004).

82. Robert F. Worth, "Collecting the world's books online," in *The International Herald Tribune* (Paris, 1–2 March, 2003).

83. *The New York Times* (14 December, 2004).

84. Genesis 11:1–9.

85. Marshall McLuhan, *Understanding Media,* I:1 (New York: McGraw-Hill, 1964).

86. Oliver Wendell Holmes, *The Poet at the Breakfast-Table* (London: Dent, 1872).

87. Gabriel Naudé, *Advis pour dresser une bibliothèque, seconde édition revue corrigée & augmentée* (Paris: Chez Rolet le Duc, 1644).

88. Marie-Catherine Rey, "Figurer l'être des hommes," in *Visions du futur: Une histoire des peurs et des espoirs de l'humanité* (Paris: Réunion des Musées Nationaux, 2000).

89. Quoted in P.N. Furbank, *Diderot* (London: Martin Secker & Warburg, 1992).

90. Jean-François Marmontel, in his *Memoirs,* quoted in Furbank, *Diderot.*

91. *"Le but de l'*Encyclopédie *est de rassembler les connaissances éparses sur la surface de la terre; d'en exposer le système général aux hommes qui viendront après nous, afin que les travaux des siècles passés n'aient pas été des travaux inutiles pour les siècles à venir. . . . Que* l'Encyclopédie *devienne un sanctuaire où les connaissances des hommes soient à l'abri des temps et des revolutions."* Denis Diderot, in "Encyclopédie," in D. Diderot et Jean d'Alembert, *L'Encyclopédie,*

ou, *Dictionnaire raisonné des sciences, des arts et des métiers* (Paris, 1751–72).

92. Guillaume Grivel, *L'Isle inconnue, ou Mémoires du chevalier de Gastines. Recueillis et publiés par M. Grivel, des Académies de Dijon, de La Rochelle, de Rouen, de la Société Philosophique de Philadelphie etc.* (Paris: Moutard, 1783–87).

93. Quoted in Furbank, *Diderot*.

94. Ibid.

95. Rebecca Solnit, *Motion Studies: Time, Space and Eadweard Muybridge* (London: Bloomsbury, 2003).

96. Seneca, *The Stoic Philosophy of Seneca: Essays and Letters*, translated by and with an introduction by Moses Hadas (Garden City, NY: Doubleday Anchor, 1958).

97. Gustave Flaubert, *Bouvard et Pécuchet* (Paris: Mercure de France, 1923).

98. Jorge Luis Borges, "La biblioteca total," in *Sur* (Buenos Aires, August 1939), later developed as "La Biblioteca de Babel," in *Ficciones* (Buenos Aires: Sur, 1944).

99. Idem, *El congreso* (Buenos Aires: El Archibrazo, 1971).

THE LIBRARY AS POWER

100. Muhammad b. 'Abd al-Rahman al-'Uthmani, *Idah al-ta'rif bi-ba'd fada'il al-'ilm al-sharif*, Princeton University Library, Yahuda Ms. No. 4293, quoted in Jonathan Berkey, *The Transmission of Knowledge in Medieval Cairo: A Social History of Islamic Education* (Princeton, NJ: Princeton University Press, 1992).

101. Quoted in Hipólito Escolar, *Historia de las bibliotecas* (Madrid: Fundación Germán Sánchez Ruipérez, 1985).

102. Fritz Milkau, *Handbuch der Bibliothekswissenschaft*, ed. Georg Leyh (Wiesbaden: G. Harrassowitz, 1952).

103. Emile Zola, *L'assommoir*.

104. Valéry Giscard d'Estaing, *Le passage* (Paris: Laffont, 1994).

105. Juan Domingo Perón, "Discurso del Presidente de la Nación Argentina General Juan Perón pronunciado en la Academia Argentina de Letras con motivo del Día de la Raza y como homenaje en memoria de Don Miguel de Cervantes Saavedra en el cuarto centenario de su nacimiento" (Buenos Aires, 12 October, 1947).

106. Casson, *Libraries in the Ancient World*.

107. Andrew Carnegie, *The Gospel of Wealth and Other Timely Essays*, ed. Edward C. Kirkland (Cambridge, MA: Harvard University Press, 1962).

108. *Long Overdue: A Library Reader*, ed. Alan Taylor (London and Edinburgh: The Library Association Publishing and Mainstream Publishing Company, 1993).

109. Thomas Carlyle, letter dated 18 May, 1832, in *The Letters of Thomas Carlyle*, ed. Charles Eliot Norton (London: Macmillan, 1888).

110. Joseph Frazier Wall, *Andrew Carnegie* (Oxford and New York: Oxford University Press, 1970).

111. Quoted in John K. Winkler, *Incredible Carnegie* (New York: Vanguard Press, 1931).

112. Thomas Morrison, "Rights of Land," unpublished manuscript quoted in Peter Krass, *Carnegie* (Hoboken, NJ: John Wiley & Sons, 2002).

113. Quoted in Wall, *Andrew Carnegie*.

114. Krass, *Carnegie*.

115. Andrew Carnegie, speech at Grangemouth, Scotland, September 1887, quoted in Burton J. Hendrick, *The Life of Andrew Carnegie* (Garden City, NY: Doubleday, Doran, 1932).

116. Quoted in Krass, *Carnegie*.

117. Quoted in Winkler, *Incredible Carnegie*.

118. Krass, *Carnegie*.

119. Quoted in George S. Bobinski, *Carnegie Libraries* (Chicago: American Library Association, 1969).

120. Krass, *Carnegie*.

121. Andrew Carnegie, *Round the World* (New York: Charles Scribner's Sons, 1884).

122. John Updike, "I Was a Teen-Age Library User," in *Odd Jobs* (London: André Deutsch, 1992).

123. Eudora Welty, *One Writer's Beginnings* (Cambridge, MA and London: Harvard University Press, 1984).

124. H.L. Mencken, *Prejudices: Fourth Series* (New York: Alfred A. Knopf, 1924).

125. Quoted in Bobinski, *Carnegie Libraries*.

THE LIBRARY AS SHADOW

126. Archibald MacLeish, "Of the Librarian's Profession," in *A Time to Speak* (London: Faber, 1941).

127. Georges Roux, *Ancient Iraq* (London: George Allen & Unwin, 1964).

128. David Diringer, *The Book before Printing* (New York: Dover, 1982).

129. Casson, *Libraries in the Ancient World*.

130. Escolar, *Historia de las bibliotecas*.

131. Jean Bottéro, *Mésopotamie. L'écriture, la raison et les dieux* (Paris: Gallimard, 1987).

132. Casson, *Libraries in the Ancient World*.

133. He was also the celebrated author of a treatise on the prostitutes of Attica.

134. Escolar, *Historia de las bibliotecas*.

135. Primo Levi, *The Periodic Table*, trans. Raymond Rosenthal (New York: Schocken, 1984).

136. Brodsky, "To Please a Shadow," in *Less Than One*.

137. Eduardo Anguita and Martín Caparrós, *La voluntad: Una historia de la militancia revolucionaria en la Argentina 1973–1976*, Volume II (Buenos Aires: Norma, 1998).

138. Varlam Chalamov, *Mes bibliothèques*, trans. Sophie Benech (Paris: Editions Interférences, 1988).

139. "Tiene hijos que lo vieron quemar sus libros," in Germán García, *La fortuna* (Buenos Aires: Ediciones de la Flor, 2004).

140. Elisabeth Rosenthal, "Don't Count the Pope among Harry Potter Fans," in *The International Herald Tribune* (Paris, 16–17 July, 2005).

141. William Blake, "The Everlasting Gospel" a.I.13, in *The Complete Poems,* ed. Alicia Ostriker (Harmondsworth, Middlesex: Penguin, 1977).

142. Luciano Canfora, *La Bibliothèque du Patriarche: Photius censuré dans la France de Maʒarin,* trans. Luigi-Alberto Sanchi (Paris: Les Belles Lettres, 2003).

143. See Leo Löwenthal, "Calibans Erbe," in *Schriften IV* (Frankfurt am Main: Suhrkamp Verlag, 1984).

144. The same story is told by the fourteenth-century Tunisian historian Ibn Khaldun, but applied to the Islamic conquest of Persia. According to this version, when General Sa'd ben Waqqas entered the conquered kingdom, he found large numbers of books and asked Omar Ibn al-Kdattab if he should distribute this loot among the faithful. Omar replied, "Throw them into the water! If they hold a guide to the Truth, God has already given us a better one. And if they hold nothing but lies, God will have rid us of them." That, says Ibn Khaldun, is how we lost the knowledge of the Persians. In Ibn Khaldun, *Al-Muqaddima: Discours sur l'histoire universelle* (Paris: Sindbad, 1967–68).

145. Thanks to Irving Wardle for suggesting this poem by A.D. Hope, in *Collected Poems 1930–1970* (Sydney: Angus & Robertson, 1972).

146. William H. Prescott, *History of the Conquest of Mexico and History of the Conquest of Peru* (orig. 1843–1847) (New York: Random House, Modern Library, 1986).

147. Jacques Lafaye, *Albores de la imprenta: El libro en España y Portugal y sus posesiones de ultramar (siglos XV–XVI)* (Mexico: Fondo de Cultura Económica, 2002). A *maravedi* was worth 14 shillings.

148. Richard E. Greenleaf, *Zumárraga y la Inquisición mexicana 1536–1543,* trans. Victor Villela (Mexico: Fondo de Cultura Económica, 1998).

149. See Miguel León Portilla, *El reverso de la conquista* (Mexico: Editorial Joaquín Motiz, 1964).

150. Diego Durán, *Historia de las Indias de Nueva España y Islas de la Tierra Firme,* I: Introduction, quoted in Tzvetan Todorov, *La conquête de l'Amérique* (Paris: Editions du Seuil, 1982).

151. Tacitus, *Annales,* trans. after Burnouf, and annotated by Henri Bornecque (Paris: Garnier Frères, 1965).

152. Eche, *Les bibliothèques arabes publiques et semi-publiques en Mésopotamie.*

153. A large number of the Corvina books were spared because they had been stored in the royal castle of Buda, which the Turks found it unseemly to burn down. See Csaba Csapodi & Klára Csapodi-Gárdonyi, *Bibliotheca Corviniana* (Budapest: Magyar Helikon, 1967).

154. Johannes Pedersen, *Den Arabiske Bog* (Copenhagen: Gyldendal, 1946).

155. *Le Monde* (Paris, 4 September, 1995).

156. Lawrence Donegan, "Anger as CIA homes in on new target: library users," in *The Observer* (London, 16 March, 2003).

157. Richard F. Tomasson, *Iceland: The First New Society* (Minneapolis: University of Minnesota Press, 1980).

158. Joseph Kahn, "Yahoo helped Chinese to prosecute journalist," in *The International Herald Tribune* (Paris, 8 September, 2005).

THE LIBRARY AS SHAPE

159. Tom Stoppard, *The Invention of Love* (London & Boston: Faber & Faber, 1997); Act I.

160. Seneca, *The Stoic Philosophy of Seneca.*

161. *"Un bibliothécaire est toujours un peu architecte. Il bâtit sa collection comme un ensemble à travers lequel le lecteur doit circuler, se reconnaître, vivre."* Melot, *La sagesse du bibliothécaire.*

162. Angelo Paredi, *A History of the Ambrosiana.* trans. Constance and Ralph McInerny (Notre Dame, IN: University Press of Notre Dame, 1983).

163. Johannes Duft, *The Abbey Library of Saint Gall* (St. Gallen: Verlag am Klosterhof, 1990).

164. Simone Balayé, *La bibliothèque nationale des origines à 1800* (Geneva: Droz, 1988).

165. The objection was made by Count Léon de Laborde, quoted in Bruno Blasselle and Jacqueline Melet-Sanson, *La bibliothèque nationale, mémoire de l'avenir* (Paris: Gallimard, 1991).

166. Blasselle and Melet-Sanson, *La bibliothèque nationale.*

167. P.R. Harris, *The Reading Room* (London: The British Library, 1986).

168. Ibid.

169 William E. Wallace, *Michelangelo at San Lorenzo: The Genius as Entrepreneur* (Cambridge & New York: Cambridge University Press, 1994).

170. H.M. Vaughan, *The Medici Popes, Leo X and Clement VII* (London: Macmillan, 1908).

171. *Rime e lettere di Michelangelo,* ed. P. Mastrocola (Turin: UTET, 1992).

172. Quoted in Wallace, *Michelangelo at San Lorenzo.*

173. *"Quand'avvien c'alcun legno non difenda/ il proprio umor fuor del terrestre loco,/ non può far c'al gran caldo assai o poco/ non si secchi o non s'arda o non s'accenda.// Così'l cor, tolto da chi mai mel renda,/ vissuto in pianto e nutrito di foco,/ o ch'è fuor del suo proprio albergo e loco,/ qual mal fie che per morte non l'offenda?"* in Michelangelo Buonarroti, *Rime,* ed. E.N. Girardi (Bari: Laterza, 1960).

174. Giorgio Vasari, "Michelangelo Buonarroti," in *Lives of the Artists*, Vol. I, trans. George Bull (Harmondsworth, Middlesex: Penguin, 1987).

175. Georges Roux, *Ancient Iraq*, 3d edition (London: George Allen & Unwin Ltd, 1964).

176. Casson, *Libraries in the Ancient World*.

177. See Kenneth Clark, "The Young Michelangelo," in J.H. Plumb, *The Horizon Book of the Renaissance* (London: Collins, 1961).

178. Luca Pacioli, *Divine Proportion* (New York: Abaris, 2005).

THE LIBRARY AS CHANCE

179. Henry James, "The Figure in the Carpet," in *Embarrassments* (London: William Heinemann, 1896).

180. Robert Louis Stevenson, "Travel," in *A Child's Garden of Verses* (London: The Bodley Head, 1896).

181. Théodore Monod, *Méharées* (Arles: Actes Sud, 1989).

182. A.M. Tolba, *Villes de sable: Les cités bibliothèques du désert mauritanien* (Paris: Hazan, 1999).

183. Pausanias, *Guide to Greece*, trans. Peter Levi (Harmondsworth, Middlesex: Penguin, 1971); Vol. II, VI:6.

184. Jacques Giès and Monique Cohen, "Introduction" to *Sérinde, Terre de Bouddha* (Paris: Réunion des Musées Nationaux, 1995).

185. Susan Whitfield and Ursula Sims-Williams (ed.), *The Silk Road: Trade, Travel, War and Faith* (London: British Library, 2004).

186. Pieces shown in Giès and Cohen, *Sérinde, Terre de Bouddha*, and in Whitfield and Sims-Williams, *The Silk Road*.

187. Liu Jung-en, ed., introduction to *Six Yuan Plays* (Harmondsworth, Middlesex: Penguin, 1972).

188. Mark Aurel Stein, *Serindia*, Vol. I (Oxford: Oxford University Press, 1921).

189. Quoted in Whitfield and Sims-Williams, *The Silk Road*.

190. Battista Guarino, "A Program of Teaching and Learning," in *Humanist Educational Treatises,* ed. and trans. Craig W. Kallendorf (Cambridge, MA, and London: Harvard University Press, 2002).

191. Dora Thornton, *The Scholar in His Study: Ownership and Experience in Renaissance Italy* (New Haven & London: Yale University Press, 1997).

192. Jacob Burckhardt, *The Civilization of the Renaissance in Italy,* trans. S.G.C. Middlemore (London, 1878).

193. Cicero, "Cicero to Atticus, April 59," in *Selected Letters,* trans. D.R. Shackelton Bailey (London: Penguin, 1986).

194. "Cicero to Atticus, 10 March 45," ibid.

195. Virginia Woolf, *A Room of One's Own* (London: The Hogarth Press, 1929).

196. N. Sanz and Ruiz de la Peña, *La Casa de Cervantes en Valladolid* (Valladolid: Fundaciones Vega-Inclán, 1993).

197. Miguel de Cervantes Saavedra, *El ingenioso hidalgo Don Quijote de la Mancha,* ed. Celina S. de Cortazar and Isaías Lerner (Buenos Aires: EUDEBA, 1969); I:VI.

198. Jorge Luis Borges, "Poema de los dones," in *El hacedor* (Buenos Aires: Emecé, 1960).

199. Jorge Luis Borges, "Autobiographical notes," in *The New Yorker* (New York, 19 September, 1970).

200. Borges, "Al iniciar el estudio de la gramática anglosajona," in *El hacedor.*

201. Seneca, *The Stoic Philosophy of Seneca.*

202. William Blake, "Milton," Pl.35, 42–45 in *The Complete Poems,* ed. Alicia Ostriker (Harmondsworth, Middlesex: Penguin, 1977).

203. Badr al-Din Muhammed Ibn Jama'a, *Tadhkirat al-sami,'* quoted in Berkey, *The Transmission of Knowledge in Medieval Cairo.*

204. Nasir al-Din Tusi, *Risala,* ibid.

205. Quoted in Robert Irwin, *Night & Horses & the Desert: An Anthology of Classical Arabic Literature* (London: Allen Lane/The Penguin Press, 1999).

THE LIBRARY AS MIND

206. Niccolò Machiavelli, *The Literary Works of Machiavelli,* ed. John Hale (Oxford: Oxford University Press, 1961).

207. Philippe Ariès, *Essais sur l'histoire de la mort ven occident: du moyen âge à nos jours* (Paris: Seuil, 1975).

208. Revelation 20:12.

209. See Berkey, *The Transmission of Knowledge in Medieval Cairo.*

210. Toni Cassirer, *Mein Leben mit Ernst Cassirer,* Hildesheim, 1981, quoted in Salvatore Settis, "Warburg *continuatus,*" in *Le pouvoir des bibliothèques: La mémoire des livres en Occident,* ed. Marc Baratin and Christian Jacob (Paris: Albin Michel, 1996).

211. Ernst Cassirer, "Der Begriff der symbolischen Form im Aufbau der Geisteswissenschaften," in *Vorträge der Bibliothek Warburg,* I, 1921–1922 (Leipzig & Berlin, 1923).

212. *"Ein kleiner Herr mit schwarzem Schnurrbart der manchmal Dialektgeschichten erzählt,"* quoted in Ernst Gombrich, *Aby Warburg: An Intellectual Biography* (London: The Warburg Institute, University of London, 1970). I have revised Gombrich's English translation.

213. *"dadurch offenbar das Mittel gefunden, mich von einer erschüttern-den Gegenwart, die mich wehrlos machte, abzuziehen. . . . Die Schmerzempfindung reagierte sich ab in der Fantasie des Romantisch-Grausamen. Ich machte da die Schutzimpfung gegen das aktiv Grausame durch . . . ,"* in Aby Warburg, *Notes for Lecture on Serpent Ritual,* 1923, pp. 16–18, quoted in Gombrich, *Aby Warburg.*

214. Ron Chernow, *The Warburgs* (New York: Random House, 1993).

215. Johann Wolfgang von Goethe, *Dichtung und Wahrheit,* II:8 in *Goethes Werke,* Band IX, Autobiographische Schriften I, Ed. Liselotte Blumenthal (Munich: Verlag C.H. Beck, 1994).

216. Ernst Cassirer, "Der Begriff der symbolischen Form im Aufbau der Geisteswissenschaften."

217. As Gombrich notes.

218. *"Das Gedächtnis als organisierte Materie,"* in Ewald Hering, *Über das Gedächtnis als eine allgemeine Funktion der organisierten Materie* (Lecture, Akademie der Wissenschaften in Vienna, 30 May, 1870), 3 ed. (Leipzig, 1921).

219. The story of the controversy is told by Salvatore Settis in "Warburg *continuatus,"* in *Quaderni storici,* 58/a XX, no. 1, (April 1985).

220. Fritz Saxl, "The History of Warburg's Library (1886–1944)," appendix to Gombrich, *Aby Warburg.*

221. *"Aalsuppenstil,"* quoted in Gombrich, *Aby Warburg.*

222. Richard Semon, *Die Mneme als erhaltendes Princip im Wechsel des organischen Geschehens,* 2d ed. (Leipzig: W. Engelman, 1908).

223. *"Gespenstergeschichte für ganz Erwachsene."* Aby Warburg, *Grundbegriffe,* I, p.3, quoted in Gombrich, *Aby Warburg.*

224. *"das Nachleben der Antike,"* quoted in Gombrich, *Aby Warburg.*

225. *"Wie ein Seismograph hatten seine empfindlichen Nerven die unterirdischen Erschütterungen schon dann verzeichnet, als andere sie noch völlig überhörten."* Carl Georg Heise, in *Persönliche Erinnerungen an Aby Warburg* (Hamburg: Gesellschaft der Bücherfreunde, 1959).

226. *"Du lebst und tust mir nichts."*

227. *"Die Wiederbelebung der dämonischen Antike vollzieht sich dabei, wie wir sahen, durch eine Art polarer Funktion des einfühlenden Bildgedächtnisses. Wir sind im Zeitalter des Faust, wo sich der moderne Wissenschaftler—zwischen magischer Praktik und kosmologischer Mathematik—den Denkraum der Besonnenheit zwischen sich und dem Objekt zu erringen versuchte."* Aby Warburg, *Gesammelte Schriften,* II:534, quoted in Gombrich, *Aby Warburg.*

228. I'm grateful to Professor W.F. Blisset for this information.

229. *"warum das Schicksal den schöpferischen Menschen in die Region der ewigen Unruhe verweist, ihm überlassend ob er seine Bildung im Inferno, Purgatorio oder Paradiso findet."* Aby Warburg, in *Schlussübung,* Notebook 1927–28, pp. 68–69, quoted in Gombrich, *Aby Warburg.*

230. Aby Warburg, *Le rituel du serpent: récit d'un voyage en pays pueblo,* introduction by Joseph Leo Koerner, text by Fritz Saxl and de Benedetta Cestelli Guidi, trans. Sibylle Muller, Philip Guiton and Diane H. Bodart (Paris: Macula, 2003).

231. *"Die Bilder und Worte sollen für die Nachkommenden eine Hilfe sein bei dem Versuch der Selbstbesinnung zur Abwehr der Tragik der Gespanntheit zwischen triebhafter Magie und auseinandersetzender Logik. Die Konfession eines (unheilbaren) Schizoiden, den Seelenärtzen ins Archiv gegeben."* Aby Warburg, *Note 7,* quoted in Gombrich, *Aby Warburg.*

232. *"Annahme des Kunstwerkes als etwas in Richtung auf den Zuschauer feindlich Bewegtes."* Aby Warburg, in *Fragmente* (27 August, 1890).

THE LIBRARY AS ISLAND

233. See William V. Harris, *Ancient Literacy* (Cambridge, MA, and London: Harvard University Press, 1989).

234. W. Jaeger, *Aristotle,* trans. R. Robinson (Oxford: Clarendon Press, 1948).

235. Plato, "Phaedrus," trans. R. Hackforth, in *The Collected Dialogues* (Princeton, NJ: Princeton University Press, 1961).

236. "They read your will: they choose it to be theirs: they cherish it. They read it without cease and what they read never passes away. For it is your own unchanging purpose that they read, choosing to make it their own and cherishing it for themselves." Saint Augustine, *Confessions,* translated by and with an introduction by

R.S. Pine-Coffin (Harmondsworth, Middlesex: Penguin, 1961);
Book XIII:15.

237. Johann Wolfgang von Goethe, *Maximen und Reflexionen,*
no. 838 in *Goethes Werke,* ed. Hans Joachim Schrimpf (Munich:
Verlag C.H. Beck, 1981); Vol. XII.

238. Ecclesiastes 12:12.

239. Adolfo Bioy Casares, "Libros y amistad," in *La otra aventura*
(Buenos Aires: Galerna, 1968).

240. Walter Benjamin, *The Arcades Project,* trans. Howard Eiland
and Kevin McLaughlin (London: Harvard University Press, 1999).

241. Nicholas de Cusa, *"De docta ignorantia,"* in *Selected Spiritual
Writings,* translated and introduced by H. Lawrence Bond (New
York: Paulist Press, 2005).

242. Julie Flaherty, "New Testament on a Chip," in *The New York
Times* (New York, 23 June, 2003).

243. Announced on the BBC evening news, 26 May, 2003.

244. The Venerable Bede, *The Ecclesiastical History of the English
Nation,* Book II, chapter XIII, in *Opera Historica,* Vol. I, ed. J.E.
King (Cambridge, MA, and London: Harvard University Press and
William Heinemann Ltd, 1971).

245. Bill Gates, *The Road Ahead* (New York: Penguin, 1996).

246. Walter Benjamin, *Schriften,* edited by and with an introduction
by Hannah Arendt (Frankfurt am Main: Suhrkamp Verlag, 1955).

247. *The International Herald Tribune* (Paris, 18 January, 1999).

248. Will Eisner, interview on France Info Radio, broadcast 19
December, 2004.

249. Paul Duguid, "PG Tips," in *The Times Literary Supplement*
(London, 11 June, 2004).

250. Garrick Mallery, *Picture Writing of the American Indians*
(Washington, 1893).

251. "Mucho más que libros," *Semana* (Bogotá, 4 June, 2001).

252. Personal interview, Bogotá, 25 May, 2001.

253. Philip Friedman, *Roads to Extinction: Essays on the Holocaust,*
ed. Ada June Friedman (New York and Philadelphia: The Jewish
Publication Society of America, 1980).

THE LIBRARY AS SURVIVAL

254. Tuvia Borzykowski, *Ben kirot noflim,* trans. Mosheh Basok
(Tel Aviv: Ha-Kibbuts ha-Meuhad, 1964).

255. William L. Shirer, *The Rise and Fall of the Third Reich: A History
of Nazi Germany* (New York: Simon and Schuster, 1960).

256. Quoted in Friedman, "The Fate of the Jewish Book," in *Roads
to Extinction.*

257. Donald E. Collins and Herbert P. Rothfeder, "The Einsatzstab
Reichsleiter Rosenberg and the Looting of Jewish and Masonic
Libraries During World War II," in *Journal of Library History* 18,
1983.

258. Founded by the exiled son-in-law of Samuel Fischer, the celebrated German publisher.

259. Quoted in Friedman, "The Fate of the Jewish Book," in *Roads
to Extinction.*

260. Nili Keren, "The Family Camp" in *Anatomy of the Auschwitz
Death Camp,* ed. Yisrael Gutman and Michael Birnbaum
(Bloomington, IN: Indiana University Press, 1994), quoted in David
Shavit, *Hunger for the Printed Word: Books and Libraries in the Jewish
Ghettos of Nazi-Occupied Europe* (Jefferson, NC, and London:
McFarland & Co., 1997).

261 Shavit, *Hunger for the Printed Word.*

262. *"Mensh, oyf tsu shraybn geshikhte darf men hobn a kop un nisht
keyn tukhes,"* quoted in Yitzhak Zuckerman, "Antek," in *A Surplus of
Memory: Chronicle of the Warsaw Ghetto Uprising,* trans. and ed.
Barbara Harshav (Berkeley and Los Angeles: University of
California Press, 1993).

263. Quoted in Shavit, *Hunger for the Printed Word.*

264. Deborah Dwork, *Children with a Star: Jewish Youth in Nazi Europe* (New Haven, CT: Yale University Press, 1991).

265. Moshe Kligsberg, *"Die yidishe yugent-bavegnung in Polyn tsvishn beyde vel-milkhumes (a sotsyologishe shtudie),"* in *Studies in Polish Jewry 1919–1939*, ed. Joshua A. Fishman (New York: YIVO Institute for Jewish Research, 1974).

266. Graham Greene, *The Heart of the Matter* (London: Heinemann, 1948).

267. Diary of Johann Paul Kremer (entry for 2 September, 1942), ed. Kazimierz Smolen, in *KL Auschwitz seen by the SS*, second edition (O'swieçim, 1978), quoted in Martin Gilbert, *The Holocaust* (London: William Collins, 1986).

268. Martin Buber, *Die Erzählungen der Chassidim* (Frankfurt am Main: Manesse Verlag, 1949).

269. Victor Hugo, *Inferi: La légende des siècles* (Paris, 1883).

270. Romain Gary, *La danse de Genghis Cohn* (Paris: Gallimard, 1967).

271. *Nunca Más: A Report by Argentina's National Commission on Disappeared People* (London and Boston: Faber & Faber in association with Index on Censorship, 1986).

272. Amin Maalouf, *Les croisades vues par les Arabes* (Paris: Editions Jean-Claude Lattès, 1983).

273. Carole Hillenbrand, *The Crusades: Islamic Perspectives* (New York: Routledge, 2000).

274. Dante, *Inferno*, XXXIV, 129–132.

275. Quoted in Gilbert, *The Holocaust*.

THE LIBRARY AS OBLIVION

276. Virgil, *Eclogues, Georgics, Aeneid I-VI*, ed. and trans. H. Rushton Fairclough (Cambridge, MA, and London: Harvard University Press, 1974).

277. Robert Musil, *Der Mann ohne Eigenschaften* (Berlin: Ernst Rowohlt, 1930).

278. Flann O'Brien, "Buchhandlung," in *The Best of Myles* (London: Picador, 1974).

279. Edward Gibbon, *The History of the Decline and Fall of the Roman Empire*, edited by and with an introduction and appendices by David Womersley (London: Allen Lane/The Penguin Press, 1994); Vol. I, chapter 7.

280. Harald Weinrich, *Lethe. Kunst und Kritik des Vergessens* (Munich: C.H. Beck'sche Verlagsbuchhandlung, 1997).

281. "Shah Muhammad, libraire," in *Le Monde* (Paris, 28 November, 2001). Curiously, a year after this article appeared, the Norwegian journalist Åsne Seierstad published her account of an Afghani bookseller's life under the title *The Bookseller of Kabul*. Seierstad's hero is given the name Sultan Khan but many of the incidents and quotations are the same.

282. Andrew Murray, foreword to *Presbyterians and the Negro: A History* (Philadelphia: Presbyterian Historical Society, 1966).

283. Booker T. Washington, *Up from Slavery* (1901).

284. Janet Duitsman Cornelius, *"When I Can Read My Title Clear": Literacy, Slavery, and Religion in the Antebellum South* (Columbia, SC: University of South Carolina Press, 1991).

285. Eliza Atkins Gleason, *The Southern Negro and the Public Library* (Chicago: University of Chicago Press, 1941).

286. James Baldwin, *Go Tell It on the Mountain* (New York: Alfred A. Knopf, 1953).

287. Nina Berberova, *La disparition de la bibliothèque de Turgeniev* (Arles: Actes Sud, 1999).

288. Interview with Dr. Irene Kupferschmitt, Montreal, 3 May, 2004. Unpublished.

289. Robert Fisk, "Library books, letters and priceless documents are set ablaze," in *The Independent* (London, 15 April, 2003).

290. Irwin, *Night & Horses & the Desert*.

291. Jabbar Yassin Hussin, *Le lecteur de Bagdad* (Aude: Atelier du Gué, 2000).

292. Johannes Pedersen, *Den Arabiske Bog* (Copenhagen: Gyldendal, 1946).

293. Milbry Polk and Angela M.H. Schuster (ed.), *The Looting of the Iraq Museum, Baghdad: The Lost Legacy of Ancient Mesopotamia* (New York: Harry N. Abrams, 2005).

294. Luciano Canfora, *Il copista come autore* (Palermo: Sellerio editore, 2002).

295. Jean Bottéro, *Mésopotamie.*

THE LIBRARY AS IMAGINATION

296. Henry Fielding, *Amelia*, I:10 (1752), Vol. VI and VII of *The Complete Works of Henry Fielding, Esq.* (London: William Heinemann, 1903).

297. Ginzberg, *The Legends of the Jews;* vol. I, p. 5.

298. "The sun itself is but the dark simulacrum, and light but the shadow of God." Sir Thomas Browne, *The Garden of Cyrus,* II.

299. Dylan Thomas, "Do Not Go Gentle into That Good Night," in *Collected Poems 1934–1952* (London: Dent, 1952).

300. Shakespeare, *Othello,* V:2.

301. Van Wyck Brooks, *The Flowering of New England: 1815–1865* (New York: E.P. Dutton & Co., 1936).

302. Christmas Humphreys, *Buddhism* (Harmondsworth, Middlesex: Penguin, 1951).

303. In conversation with the author.

304. Borges, "Autobiographical Notes," in *The New Yorker.*

305. Idem., "Poema de los dones," in *El hacedor.*

306. Idem., "Examen de la obra de Herbert Quain," "El acercamiento a Almostásim," "Tlön, Uqbar, Orbis Tertius," in *El jardín de senderos que se bifurcan* (Buenos Aires: Sur, 1941); "El milagro secreto," in *Ficciones;* "El libro de arena," in *El libro de arena* (Buenos Aires: Emecé, 1975).

307. François Rabelais, *Gargantua and Pantagruel,* trans. Sir Thomas Urquhart and Pierre Le Motteux (1693–94), introduction by Terence Cave (New York & Toronto: Alfred A. Knopf, 1994).

308. Henri Lefebvre, *Rabelais* (Paris: Editeurs français réunis, 1955).

309. Antonine Maillet, *Rabelais et les traditions populaires en Acadie* (Laval: Les Presses Université de Laval, 1971).

310. Lucien Febvre, *Le problème de l'incroyance au seizième siècle: La religion de Rabelais* (Paris: Albin Michel, 1942).

311. Jean Plattard, *La vie et l'oeuvre de Rabelais* (Paris: Boivin, 1930).

312. Mijail Bajtin, *La cultura popular en la edad media y en el Renacimiento: El contexto de françois rabelais,* trans. Julio Forcat and César Conroy (Madrid: Alianza Editorial, 1987).

313. Edwin H. Carpenter, Jr., *Some Libraries We Have Not Visited: A Paper Read at the Rounce & Coffin Club, August 26, 1947* (Pasadena, CA: Ampersand Press, 1947).

314. Sir Thomas Browne, "Tract XIII," in *Certain Miscellany Tracts* (London, 1684).

315. Carpenter, *Some Libraries We Have Not Visited.*

316. *"Qu'est-ce que tu fais, Paul?" "Je travaille. Je travaille de mon métier. Je suis attaché au catalogue de la Nationale, je relève des titres." "Oh. . . . Tu peux faire cela de mémoire?" "De mémoire? Où serait le mérite? Je fais mieux. J'ai constaté que la Nationale est pauvre en ouvrages latins et italiens du XVe siècle. . . . En attendant que la chance et l'érudition les comblent, j'inscris les titres d'oeuvres extrèmement intéressantes, qui auraient dû être écrits . . . qu'au moins les titres sauvent le prestige du catalogue. . . ." "Mais . . . puisque les livres n'existent pas?" "Ah!" dit-il, avec un geste frivole, "je ne peux pas tout faire!"* Colette, in *Mes apprentissages* (Paris: Ferenczi et fils, 1936).

317. Rudyard Kipling, "The Finest Story in the World," in *Many Inventions* (London: Macmillan & Co., 1893).

318. The *Necronomicon* is first mentioned in a 1922 Lovecraft story, "The Hound"; the location of a copy is detailed in "The

Festival" (1923). Both stories are collected in L.P. Lovecraft and Others, *Tales of the Cthulhu Mythos* (Sauk City: Arkham House, 1969).

319. H.P. Lovecraft, *A History of the Necronomicon,* (Oakman, AL: Rebel Press, 1938).

320. H.P. Lovecraft and August Derleth, "The Shadow Out of Space," in *The Shuttered Room* (London: Victor Gollancz, 1968).

321. Verne, *Vingt mille lieues sous les mers.*

322. Shakespeare, *As You Like It,* II:1.

323. Carlo Collodi, *Le avventure di Pinocchio,* ed. Ornella Castellani Pollidori (Pescia: Fondazione nazionale Carlo Collodi, 1983).

324. Information provided by the director of the Provincial Archives of Oulu, Ms. Vuokko Joki.

325. Timothy W. Ryback, "Hitler's Forgotten Library: The Man, His Books and His Search for God," in *The Atlantic Monthly* (May 2003).

THE LIBRARY AS IDENTITY

326. The idea was proposed by K.W. Humphreys in his splendid Panizzi lectures. See K.W. Humphreys, *A National Library in Theory and in Practice* (London: The British Library, 1987), which I have closely followed for this chapter.

327. U. Dotti, *Vita di Petrarca* (Rome and Bari: Laterza, 1987).

328. Quoted by Humphreys in *A National Library in Theory and in Practice.*

329. Ibid.

330. Harris, *The Reading Room.*

331. Quoted by Humphreys in *A National Library in Theory and in Practice.*

332. *Report from the Select Committee on the British Museum together with the Minutes of Evidence, appendix and index* (London: House of Commons, 14 July, 1836), quoted by Humphreys in *A National Library in Theory and in Practice.*

333. Edward Miller, *Prince of Librarians: The Life and Times of Antonio Panizzi* (London: The British Library Publications, 1988).

334. Edmund Gosse, "A First Sight of Tennyson," in *Portraits and Sketches* (London: William Heinemann, 1912).

335. Quoted by Ann Thwaite in *Edmund Gosse: A Literary Landscape* (London: Martin Secker and Warburg, 1984).

336. Quoted by Humphreys in *A National Library in Theory and in Practice.*

337. Quoted by Harris in *The Reading Room.*

338. Judith Flanders, "The British Library's Action Plan," in *The Times Literary Supplement* (London, 2 September, 2005).

339. Lucien Febvre and Henri-Jean Martin, *L'apparition du livre* (Paris: Albin Michel, 1958).

340. Maud Stéphan-Hachem, *La Bibliothèque Nationale du Liban, entre les aléas de l'histoire et l'acharnement de quelques-uns.* (Paris: Bulletin des bibliothèques de France, ENSSIB, January 2005).

341. Blaine Harden, "For Immigrants, U.S. Still Starts at a Library," in *The International Herald Tribune* (Paris, 29 April, 1998).

THE LIBRARY AS HOME

342. Bram Stoker, *Dracula,* introduction, notes and bibliography by Leonard Wolf (New York: Clarkson Potter, 1975), chapter 3.

343. Ibid., chapter 2.

344. Mary Shelley, *Frankenstein,* introduction and notes by Leonard Wolf (New York: Clarkson Potter, 1977); Vol. II, chapter 4.

345. Ibid., volume III, chapter 7.

346. Ibid., volume II, chapter 4.

347. Ibid., chapter 6.

348. These words ("Did I request thee, Maker, from my clay/ To mould me man? Did I solicit thee/ From darkness to promote me?") are from *Paradise Lost,* Book 3, and were set as an epigraph on the title page of the first volume of Shelley's *Frankenstein.* Leonard

Wolf, annotator of Mary Shelley's novel, has this to say about the monster's touching, perfect words: "As an epigraph (or an epitaph) for humanity, 'Pardon this intrusion' is unsurpassed."

349. Shelley, *Frankenstein*, volume II, chapter 7.

350. Seneca, "On the Shortness of Life," in *The Stoic Philosophy of Seneca.*

351. Plutarch, *Moralia*, Vol. IV, ed. and trans. Frank Cole Babbitt (Cambridge, MA, and London: Harvard University Press and William Heinemann Ltd, 1972).

352. Dante, *De vulgari eloquentia*, introduction, translation and notes by Vittorio Coletti (Milan: Garzanti, 1991).

353. Erasmus von Rotterdam, "Adagen" (*Festina lente*), in *Ausgewählte Schriften*, ed. W. Welzig (Darmstadt: Wissenschaftliche Buchgesellschaft, 1967–1969); II:I:I.

354. Steven Wilson, *Related Strangers: Jewish-Christian Relations, 70 to 170 CE* (Philadelphia: Fortress Press, 1995).

355. *"Alors que dans la modalité du temps, elle présentifiait l'Antiquité grecque et arabe comme modèles culturels exemplaires, dans celle de l'espace, elle s'acharnait à réunir ce qui était dispersé et à rapprocher ce qui était éloigné." "Rendre visible l'invisible . . . ce souci de possession du monde."* Touati, *L'armoire à sagesse.*

356. *"Défiez-vous de ces cosmopolites qui vont chercher loin dans leurs livres des devoirs qu'ils dédaignent de remplir autour d'eux. Tel philosophe aime les Tartares, pour être dispensé d'aimer ses voisins."* Jean-Jacques Rousseau, *Émile ou de l'éducation*, Book I.

357. Thomas Traherne, *Centuries of Meditations* (London, 1908); I:29.

358. Hermann Broch, *Der Tod des Vergil* (1945).

359. Sir Thomas Browne, *Religio Medici*, edited with an introduction by Geoffrey Keynes (London: Thomas Nelson & Sons, 1940); I:6.

360. Richard Rorty, "The Inspirational Value of Great Works of Literature," in *Raritan*, volume 16, no. 1 (New Brunswick, NJ: 1996).

361. Naudé, *Advis pour dresser une bibliothèque.*

362. *El libro de los veinticuatro filósofos,* ed. Paolo Lucentini, trans. Cristina Serna and Jaume Pòrtulas (Madrid: Siruela, 2000).

363. I thank Edgardo Cozarinsky for this information. Vladimir Nabokov/Elena Sikorskaja, *Nostalgia,* letter of 9 October, 1945 (Milano: Rosellina Archinto, 1989).

364. *"La présence de la bibliothèque est le signe que l'univers est encore tenu pour pensable."* Jean Roudaut, *Les dents de Bérénice: Essai sur la représentation et l'évocation des bibliothèques* (Paris: Deyrolle Éditeur, 1996).

365. The First Epistle General of John, 2:16.

366. Penelope Fitzgerald, *The Blue Flower* (London: HarperCollins, 1995).

367. Northrop Frye, *Notebooks.*

Image Credits

Title page (Pp. ii–iii) Aby Warburg's Library, Author's collection; P. 1 inscription, Author's collection; P. 8, *top* library at Le Presbytère, Author's collection; *bottom* library of the Colegio Nacional de Buenos Aires, Author's collection; P. 10 stained-glass window, Author's collection; P. 11 Long Hall library, Author's collection; P. 13 boat palace, photograph provided by www.downtheroad.org The Ongoing Global Bicycle Adventure; P. 16 Montaigne's tower, photograph, Michael Sympson; P. 21 tower of Babel, Copyright © The British Library, Egerton, 1894; P. 23 Library of Alexandria, Mohamed Nafea / Bibliotheca Alexandrina; P. 38 Pepys's bookcase, courtesy of http://www.furniturestyles.net/european/english/misc/oak-bookcase-pepys.jpg; P. 46 *literatura de cordel,* Author's collection; P. 48 Yongle Dadian, © Wason Collection on East Asia, Cornell University; P. 57 scroll shelf, Author's collection; P. 58 Melvil Dewey, © 2003, from Encyclopedia of Library and Information Science by Winifred B. Linderman. Reproduced by permission of Routledge/Taylor & Francis Group, LLC; P. 69 library steps, reprinted from Percy D. Macquoid, *Dictionary of English Furniture,*

(Wappingers' Falls, N.Y., 2000), p. 390; P. 72 Patrice Moore's apartment, courtesy of http://www.gothamist.com/archives/2004/01/06/disposophobia.php; P. 74 Library of Congress, Jim Higgins, Library of Congress; P. 76 Domesday Book, The National Archives, ref. E31/1, E31/2; P. 80, *left* title page, Author's collection; *right* a *stupa*, © The Trustees of the Chester Beatty Library, Dublin; P. 87 "Writing," The Thomas Fisher Rare Book Library/ University of Toronto; P. 93 library at Wolfenbüttel, Ölgemälde der Rotunde, Innenansicht; P. 95 Ashurbanipal, © The Trustees of the British Museum; P. 101 Carnegie cartoon, provided courtesy HarpWeek; P. 103 bookplate, photograph, G. Blaikie; P. 108 a book burning in Warsawa, Indiana, Times-Union (Warsaw, IN); P. 111 book burning cartoon, Author's collection; P. 113 warning sign, Author's collection; P. 119 Archbishop Juan de Zumárraga, courtesy of http://www.latinamericanstudies.org/juan-zumarraga.htm; P. 130 Toronto Reference Library, Toronto Public Library (TRL); P. 132, *top* the King's Library, copyright © The British Library, 60.g.12; *bottom* Biblioteca de Catalunya, photograph, Søren Lauridsen, 2006; Pp. 134–35 (*top*) Freie Universität, © Foster and Partners; P. 135 Bibliothèque Nationale de France, © Dominique Perrault/SODRAC (2006); P. 136, *top* ground plan of the library at Wolfenbüttel, Lambert Rosenbusch, Wolfenbüttel, Former Rotunda of the Library, Figure of Proportion after Serlio, Primo Libro de Geometria p 13v, Nicolini Vinetia (1551) Industrial Design 04, Thomas Helms Verlag Schwerin 2000, p7; *bottom* layout for library in a Carolingian monastery, Author's collection; Pp. 140–41 Boullée's ideal design for a library, Author's collection; P. 142 Salle Labrouste, photography by Diane Asseo Griliches © *Library: The Drama Within* (University of New Mexico Press, 1996); P. 146 Reading Room, Author's collection; P. 147 Panizzi's sketch, Author's collection; P. 148 stalls, Author's collection; P. 150 Michelangelo's sketch, Author's collection; Pp. 154–55 staircase,

Biblioteca Medicea Laurenziana, n. 226/2006, Vesibolo (Scala di Michelangelo)/Microfoto; P. 158 ground plan of Pergamon Library, Author's collection; P. 166 Habott Library, David Sauveur/Agence VU; P. 169 Dunhuang Caves, courtesy of www.worldtravelgate.net; P. 172 Diamond Sutra, copyright © The British Library, Or 8210/P. 2; P. 181 Kipling portrait, Library of Congress, The Carpenter Kipling Collection, (LC-USZ62–59457); P. 195 Last Jugement fresco, photograph, Thomas Hallon Hallbert; P. 198 Aby Warburg, photograph: Warburg Institute; P. 210 Mnemosyne panel, Aby Warburg, Mnemosyne Atlas, panel 32: 'Moreska,' photograph: Warburg Institute; P. 216 Robinson Crusoe, Author's Collection; P. 231 Biblioburro, © Oscar Monsalve, 2005; P. 236 German prayer book, Author's collection; P. 241 Birkenau, Russian State Archives of Film and Video Documents; P. 248 Jacob Edelstein, The image of Jacob Edelstein, neg. 5144 © The Jewish Museum in Prague; P. 249 library in Theresienstadt Ghetto, Author's collection; P. 258 Shah Muhammad Rais, photograph, Ole Berthelsen, TV 2 Nettavisen, Norway; P. 260 Booker T. Washington, Cheynes Studio, Hampton, Virginia, 1903; P. 261 Cossitt Library, Special Collections, University of Maryland Libraries; P. 263 library in Baghdad, Joel Preston Smith, www.joelprestonsmith.com; P. 265 Code of Hammurabi, courtesy of http://employees.oneonta.edu/farberas/arth/Images/ARTH200/ politics/hammurabi.jpg; P. 273 Borges, © Eduardo Comesana; P. 275 Gargantua, C Lebrecht Music & Arts; P. 278 Rabelais's house, Author's collection; P. 281 Sir Thomas Browne, Gwen Raverat, Sir Thomas Browne, 1910, © DACS/SODART 2006; P. 282 Dickens, Library of Congress, Prints & Photographs Division, (LC-USZ62–117829); P. 283 Paul Masson, Author's collection; P. 286 Captain Nemo's library, Author's collection; P. 289 Hitler's bookplate, Third Reich collection, Rare Books and Special Collections Division, Library of Congress; P. 297 Sir

Anthony Panizzi, Picture History, Elliott & Fry, 1870; P. 304 books of the Lebanon National Library, Author's collection; P. 309 Dracula, Author's collection; P. 313 Frankenstein, Author's collection.

Page numbers in italic denote illustrations. For any specific library that is cited, *see* Library, [*name*] (*e.g.* Library, Bodleian)

quoting, functions of, 224

Weil, Simone, 31–32

Weinrich, Harald, 257

Wells, H. G., 238

Welty, Eudora, 102, 104

Whitman, Walt, 97

William III, 295

Winchester, Sarah, 86

Woolf, Virginia, 17–18, 180

words, as calling forth light,
    270–71

workshop. *See* the study

World Wide Web. *See* the Web

writers, their wants and needs,
    178–90

Xenophon, 285

Yahoo! (Internet Company), 126

Yongle Dadian. *See*
    encyclopedias

Zola, Emile, 94, 237, 245

Zweig, Stefan, 237

Zumárraga, Juan de, 118–22, *119*

The principle text of *The Library at Night* is set in Monotype Fournier, designed by Pierre Simon Fournier *le jeune*. He was both an originator and a collector of types. Among his contributions to the art of print communication were his creation of ornaments, decorative initials and his standardization of type sizes. In 1764 and 1766 he published his *Manuel typographique*, a treatise on the history of French types and printing, on typefounding and on what many consider his most important service to the printed word—the measurement of type by the point system.

The display heads and epigraphs are set in Twentieth Century, designed by Sol Hess between 1936 and 1947 and added to the Monotype font library in 1959. Twentieth Century is based on the geometric shapes and unadorned aesthetic of the Bauhaus movement in Germany in the early 1920s.

ALBERTO MANGUEL is an internationally acclaimed anthologist, translator, essayist, novelist and editor and the bestselling author of several award-winning books, including *A Dictionary of Imaginary Places* and *A History of Reading*. He was born in Buenos Aires, moved to Canada in 1982 and now lives in France, where he was named an Officer of the Order of Arts and Letters.